Parenting For Dummies 2nd Edition

W9-BLT-138

Cheat Sheet

Important Numbers

Police: _____

Fire: _____

Doctor: _____

Ambulance: _____

Hospital: _____

Poison Center: _____

Neighbors: _____

_____

School: _____

_____

Other: _____

_____

The Parenting Commandments

Thou shalt not make anything more important than thy children.

Thou shalt work to have great patience during times of stress.

Thou shalt feed thy children healthy, nutritious foods.

Thou shalt love and nurture thy children.

Thou shalt work to protect and keep thy children safe.

Thou shalt communicate openly and honestly with thy children.

Thou shalt make thyself a good example at all times.

Thou shalt treat thy children with respect.

Thou shalt not shake or physically try to hurt thy children.

Thou shalt be a good friend and supporter to thy co-parent.

General Parenting Tips

1. You're not going to do everything right. When you find you've handled a situation wrong, correct the error, brush yourself off, and try again.

2. Being a good parent takes time and practice.

3. Parenting is a series of trial and errors. You'll learn from your mistakes. Aside from the rules on being consistent, following-through, and keeping communications positive, there are very few definite rules on parenting. You have to find what works for yourself and your children.

4. Don't give up on your children. Following the parenting rules in this book can be hard. Be persistent and keep on trying. Your kids need you to be strong.

5. Have fun with your kids. The time when your kids just want to sit and play with you is relatively short. Don't lose that time. Play with your kids as much as you can. One day, they'll be off running around with their own set of friends and you'll be begging them for their time.

6. Turn off the TV and read. Reading, talking, walking, and playing are so much more fun than the mesmerizing effects of the TV.

For Dummies: Bestselling Book Series for Beginners

Parenting For Dummies,® 2nd Edition

Cheat Sheet

The Crying Baby Flowchart

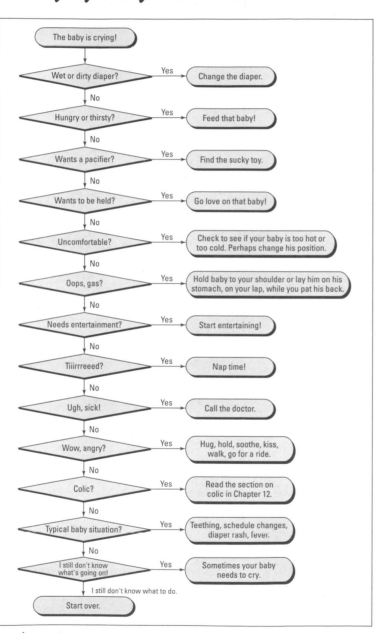

The baby is crying!

Wet or dirty diaper? — **Yes** → Change the diaper.

No

Hungry or thirsty? — **Yes** → Feed that baby!

No

Wants a pacifier? — **Yes** → Find the sucky toy.

No

Wants to be held? — **Yes** → Go love on that baby!

No

Uncomfortable? — **Yes** → Check to see if your baby is too hot or too cold. Perhaps change his position.

No

Oops, gas? — **Yes** → Hold baby to your shoulder or lay him on his stomach, on your lap, while you pat his back.

No

Needs entertainment? — **Yes** → Start entertaining!

No

Tiiirrreeeed? — **Yes** → Nap time!

No

Ugh, sick! — **Yes** → Call the doctor.

No

Wow, angry? — **Yes** → Hug, hold, soothe, kiss, walk, go for a ride.

No

Colic? — **Yes** → Read the section on colic in Chapter 12.

No

Typical baby situation? — **Yes** → Teething, schedule changes, diaper rash, fever.

No

I still don't know what's going on! — **Yes** → Sometimes your baby needs to cry.

I still don't know what to do.

Start over.

For more information about Wiley Publishing, call 1-800-762-2974.

For Dummies: Bestselling Book Series for Beginners

Parenting
FOR
DUMMIES®
2ND EDITION

by Sandra Hardin Gookin
Edited by Dan Gookin

Contributing editors:
Mary Jo Shaw, MD
Timothy Cavell, PhD

WILEY

Wiley Publishing, Inc.

Parenting For Dummies,® 2nd Edition

Published by
Wiley Publishing, Inc.
111 River Street
Hoboken, NJ 07030-5774
www.wiley.com

Copyright © 2007 by Wiley Publishing, Inc., Indianapolis, Indiana

Published by Wiley Publishing, Inc., Indianapolis, Indiana

Published simultaneously in Canada

For general information on our other products and services, please contact our Customer Care Department within the U.S. at 800-762-2974, outside the U.S. at 317-572-3993, or fax 317-572-4002.

For technical support, please visit www.wiley.com/techsupport.

Wiley also publishes its books in a variety of electronic formats. Some content that appears in print may not be available in electronic books.

Library of Congress Control Number: 2006927652

ISBN 0-7645-5418-2

Manufactured in the United States of America

10 9 8 7 6 5

2B/RV/QS/QX/IN

WILEY is a trademark of Wiley Publishing, Inc.

About the Authors

Sandra Hardin Gookin is the mother of four boys. She holds a degree in speech communications from Oklahoma State University, and her background in communications has been the basis for her theories on parenting. That, plus lots of experience in parenting methods that not only work but are painless.

Sandy also is an accomplished computer book author. She has written such books as *Windows XP Home Edition, I Didn't Know You Could Do That,* and *PCs For Dummies Quick Reference*. When Sandy isn't busy writing and parenting, she's an actress and theater director.

Dan Gookin has written more than 75 books about computers, and his works have been translated into 34 languages. Dan wrote the first "For Dummies" book (and many after that), so the light, humorous, and informative style of "For Dummies" books is Dan's style. His most recent titles include *PCs For Dummies, 8th Edition* and *Naked Windows XP*.

Dan and Sandy currently live with their several boys in the as-yet-untamed state of Idaho.

Dedication

This book is dedicated to our four boys, Jordan, Simon, Jonah, and Jeremiah. Thank you for being the subject of inspection and prodding and poking and just a whole lot of fun. You make life worth living and you turn every day into an adventure.

Author's Acknowledgments

It takes a lot of people to make a book. People you wouldn't even know about, such as my parents; thank you Mom and Dad for helping with the kids when I had to lock myself in my office to get this book done so Norm, my editor, wouldn't yell at me. Thank you also to contributing editors, Dr. Tim Cavell and Dr. Mary Jo Shaw. Your brilliance in your fields of expertise was very much appreciated.

Special thanks to Matt Wagner, my literary agent, for pushing this book through to its second edition. I am grateful for your persistence and patience.

And thank you to Norm Crampton, Editor Supreme, and Neil Johnson, my copy editor, for their ability to make me look smarter than I really am.

There are many people who contributed to this book whose names I don't know — parents I've observed who were wonderful and kind to their kids and who gave me inspiration. I thank you all.

Publisher's Acknowledgments

We're proud of this book; please send us your comments through our Hungry Minds Online Registration Form located at www.dummies.com.

Some of the people who helped bring this book to market include the following:

Acquisitions, Editorial, and Media Development

Project Editor: Norm Crampton

Acquisitions Editor: Pam Mourouzis

Copy Editor: Neil Johnson

Technical Editors: Beth Ann Martin, MD; Timothy Cavell, PhD

Editorial Manager: Christine Beck

Editorial Assistant: Melissa Bennett

Cover Photos: © IT Int'l/eStock Photography/Picture Quest

Production

Project Coordinator: Erin Smith

Layout and Graphics: Stephanie D. Jumper, Jackie Nicholas, Jeremey Unger, Mary J. Virgin, Erin Zeltner

Proofreaders: Laura Albert, John Greenough, Andy Hollandbeck, Linda Quigley, TECHBOOKS Production Services

Indexer: TECHBOOKS Production Services

Publishing and Editorial for Technology Dummies

    Richard Swadley, Vice President and Executive Group Publisher

    Andy Cummings, Vice President and Publisher

    Mary Bednarek, Executive Acquisitions Director

    Mary C. Corder, Editorial Director

Publishing for Consumer Dummies

    Diane Graves Steele, Vice President and Publisher

    Joyce Pepple, Acquisitions Director

Composition Services

    Gerry Fahey, Vice President of Production Services

    Debbie Stailey, Director of Composition Services

Contents at a Glance

Cartoons at a Glance

By Rich Tennant

The 5th Wave — By Rich Tennant

"DON'T TOUCH ANYTHING. DON'T PICK ANYTHING OFF THE FLOOR AND EAT IT. DON'T PLAY WITH YOUR EARS. DON'T FOOL AROUND WITH BILLY MAGUIRE'S RETAINER. DON'T GRAB ANYONE'S HAIR. DON'T FORGET TO SAY PLEASE AND THANK YOU. DON'T PICK YOUR NOSE, TALK LOUD OR PLAY WITH TOO MANY TOYS. AND HAVE A WONDERFUL TIME."

page 185

The 5th Wave — By Rich Tennant

"I FIND IT EASIER TO SAY 'NO,' IF I IMAGINE THEM SAYING, 'MOMMY, CAN I HAVE THE LATEST OVER-HYPED, OVER-PRICED, COMMERCIAL EXPLOITATION OF AN OBNOXIOUSLY ADOR-ABLE CARTOON CHARACTER.'"

page 341

The 5th Wave — By Rich Tennant

PARENTAL TRAINING COURSE — SOME COURSE HIGHLIGHTS:
① Driving from Idaho to Louisiana in a sub-compact vehicle with a pack of wild dingos in the back seat.
② Leading a bull safely through a china shop-using voice commands ONLY!
③ Meticulously grooming a flock of feeding vultures in less than 60 seconds using only a wet kleenex.

page 7

The 5th Wave — By Rich Tennant

YOUR CHILD'S FANTASY RESTAURANT

I'LL START WITH THE BOLOGNA AND COCOA PUFFS. FROM A PULL UPS AND A BOWL OF FRENCH JELLY SOUP. FOR AN ENTREE I'LL HAVE SPAGHETTI'OS WITH PEANUT BUTTER AND A SIDE OF CHOCOLATE HOT DOGS.

VERY GOOD SIR.

page 145

The 5th Wave — By Rich Tennant

And now, I'd like to share some of my day with you.

page 73

The 5th Wave — By Rich Tennant

"SCREAMING OR NON-SCREAMING?"

page 247

The 5th Wave — By Rich Tennant

"Mr Klein, would you mind telling me the next time you plan to smash your thumb with a hammer?"

page 327

Cartoon Information:
Fax: 978-546-7747
E-Mail: richtennant@the5thwave.com
World Wide Web: www.the5thwave.com

Table of Contents

• •

Introduction

Welcome to *Parenting For Dummies*. Here are my goals for the person who was smart enough to realize that parenting is probably more than just birthin' babies:

- I want you to learn how to develop a good relationship with your kids. I don't want you to get so wrapped up in being a "parent" that you forget that the little tyke who just spilled flour all over the floor is someone who has the same wants and desires about the way he is treated as you do.

- I want you to learn what invalidating your child's feelings is like. Saying, "Get up, you're not hurt" is telling your child that you don't believe what she is telling you.

- I want to help you to stop all the parenting sins you were taught by your parents.

- I hope your baby grows up to be a very old person someday because you were smart enough to believe all the safety warnings out there and that you didn't fall into that category of, "Oh, that'll never happen to me."

Of course, I'm hoping that you get even more from this book. More than anything, I hope that you'll embrace your job as parent with open arms and realize what a gift and honor it is to be one of the fortunate few who really do understand that your job is the most important job in the world.

About This Book

This book was written with the sincere desire to coax you to look at parenting in a way that's different from the way you may have been raised. In this book, a big emphasis is placed on communications and on developing a relationship with your child. But plenty of health and safety issues also are covered. I've tried to weed out the psychological hype and medical terminology, but you may find that I've had to include it from time to time. And, I've tried to limit the number of sappy stories about my own kids (although I have thrown in a few).

As with most *For Dummies* books, this one isn't meant to be read from front to back, although it would please me tremendously if you read the entire thing from cover to cover. Although age-specific information is included for newborns and toddlers, this book is considered more of a reference for people who work with children of all ages. Each chapter has self-contained information about parenting. You don't have to read the entire book to understand what's going on; just go to the chapter and section that interests you.

You won't learn the history of potty training in this book, or the psychological effects of bottlefeeding versus breast-feeding. But you will be equipped with excellent guidelines and helpful hints about getting your kids to bed, finding a good doctor, and making your home as safe as it can be. You know — practical stuff. The examples you'll read in this book have really happened to our family. Why would you want to read a book on parenting from people who haven't ever really parented?

Foolish Assumptions

The only assumption made in this book is that you have kids, are going to have kids, would like to have kids, know somebody who has kids, live next to somebody who has kids, or were, yourself, once a kid. Whatever the subject is when dealing with children, this is your reference.

For ourselves, you may notice that two people are listed on the cover. That's right, we're married, and we have four children (ages 7, 8, 9, and 15). So the information in the book has been practiced in real-world situations. It really works.

How This Book Is Organized

This book has seven major parts and 30 chapters. Inside each chapter are subsections that apply to the topic at hand. Even though this book is arranged so that you can pick it up and start reading from any point, this is how it reads from front to back:

Part 1: The Basic Stuff You Must Know

This first section is the backbone of the whole parenting topic. It contains information about how to be consistent, follow through with your actions, and interact with your children — the basic, important stuff. There's also a very important section on co-parenting.

Part II: Dealing with Babies

Babies are in a class by themselves, so they deserve their own special section (which we would have written in gender-neutral yellow, had we thought of it sooner). Breast-feeding and diapers and drooling and health concerns are all a little different for babies

Part III: Serving Your Child's Physical Needs

This part of the book starts getting into parenting topics like food and nutrition, bathtime, bedtime, and the dreaded potty training.

Part IV: Seeing to Your Child's Health and Safety

Safety! Nothing is more important than being organized and prepared for safety issues in your home and safety issues with childcare. This section also includes health issues such as finding a good doctor and living with dangerous elements like heat and cold.

Part V: Developing a Good Person

Your child wants to be treated with respect and like an individual human. That's tougher than it may seem. If it were easy, parents would be doing it all the time. So I've dedicated a section on communication and interaction with your child. The sensitive subject of punishment and discipline also is addressed.

Part VI: The Part of Tens

Life can be a series of checklists if you look at it that way. And this section gives you those checklists. Ten things to do every day. Ten reminders from your conscience. Ten excellent resources for parents.

Part VII: Appendixes

Checklists and questionnaires galore. Appendixes A through E are replete with helpful checklists and questionnaires to get you through the tedious tasks of shopping, packing, and interviewing day-care and medical-care providers.

Icons Used in This Book

These are hints, guides, and suggestions that you won't find in other books. They come from ourselves and other parents like us who *know* they work because we use or do them. These are things your grandmother would normally pass down to you.

A reminder so you don't forget.

A reminder of what to look out for.

Names of books, phone numbers, or products that are currently used by these parents — who think that they're great.

Quotes by people, some who are famous, most of whom are not.

Sidebars from My Guests

I have invited two guest contributors to this book. I picked these two people for a variety of reasons, but most important, because they represent the two areas of parenting that I believe are equally important: the physical health, safety, and well being, and the mental health and well being of your child.

Dr. Mary Jo Shaw is the pediatrician for my children and has been since the day they were born. Dr. Shaw has sprinkled real-life advice and guidance throughout this book. Dr. Shaw has practiced pediatrics in Coeur d'Alene, Idaho, for 14 years. She is the mother of three children.

Dr. Tim Cavell is an associate professor in the Department of Psychology at Texas A&M University. He has conducted a tremendous amount of research on what parents can do to prevent children from becoming delinquent and how to handle difficult children. I think his advice and contributions add another great element to this book.

Contacting the Author

Yes, you are free to write to me. Feel free to tell me about your personal parenting adventures, how you've overcome some situations, or just to ask for more detailed information that may not be covered in this book.

The best way to contact me is through an online account. You can expect the fastest feedback that way. Obviously, this works best when you have a computer and modem.

Via the Internet, write to

```
sandyg@wambooli.com
```

Via the U.S. Postal Service (which was devised in the 18th century, by the way), address us:

Sandy & Dan Gookin
P.O. Box 2697
Coeur d'Alene, ID 83816

Visit Our Web Site for Free Newsletters

Please visit our Web site at www.wambooli.com. You can sign up for a free weekly parenting newsletter or the free weekly computer tips newsletter. Just click on the newsletter link to subscribe to one or both of the newsletters.

Part I
The Basic Stuff You Must Know

The 5th Wave — By Rich Tennant

PARENTAL TRAINING COURSE
SOME COURSE HIGHLIGHTS:

1. Driving from Idaho to Louisiana in a sub-compact vehicle with a pack of wild dingos in the back seat.

2. Leading a bull safely through a china shop—using voice commands ONLY!

3. Meticulously grooming a flock of feeding vultures in less than 60 seconds using only a wet kleenex.

In this part . . .

The Egyptians knew that to make the whole pyramid concept work, they had to start with a strong, solid base. This base had to be all-encompassing and broad enough to handle the weight of everything that went on top of it. Making a good pyramid took a long time. Many attempts at building pyramids failed, but those aren't the structures that you see in pictures or get to tour.

This part serves as a solid base for building a parenting pyramid. The following six chapters provide you with information and guidelines that can help you construct the sturdy foundation upon which you can build a great relationship with your kids. As was true of the original pyramids, you'll run into stumbling blocks when you work on your parenting skills. But, if you have a strong foundation, your kids can pile all kinds of stuff on you, and you'll handle it just fine.

Chapter 1

The Parenting Game: Everyone's a Winner

Admit it, you're not in charge. Your children are. You know it, and worse yet, they know it. Children have a wonderful plan of attack: They draw you in, and then they pounce! They know exactly when to cry. They know precisely how to get you to say, "Yes." They know the millisecond you're no longer looking. Parenting is like playing a game of chess with an opponent who has an IQ of 300. You know they're manipulating you, but as parents you don't want to destroy your opponents — although sometimes the thought does cross your mind. You're torn between wanting to love them and the bitter realities of having to raise them properly. You want to do what you think is right without resenting your child just because he or she is manipulating you.

Welcome to *The Parenting Game*.

Although at times you may yearn for it, the object of this game isn't total victory, but rather a mutual solution that keeps everyone happy. You want to raise a child who turns into a well-adjusted adult, and you want to do it without being escorted away by men in white coats fitting you in a jacket that has sleeves long enough to wrap around you and tie behind your back. But you can't play the game without the proper parenting skills. That's precisely what this chapter shows you.

Leveling the Parenting Game Playground

No parent ever has or does everything right, so wake up and take a good whiff of that morning coffee. You won't be perfect. You will lose your temper. You will yell — loud enough at times to stir the neighbors. You will give in to the whining, if only as barter for a few brief moments of silence. And you will feed your kids cake, pie (after all, it has fruit), or various brand-name snack cakes and sugar-packed breakfast cereals for dinner *at least* once. That's all okay. No parent is perfect, so all that you can do is your level best. If your kids grow up to be happy, wholesome, and productive adults, people who are valued in the community, and you wind up having a wonderful relationship with them, then you've won.

So, the object of the game is discovering how to perfect your parenting and relationship skills. To do that you must understand three basic things:

- ✔ Parenting is a job that you can never quit.
- ✔ Parenting means playing some new and exciting roles.
- ✔ Parenting means finding out how to develop healthy relationships with your children.

Some people say that the parenting game never ends. After all, it would be nice to have an answer to the question, "At what age will my children be completely independent?" Alas, the answer is, "Never."

The American Dream is not owning your own house. The American Dream is getting your children out of your house. — Congressman Dick Armey

Parenting: A job you can never quit

You can't just quit the parenting game. As a parent, your job doesn't start at 8 a.m. and end at 5 p.m. It's a 24-hour-a-day job. And having an outside job doesn't mean that when you get home your job is over. Nope, instead, when you come home, you instantly change into your *parenting uniform* and get right back to work. There is no time off!

Don't use silk or white as a part of your parenting uniform; puke stains.

Your job as a parent consists of several duties and responsibilities to your kids. You love them. You feed them. You take care of them when they're sick. You play with them. You educate them with what you remember of your book-learning and common sense. You discipline them. You listen to them. And, occasionally you do something really goofy on purpose just to cause them embarrassment in front of their friends (who often think you're really cool for doing it).

Despite all that, remember that you can't slack off, you can't quit, and you know that parenting isn't accompanied by many tax breaks. Parenting is your responsibility, regardless of whether you have an outside job.

Why do I keep bringing up the issue of an outside job? Because it is a major element in how parents treat their kids. People have a tough day at work and come home not wanting to deal with their children. Too bad! When you find yourself cutting short the time that you spend with your kids or ignoring them because you've already had a full day, that's when it's time to reevaluate your other job. Parenting is your first priority.

The good news is that your parenting job comes with a wonderful bonus plan. In return for your work, your kids will love you back, frustrate you, make you laugh, make you cry tears of joy and sorrow, anger you, and, eventually, make you really proud of them.

Knowing the game terminology

Kids aren't born politically correct. So, if you have any tendencies toward political correctness, now is the time to face reality and get over them. Kids call poop what it is. They're more than happy to explain it to you — repeatedly in great detail. The same is true of throw-up, barf, heave, and spit up. All are real things about which your kids are more than happy and willing to share their unique knowledge.

Believe it or not, all this is good. Children think adults are the weird ones who decide the meanings of these favored words — offensive or not. The thing to remember is that your kids are just trying to communicate. So, in this game, becoming comfortable with common, everyday, descriptive kid language, regardless of how tasteless it sometimes gets, is up to you.

The four duties of a parent

One thing you need to understand about the parenting game is that you must take on some new and important duties. Sure, you can still "be yourself," but parenting requires you to understand that regardless of whether you want to accept these new duties, they nevertheless are yours, and it's for your and your kids' benefit that you do them well.

So here are the new roles that you must play:

- A positive role model
- A teacher
- A friend and listener
- A parent

The positive role model

A *role model* is someone you look up to and try to be like. Maybe it's that woman down the street who raised five kids all to become doctors. Maybe it's a fictional character. Batman was a great role model. Even when Batgirl was about to be dipped in hot bubbling oil, he still drove the speed limit. Or maybe your role model is your own mother or father. Whoever, it's someone you want to be like, someone who is well liked.

You also can be a role model in a way that you don't even realize that you're being one. How you handle stress, how you communicate, how you reassure your children are important aspects of being a positive role model.

Being a positive role model is important, because your children look to you as an example of how to behave. Your actions and behavior play a significant role as your child's personality develops between birth and age 7. Regardless of what habits you have and actions you take, you can rest assured that your li'l thumb-sucker is watching your every move and gathering that that is the behavior to imitate. What you do has a direct impact — positive or negative.

A *good role model* isn't necessarily someone who is perfect in every way. If you can walk on water, that's great. Otherwise, try doing the things that you know are right. You'll no doubt get upset sometimes. That happens. The important part is to apologize later, or explain to your kids why you got upset. It's healthy for kids to know that their parents get upset or mad. Everyone does. *How* you handle being upset is what's important. In Chapter 23, I discuss communicating with your child, which includes listening to what your child really has to say and letting your child know that what he or she says is being heard.

A *bad role model* doesn't necessarily mean being a bad person. Bad role models typically are workaholics, alcoholics, drug users, or people who put material things ahead of their families — the oblivious parent type.

Being a good role model means no smoking, cursing, getting drunk, lying, cheating, crossing the street on a red light, stealing, yelling, (*think of your own nasty habit and enter it here*), and so on.

That's quite a bit to ask for, isn't it? But remember that the rewards are great. You'll raise a child who grows up to be someone others want to be friends with. They'll contribute to their communities and generally be all-around great people. And that's a great gift to society.

The ever-present teacher

Everything you do and say is absorbed by your child's brain. This happens whether you want it to or not, so welcome to your second role as parent, that of *teacher*.

From the time your children are born, they watch your actions and behaviors and learn from them. That's sort of a scary thought, isn't it? Your wee ones discover things when you talk to them and do things with them. You'll teach them how to respond to spilled milk, how to react to a joke, what to do when they fall down — and all the other things that we deal with in life.

If you're calm, relaxed, and don't overreact to broken dishes and other such events, your children are likely to be calm and relaxed. On the other hand, if you're nervous and tense, your children are likely to be nervous and tense.

As a parent/teacher, you have two general areas in which you need to spend time teaching your children:

- ✔ Relationships
- ✔ Education

Relationships

Teaching your child how to be his own person requires you to understand what that means. So, you must enable your child to be his own person, have his own ideas, recognize and respect the fact that your and his ideas can be different. Yes, a child can have his own ideas about life. Although those ideas may differ from what you think or what you know to be true, they nevertheless are still his ideas.

The strongest relationships that parents and children can have with other people are the kind in which both can come together, accepting that they are different and that they have different thoughts and ideas and respecting those differences. Achieving this balance takes a considerable amount of work on a parent's part, because kids instinctively consider their way of thinking right and that everyone else must think that way too.

Education

Whether your kids attend public schools or are schooled in your home, you'll need to help them with their homework and other educational needs. Take the time to explain how things work, and let your children help you cook and clean, grow some flowers. This is all part of education.

A scholar is of all persons the most unfit to teach young children. A mother is the infant's true guide to knowledge. — Edward Bulwer-Lytton

The good listener

Listening probably is one of the weakest and most underused skills that people have. Listening, paying close attention to, and focusing on your child are the greatest gifts that you can give to him. A technique known as *mirroring* — in which you repeat back what your child (or partner for that matter) says or summarize those same thoughts — is great to use when you and your child are talking. Mirroring not only clarifies what is being said, it also keeps you on track with the conversation and serves as an acknowledgement for your child that you're actually paying attention. It's also a wonderful skill to use in conversations with your friends and other family members.

The parent

How can parents *befriend* their children and still function as parents? This question is a tough one to answer and a difficult issue to approach. You want to be friends with your children, spending time together, doing things together, paying attention to each other, and helping them to grow up to be healthy, strong, independent people. But you don't want to cross the line and forget about being a parent.

Another book that I suggest that you read is called *The Emotional Incest Syndrome, What to Do When a Parent's Love Rules Your Life*, by Dr. Patricia Love. I admit that the title, to me at least, is a tad scary. But the reason that I suggest this book is to show you what to avoid. "Too much of a friend" can be defined as a parent who shares confidential information with a child or makes the child think of himself and that parent as "best friends." Becoming too much of a friend leads a child to believe that he must help you to take care of your needs instead of you enabling him to grow and take care of his own needs. The friend versus parent conflict isn't all doom and gloom because good parents can and do make things fun, the way that a good friend does. But beware of bad but not-so-obvious habits that you don't want to develop, such as *invalidating* a child with a problem, which you probably learned from your parents. Examples include telling a child to stop whining because nothing really is wrong with him or telling him to get up because he isn't really hurt.

Being a good parent to your children also means accepting them for who they are, which typically is what a friend does. It isn't harping on or pointing out their weaknesses, but rather helping them build up the things they're good at. By encouraging them, you not only prove that you're a good friend, you also help them develop their self-confidence.

Always praise your kids and, while you're at it, praise everyone else's kids. Of course, that means being realistic where praise is concerned. A kind word or a pat on a back can be considered praise. A snide comment to a child — even if you're doing it as a joke among your own friends — has two negative results: It belittles the kid, and it shows other kids that it's okay to make snide comments that can belittle someone.

A good friend remembers what we were and sees what we can be. — Janette Oke

Let your kids "help" you. Even if that means letting them stir flour all over your counter when you're cooking. Going to the store and cleaning house *together* can also be fun. Such a strategy not only shows your children that work can be fun, it also helps them discover essential skills and enables you to spend time developing your relationship with your child.

Think about your best friend. Ask yourself how this person became your best friend? You probably just spent a lot of time together, had fun, and, the next thing you knew, you were friends. The same thing can happen with your children. Raising kids isn't the time to be selfish with your time or energy. It's the time when you *make time* to be with and do things with your kids.

If your children are your friends, they're more likely to open up to you with their problems and concerns about school, peer pressure, or other things that bother them. Likewise, you'll be more approachable when your kids look to you not only as a parent but also a friend.

Introducing the Five Basic Parenting Skills

Five basic skills are involved in *The Parenting Game*. When you master these skills, you should be able to handle most situations that arise. The five basic skills are

- ✔ Speaking and listening with care
- ✔ Being consistent
- ✔ Following through
- ✔ Remaining patient
- ✔ Learning to manage behavior

These rules are all that you need to become an effective, happy parent and to raise those *perfect* kids you see in the catalogs. But the one evil twist to these rules is that you must be consistent with them. Yes, you even must learn to be consistent at being consistent. You can't choose to follow these rules one day and not the next. You'll lose the parenting game if you don't tackle these skills with gusto!

Your responsibility as a parent is not as great as you might imagine. You need not supply the world with the next conqueror of disease or major motion picture star. If your child simply grows up to be someone who does not use the word "collectible" as a noun, you can consider yourself an unqualified success.
— Fran Leibowitz

Speaking and listening with care

You need an effective way to express your ideas, wants, and desires to your kids. That's communication. Speak clearly, precisely, and without a lot of babbling. But taking the time to listen also is important. In any relationship — even with your hair stylist — if you don't, won't, or can't communicate effectively, you're doomed. Doomed! Doomed! Doomed!

Being specific is the opposite of being vague, and most people are vague. Don't you hate talking to people who seem neither here nor there about what they want? Vagueness may be a blessing when you're a politician, but it can be hazardous in *The Parenting Game.*

You must be specific about your wants and desires when you talk to your children, keeping in mind that they don't always have the same frame of reference that you do. So, when you say, "Go clean your room," you must be specific about what "clean" means. You may mean as clean as an operating room before surgery, but they may think that you mean that they need only to make the path from the doors to their rooms to their beds and closets just a little wider.

Babble. *Abba blabba abba dabba blah* is a disease. Kids don't like to hear you babble, or nag, or complain. They'd rather you just get to the point. If you're too long-winded, their minds wander off to battle against *The Forces of Evil,* and they won't hear half of what you're saying. But communication also means listening. It's a two-way street: You talk. You listen. Without listening, talking isn't communication. It's filling the room with noise while you recycle air through your lungs. Kids pick up on this real quickly.

Communication is more than just talking to your kids. It's being a great listener, too.

The basic rules of communication are that you be specific about what you want and that you don't babble when you say it.

> ✔ Be specific!
> ✔ Get to the point!

Yes, sometimes it helps to phrase things in cryptic lawyer-speak. But when you say, "We're going to the grocery store, so I want you to behave," do you mean, "We are going to the store. Do not touch anything, do not ask for anything, do not yell or scream, do not poke the hamburger meat, and please sit quietly in the cart"? Be specific about what you want. "Behave" may mean something different to you than it does to your kids.

I must point out, in all fairness, that just because you get to the point and are specific about your requests, children don't always listen. They have their own wants and desires, too, and they may not be the same as yours.

Speaking to a young child is easy. He reaches for an apple, you say, "No." He starts to touch the apple again, and you say, "No." This activity may go on until you figure out that what you need to do is move him away from the apples. In fact, it's your fault that you put him near the apples, because it's in his nature to want to play with the apples.

Just don't babble: "Sweetheart, please don't touch the apples. If you touch the pretty red apples, they may all fall on the ground causing your dear, sweet mother an enormous amount of embarrassment." What he hears is: "Sweetheart, blah apples blah blah. . . ."

Communication is the key to your relationship with your children, and this little section is just the tip of the iceberg. Refer to Chapter 23, "Communicating with Your Child," and read it carefully. Good communication is the foundation of a good relationship.

For a fun book to read to your kids that shows how words can mean different things, try *The King Who Rained* by Fred Gwynne (The Trumpet Club).

Waver not, lest ye topple (being consistent)

Think of a top. It spins until it wobbles, and then it falls down. As it spins, it's being consistent. When it slows down, it stops being consistent. It wobbles and falls. Being consistent is setting rules and guidelines and not going back on or changing those rules. It means not being wishy-washy with your kids. Even when the whining gets to you (and, believe me, it *will*), you need to be firm.

Be consistent — don't get tired and start to wobble.

That is perhaps the toughest part of being a parent. When your child crawls on the dining room table, you take him down *every time* he crawls back up. Don't pretend after a while that you don't see him. You may be tired of the game, but he has the energy of the Energizer Bunny and just keeps on going. Every time you take him off the table you're being consistent.

Being consistent sounds easy, like one of the easiest rules of *The Parenting Game*. But your kids have one up on you. They're cute; they cry; they beg; tiny arms reach up; tear-filled eyes beg for mercy; and boo-boo lips protrude. But don't give in. Be strong. Be consistent. Your kids really want that from you. They need it. They want to know the guidelines and they want you to be consistent about enforcing them.

A thousand or more examples of when you need to be consistent exist. Bedtimes need to be consistent, and so do meal times, homework times, rules about behavior, rules about how your household is set up (what furniture is okay to abuse and what isn't), and the list goes on.

Being consistent and following through are sort of like cousins marrying; the two concepts are related in a weird kind of way. If you're not consistent, and you don't practice follow-through, you'll have problems with your kids.

Do what you say, and think before you say it (the art of follow-through)

Before follow-through can happen, you must give children a choice. Giving children choices keeps you from being a bully and enables the child to make a choice. *Follow-through* means doing what you said you were going to do if your child makes a choice to follow an action. It means sticking to your original word, an important offshoot of being consistent. The key here is thinking before you say something because follow-through doesn't always mean bad stuff. Do you really mean, "Sit down or you won't get any dinner?" And did you really mean it when you said, "Make straight A's and we're going to Europe!" You had better mean it if you expect to live up to your follow-through.

Hold, hover, shepherd, and guide — Dr. Tim

The images that occupy your mind and your words can say a lot about how you think about the job of parenting. Are you actively "bending the twig" or are you passively "watching the seedling sprout and blossom"? But these images also can mislead you if you don't periodically readjust the picture to fit the changing needs of your children. I suggest four images to keep in mind. They're quite simple but they may remind you of how the job of parenting changes over time.

Hold. Infants, of course, need to be held. We hold our babies when we suckle them, bathe them, and soothe them. Thus, the classic image of the infant cradled in the arms of mother or father is a fitting one.

Hover. Toddlers and some preschoolers are more mobile and independent than infants. You can no longer hold onto them and meet all their needs. But their newfound mobility and independence can also be their undoing. They are vulnerable to all sorts of hazards, from falling and hitting their head to walking blindly through a busy parking lot. They need you to hover and to intervene when their small adventures put them in harm's way.

Shepherd. Elementary school children (and some adolescents) have a different set of needs, and the picture that emerges is that of the shepherd. The time to hover has passed; you must now stand straight up and follow them as they move forward across well-worn paths. But like the shepherd, you provide safety and security. You make sure they don't stray down the wrong path, and you recognize that keeping them in the fold, committed to the flock, is of the utmost importance.

Guide. Adolescents (and some young adults) require yet a different kind of parent. No longer can you follow their every movement because adolescents take paths that you don't see or know about. Your role and influence have narrowed. But narrow does not mean insignificant. You are like a guide whose expert advice in specialized areas can be immensely helpful to those who are lost or uninformed. So your task is to be the best guide you can be — wise and welcoming, strong and humble, grounded and content. You lead your own life, but you are also ready for the times when your children look your way or seek your advice on matters of grave importance.

Don't say, "Do that one more time and you'll regret it." It sounds nice because it gives you an out; you're not bound to do anything linked to that threat. But it's better if you say instead, "If you choose to do that one more time, then I'm not allowing AJ to spend the night tonight." Then if the child *chooses* to do the dastardly deed one more time, your follow-through is to say, "You chose to do (whatever). Because you made that choice, AJ doesn't get to spend the night." Then follow through by not allowing AJ to spend the night.

Following through on a punitive measure not only gives the child a choice, it also puts the behavior in their hands. They made a choice so your follow-through is based on that choice. So be sure that you:

- *Think* before you say something.
- Consistently follow through or your children never will believe you again.

Making your punishment realistic also helps. For example, instead of saying "Do that one more time and I'll ground you for a *millennium*," say, "Do that one more time and you won't get to have friends over for a *week*." Then follow through for a week and don't allow friends to come over. If you tell your 6-year-old that you'll take his ball away if he throws it again in the house, take his ball away the next time he throws it in the house.

For more information about following through with what you say, please see Chapter 4, "Following Through."

Learning the virtue of patience

Who couldn't use more patience? I suppose we all could. But what is patience, anyway? Broken down into parenting terms, it means not allowing the things that children do to bug you. After all, children are being themselves.

Having patience really means planning ahead, understanding the way children operate, and understanding your own issues and problems enough so that you can recognize that the things kids do that bug you are actually your own problems. They are just being kids and are programmed to do and act a certain way. Patience actually means understanding these things ahead of time and working with the situations that you find are bugging you.

How do you get to the point where crying babies, poopy diapers that have overflowed onto your nice white Battenburg bedspread, being late, and a toddler who seems to be dragging his feet don't bother you any more? These are the realities of kids, so how do you work with their reality so they don't drive you crazy? Patience means:

- Taking more time than is necessary to do something.
- Letting your daughter take two hours to pick out the most perfect Barbie doll so she can go home and cut off Barbie's hair.

✔ Understanding that kids are kids and are designed to behave the way they do. Your caterwauling or bullying them otherwise is futile.

✔ Taking a good look at yourself as you develop a way of taking the time to practice how you're going to answer the ageless and ongoing question, "Why does this bug me?"

To learn more about making patience a part of your character, read Chapter 5, "The Art of Keeping Your Cool."

Behavior-management skills

Idle hands get into trouble. So do neglected hands. If your children are bored with nothing to do, or if they're craving your attention, they'll find their own means of entertainment and ways to attract your attention. They'll sort all your CDs; crawl into the fireplace, get sooty, and then crawl on the carpet; they'll even paint the cabinets with peanut butter. But these activities aren't the kid's fault. They're simply innocent, time-consuming acts of kids being kids and being creative. When they get older, their boredom leads to a loss of energy and depression, which ultimately can lead to kids cruising Main Street or sitting on top of cars in vacant parking lots. The extreme side of boredom and attention-grabbing techniques may even lead to drinking, premarital sex, and experimentation with drugs. Kids as young as 7 and 8 are being approached by drug dealers these days. That really is scary stuff!

Behavior management means keeping your children busy and occupied *most* of the time. Giving them their own free time is a good idea. That way they can use their imaginations to create their own fun; however, if you help organize their time and give them your attention, they won't spend time getting into things they shouldn't. And, while you're at it, praise them when they do something great like helping you pick up toys or doing something kind for a sibling. Praise reinforces your kids' perception that what they just did made you happy. Because kids like pleasing their parents, they'll do the things that make you happy again just to get more praise from you.

WARNING: The perils of negative attention

Your kids will do anything they can to get your attention. Even if that means *negative attention*. If you don't spend time with your children and give them positive attention, they'll do whatever it takes to get your attention. If they find that pouring water on the floor is what it takes to get you to spend time with them, they'll do it. As small children, these acts are innocent enough. But as your children get older, they'll do dangerous things, like drugs and alcohol.

You may see this as manipulation, which wouldn't be far from the truth. But, remember that children are masters of manipulation. Therefore staying on top of their manipulation is your job. Manipulating your children's behavior, or behavior management, keeps your children happy, safe, and out of *trouble* by enabling you to be a part of their daily activities, attitudes, and environment.

So behavior management involves some simple concepts:

- ✔ Keeping idle hands busy
- ✔ Giving lots of attention
- ✔ Offering praise

Chapter 6, "Behavior Management," discusses how rewarding good behavior, constant praise, plenty of hugs and kisses, and organized play can keep your child out of mischief.

Finding Your Sense of Humor in the Lost and Found

I can't think of anything or anyone more entertaining than children. They're simply funny. They're goofy. Perhaps that's why so many good books, movies, and even comic strips are based on children and the things they do. Humor can be found in everything, although it may not be obvious to you when it happens.

Without being evil, children have an uncanny ability to push all your buttons. You really need to be able to laugh at the things that ordinarily would drive you up the wall. In other words, relax. Don't concern yourself with the fact that your 2-year-old has poured baby powder all over the place. Instead, grab the camera. It's going to be a funny story in a few hours so you may as well snap it for the album before cleaning the little one up.

Anger usually is a parent's first reaction because what kids do is unexpected and it's also usually the parent who has to clean it up. So what? Stop, take several deep breaths, look at that sweet face, and smile. Anger is wasted energy and that energy should be spent somewhere else.

Let your kids be kids. They goof up. They make messes. Accept that fact and never assume they're doing something "just to get you." Part of the joy of being a parent is sitting back and watching your kids do all the goofy things your parents accused you of doing when you were a kid. (Besides, you can't tell the funny story when it has the sad ending of "and then I beat the *crap* out of him.")

Stop before you react to anything and take a deep breath. Deep breathing (or maybe it's just stopping and letting your brain work for a minute) helps you realize that whatever you're looking at isn't really that awful. You may even get so mad that you have to excuse yourself and tell your children that you're upset and you'll have to discuss the situation later when you've had time to cool down. Make sure you resolve the situation that day. If you let too much time go by, your kids will have forgotten the whole thing.

Concern for your children is good. But don't be so protective of your children that you forget how fun kids can be. Laughing is great. It makes you feel good, it relieves stress, and it makes life a lot more fun.

Is There an End to this Game?

The Parenting Game never actually ends. Soon your kids will be older and have kids of their own. Then you'll start all over with the *I-told-you-so's,* which are a grandparent's right (and which you're probably getting enough of right now).

Being a parent is difficult, especially for first-time parents. Even with someone like me who has four kids, it still takes an effort to remember and follow through with the basic parenting rules. Trying to be consistent, always thinking about the proper ways to communicate with your child, cleaning up messes, and working to keep your little ones busy isn't easy.

Moms especially seem to have it in their minds that they're supposed to be *Super Mom,* able to handle it all with ease, with a smile on their faces and a clean house, and, worse yet, looking good while doing it. More and more dads are put in this position too. Hey guys — you can't do it all. You can try, and that's the whole point of this book. But you'll drive yourself insane if you think you're going to be perfect all the time.

All the parents of the world are going through the same things you're going through, so you're not alone. Everyone will have the same problems you have and get to a point where they just want to throw their hands up and give up. Just keep your sense of humor, whatever you do.

The day you bring your little bundle of joy home from the hospital is the happiest day of your life. However, the new Mommy is exhausted, sore, and probably feeling a little emotionally unstable thanks to her hormones. Daddy is tired too. You both will sit and look at your new baby and wonder, "Now what?" Then that little, beautiful baby opens its little cherub mouth and begins to wail. So what do you do? Smile. Continue smiling through all the years that you're lucky enough to be a parent.

Chapter 2

Guidelines for Co-parenting (The Two-Party System)

- -

In This Chapter

▶ Having fun as parents
▶ Sharing housework
▶ Sharing child care
▶ Recognizing the Super Mom Syndrome
▶ Surviving single parenting

- -

Co-parenting is about teamwork and having time to take care of *you* so that you can do your parenting job as well as you possibly can. It's about planning ahead so that you and your partner can act as full-time parents together, working toward a family environment. In turn, having a strong family environment gives kids a strong foundation for finding out who they are, thus making them secure individuals.

But what if you're a single parent? This chapter still is for you. Your co-parent can be a roommate, a grandmother or grandfather, uncle, aunt, rent-a-spouse. It can be anyone in your life who can be there to help you raise your kids. It doesn't necessarily have to mean a Mom and Dad, although that is the ideal situation. I have some specific advice for single parents in "Surviving Single Parenting" later in this chapter.

Parent + Parent = Teamwork

Parenting is women's work. Wrong! Many men these days are proving just how wrong that tiresome belief is. But parenting *is* teamwork. The trick is making this parenting team work together when both parents have different backgrounds, experiences, and expectations about parenting. And I don't care how much you think you've talked things out before having kids, you won't be able to cover everything. Things definitely change (often unexpectedly) for first-time parents when their child actually arrives. You may make statements like, "Oh yeah, I'll go back to work after the baby gets to be a couple of months old," and then find that you can't do it. You can't bear the thought of leaving your child in the hands of some stranger.

I could go on and on with stories, all true, of parents who've discussed and planned and organized, only to then have it all turn out differently once the baby comes home.

The following sections are not so much a list of strict rules, but suggestions about:

- ✔ Keeping a strong, healthy partner relationship
- ✔ Keeping the dynamics of the family going
- ✔ Developing parenting guidelines that you both can live with

The business of having fun together

Many statements about parenting are contradictory and even quite the opposite of the truth. A line from the movie *Honey, I Blew Up The Kids* is one example that goes, "Daddies are for fun; Mommies mean business." Who came up with this? I don't know any Mom who'd ever say, "Oh yes, I guess playing with the children would be nice, but I'd much rather discipline the children, put cranky babies to bed, or (my favorite) change those really explosive diapers." Do you know what happens when Daddies never partake in the really tough stuff? Mommies become resentful. And Daddies — I hope you know by now — that is never a good thing.

I've heard Moms and Dads say how they feel like a single parent because their partners won't help with any of the difficult parts of raising children. You both must be involved in every aspect of raising your kids. Mommies and Daddies are for fun. Mommies and Daddies can mean business.

Why is having fun a business? Because unless you schedule your activities, work and play alike, nothing happens. Putting the kids to bed can be a great time that can turn into wonderful memories, that is if you do it together. It also takes less time when you work together to complete family chores so that you can schedule fun time together, as a family and as a couple.

"Hey honey, let's put the kids to bed, then meet me downstairs by the fireplace. I'll bring the wine, you bring the snacks!"

Sharing of thy housework

Sharing housework is a sore subject with many families. One partner usually feels like he or she is doing *all* the work, or another may always complain about the house not being tidy. The housework issue doesn't necessarily mean that you have to divide the chores up equally so that everyone has five each. It means that you divide the chores up equitably (which means fairly or reasonably). Sit down and make a list of things that you're all willing and able to do. If you hate vacuuming, let your partner do it. If your partner detests the laundry, you do it. If you both hate doing the dishes, then do them together and get that chore out of the way. And, remember, the time will come when your children can do the dishes for you. If you become bored with your regular chores, keep things interesting by making changes to your chore schedule every week or so.

Personally, I'm task-oriented and I'm raising my family to be that way too. I don't like to be a nagger, so I've come up with a written checklist that people can mark so that we all know that the chores are getting done. Your chore chart can look similar to the one shown in Table 2-1.

Table 2-1	The Co-parenting Chore Chart						
	Mon	**Tue**	**Wed**	**Thur**	**Fri**	**Sat**	**Sun**
Parent #1							
Make the bed							
Vacuum							
Wipe off kitchen counters							
Fold the laundry							
Parent #2							
Sweep/mop the kitchen							
Take out the trash							
Feed the dog							
Wash a load of clothes							

To add to the whole housework issue, come up with an agreeable plan as to what a "clean house" means to both of you. What is the standard that you're both willing to live with. Keep in mind that with kids, having a clean house all the time may be a pipe dream that may not ever happen. So, pick your battles. In our house, the living room and kitchen must be tidy. Bedrooms are allowed to slip a bit.

How to be of one common mind without brain surgery

Many young couples who discuss parenting strategies before they get married often find that things are different when the child actually arrives, which is to be expected. Unless you've spent a lot of time around kids, your list of rules and regulations generally is based on your observations of what others are doing. A common declaration of couples contemplating parenthood is: "Gee, I'll never do that when I have a kid!" Yeah, right.

So when baby finally arrives, you can expect that as co-parents you're likely to disagree about how to handle certain situations with your child. Remember that you must treat those situations delicately. You don't want to turn a coloring-on-the-walls incident into a raging debate about who's going to end up sleeping on the couch, especially when your little one is standing there absorbing everything you're saying.

Here are some suggestions for handling mutual decision-making:

✔ **Don't argue about discipline.**

Especially in front of your kids. They interpret this as one parent taking their side while the other doesn't. They store this information away and eventually use it against you — not in an evil kind of way, but they remember it and bring it up later.

✔ **Respect each other's parenting ideas.**

Child-raising ideas come from your background. They're based on how you were disciplined and your life experiences. You may have even picked up some ideas by how you've seen others handle their children. Your partner has a background too, complete with his or her ideas and expectations. Be open to what your partner has to suggest. Don't always assume that your way is the right way. And women, don't assume that because you're the mommy, you know what's best.

✔ **Agree on the decision.**

If both parents agree on a solution to a problem or a rule to enforce, then the solution will be enforced. If one parent disagrees, that parent won't enforce the rule. It's that simple. People do only what they want to do, and parents who don't believe in a particular course of action won't go that route. So, when confronted with a situation that requires a solution, both parents must agree on that solution. If you can't agree, then come up with another solution.

✔ **Talk out disagreements.**

You both need to feel comfortable with the outcome and agree to household rules and how to handle incidents in which those rules are broken. When you're inconsistent with the rules, your child will likely become confused, probably decide not to listen to either one of you, or — worse yet — play you both off of each other. You know the scene, "But Dad, Grandma always lets me jump on the bed."

✔ **Never jump into ongoing situations.**

If you walk into a room where your partner already is handling a situation, try to keep quiet. Things aren't always as they appear, and you probably don't know exactly what's going on.

✔ **Don't gang up on your child.**

If you both see something happening that shouldn't, let one parent deal with it. Neither of you wants to appear as though you're ganging up on your child. If you see that your partner is having trouble, offer to step in and help.

Sharing child care (or, it took Adam and Eve to raise Cain)

When you're busy with the kids, it may seem there's little that your partner can do to help. Wrong! Although they may seem small, to nevertheless be a ton of help, your partner can:

✔ **Pick up the clutter.**

Pick up toys, blankets, bottles, or towels that you see lying around the house. It always baffles me that whole families can walk over a napkin on the floor, as if someone had placed it there as a sacrificial piece of garbage and only certain holy hands are allowed to touch it.

✔ **Share the child-care duties.**

Take turns changing diapers, putting the kids to bed, giving baths, feeding (obviously with the exception of breast-feeding, which could be painful for Dad), burping baby, helping with homework — and whatever else needs to be done to take care of your kids. If any of these tasks become an issue between the parents, then put them on a chart like the one in Table 2-1. On Mondays, Wednesdays, and Fridays, Mom helps with homework while Dad fixes dinner. On Tuesdays and Thursdays, those roles are reversed. You both brought these kids into the world, neither of you needs to think these tasks belong to only one parent.

✔ **Give Mom some special time.**

If you really want to make Mom happy, give her some special time in the morning to have to herself so she can shower, put on makeup, get dressed — or whatever her morning ritual is. This luxury often is overlooked, especially when it involves a newborn that only Mom can feed. New mothers can go through most of the day before they have a chance to get cleaned up. They'll feel much better if they can have a few minutes to themselves to wash off the baby puke and leaked breast milk.

✔ **Give your partner some free time alone every now and then.**

As much as we love our children, sometimes getting away for an hour or so to spend time alone is good. This goes for both parents.

Sharing the ties that bind

It's unfortunate that some dads feel left out of bonding because they aren't able to breast-feed. Some fathers think that newborns are a time for Mom and baby. On the contrary, dads must become involved with their newborns with as much interest and vigor as moms do. A dad can spend just as much time with his baby if he takes some time and incorporates a little imagination. Dad can

✔ Lie down with Mom and baby while she nurses. It's a nice, cozy time with baby in the middle and Mom and Dad on either side.

✔ Bottle-feed the baby (with the help of a breast pump from Mom).

✔ Join Mom in playing with baby together.

✔ Be the official baby-bath parent.

I asked my students what they preferred to receive from their parents, money or time. They all chose time. — Jonnie Johnson, 7th Grade Teacher

As your children grow older, you'll still want to spend that bonding time with them. Make dates with your children where just Mom and child or Dad and child can go out and do things together. This is a great time to grow closer to and spend uninterrupted time talking to your child. These outings don't always have to be costly. Go out and run errands, go grocery shopping, or just go for a walk or bicycle ride.

Look! Over at the Mall — Driving the Minivan — It's Super Mom!

The term *Super Mom* is a 1980s coinage, a term given to mothers who tried to do everything and be the best at everything. Super Mom tried to be a super employee, a super wife, and a super housekeeper. Super cool!

Mom and Dad differences — Dr. Tim

Gender is overrated as an indicator of how someone parents. And as old-fashioned, stereotyped sex roles fade away, gender matters even less for parenting. That doesn't mean that moms and dads won't ever differ. Children discover some things primarily from Mom and other things mainly from Dad. Moms usually provide more examples of attending to others' needs and being emotionally attuned; dads usually provide more examples of being assertive, outspoken, and competitive. And examples that moms provide usually affect girls more than boys (and vice versa for dads' examples). This is especially true when a child struggles with questions about how they rate among their peers.

Of course, much more is known about moms than dads. Who knows? Maybe someone will discover that dads bring special talents to the parenting table. For example, some studies show that children, especially boys, have better peer relationships when they play with their dad in active, physical ways. Why? Maybe because dads teach kids stuff they can use, like the rules for a game, how not to be so serious when playing, or how to lose gracefully. As a therapist, I've found that father-son play is helpful for boys who are shy and picked on by other kids. For those boys, it's important that Dad "has their back." Girls also can benefit from close relationships with their dads. One study found that girls who spent a lot of quality time with their dads were less sad and more competitive! How cool is that?

Unfortunately, Super Mom found that she wasn't effective at doing any of these things — not because of lurking kids with Kryptonite but because she was trying to do too much. The solution for Super Mom was to let something go. Some let their bedrooms be a mess. Some left work at 5 o'clock so they could be at home with their families instead of putting in overtime.

The Super Mom Syndrome isn't limited to the '80s. It's still happening today. The only change is that it isn't limited to mothers. Fathers have joined the ranks of the overachievers.

Having priorities is the cure to this disease. Number one on your list should be your family. Everything else should be secondary. Because you can't ignore everything else (although ignoring laundry would be nice), it's time to look at things differently. Thus you must:

 ✔ **Get help from your family.**

   No one person in a family should be responsible for doing everything. Those days when Mom was stuck in the kitchen working while Dad read the paper and kids were riding bikes are enshrined in *Leave It to Beaver* episodes. Today, our lives are so busy that everyone needs to be involved in cooking, cleaning, yardwork, and grocery shopping. Working together establishes a sense of togetherness, and it means that you'll have more time to play together too.

✔ **Leave work when it's time to go.**

It's a job. If your job is like most, the work still will be there when you return tomorrow.

✔ **Get organized.**

Arrange your daily house and work chores so that you don't waste time on anything. Make up chore lists for everyone in the family so they know what they're supposed to do. Lay clothes out for the next day. Make lunches the night before. Write dinner menus for the whole week. Have a specific place to put backpacks, coats, and briefcases so you don't waste time hunting for them every morning.

✔ **Set priorities.**

You can't do everything. Pick what rooms are important to be clean. In my house, the living room and kitchen are my priorities for clean, presentable rooms. Limit social activities for you and your kids so you're not overwhelmed with too much to do. Know when to say "No" to work and to the kids. No, I won't take on that project. No, you can't have friends over tonight. No, let's not clean the basement, let's play a game instead.

Be Good to Yourself

Being the best parent you can be means being the best person you can be. When you feel your best, others around you get that good feeling from you. When you're tired and haven't been taking proper care of yourself, others, including your kids, can tell. Your patience is worn thin, your energy level is low, and you're less enthusiastic. Your attention span also tends to be shorter, and you may even be — although you'll probably deny it — a little cranky.

So that you have enough energy to be the terrific parent that you always wanted to be, make exercise, diet (meaning eating right), and rest important parts of your life. Try thinking of original excuses for each of the following:

✔ Why you can't exercise.

✔ Why you snack on junk food too much.

✔ Why you never get enough rest.

Ha! It can't be done. You can offer no excuse that hasn't already been used. Even the Aliens-abducted-me-and-forced-me-to-eat-this-doughnut excuse has been used — but no one believed me.

Exorcising the demons of laziness

Exercise doesn't mean you have to join a health club, put on spandex, and sweat to the Golden Oldies to get in shape. It means loading the kids in the stroller, pulling them in a wagon, or having them ride along on their Big Wheel, bicycle, go-cart whatever while you're walking for 20 to 30 minutes, three or four times a week. That's what health experts say you really need.

Plenty of floor exercises can involve you and your kids. Do sit-ups while holding your baby on your stomach. Do leg lifts while your toddler lies beside you with a favorite toy. Race to see how many sit-ups you and your kids can do in ten minutes. This isn't brain surgery. I'm sure you can also think of a few things to do.

The best ways to find time for exercising are

- ✔ Turning the TV off. TV can be evil. It robs you of your life.
- ✔ Having everyone help with dinner and housecleaning so that everyone can take a walk after dinner.
- ✔ Scheduling your exercise time. You're more likely to exercise when exercise is a part of your schedule.

Realize one important fact. Once you have a baby, your body may not be the same size it was before you had the baby (Dads, there's no excuse for you). Moms, your weight may return the same level it was BC (before child), but your body may be shaped differently. Women tend to spread out more in the hip area, their breasts may become larger or smaller, or their feet may grow (this happens if you wear tennis shoes or go barefoot more than you used to). It's a necessary price to pay for a great baby.

Some women return to their exact same tiny prepregnancy selves, but we don't like these women.

Jogging is a great way to hear heavy breathing again. — Quote from someone really funny

Eating right (put that donut down)

Gaining weight is easy after having a baby — not necessarily because you're overeating, but rather because you tend to stop eating well and end up snacking on foods that are high in sugars and carbohydrates.

Remember how well you ate while you were pregnant? (Yes, you were supposed to be eating right.) Don't let the busy schedule that you have with kids make you fall into that bad habit of eating only fast foods, or snacking all day on crackers. Check out the alternative listed in Table 2-2.

Table 2-2	Alternative Snack Chart
What you want to eat	*What you can eat instead*
Graham crackers	Steamed soybeans
Potato chips	Baby carrots with spinach dip
Honey Nut Cheerios	Raisins and unsalted nuts
Bagel with cream cheese	Fresh fruit
Wheat Thins with Cheez Whiz	Celery with peanut butter
Reese's Peanut Butter Cup	Reese's Peanut Butter Cup

You don't have to be Julia Child to fix well-balanced meals. Grab some bags of frozen vegetables, stick a chicken in the oven, et voilà! Dinner! Don't forget to let your family help with dinner; you don't have to do it all by yourself. Ask for help and delegate those chores.

Hurry up and get some rest

When you're young, you don't want to take a nap because when you close your eyes, you know you'll miss out on something great. As adults, however, most of us would pay cash for an opportunity to take a nap. And in a society where the majority of people are walking around with sleep deprivation, you must make a point to schedule a nap.

As a parent, you owe it to your kids and your partner to be well rested. If you can, lie down and rest when your kids do. But don't try to get them to nap when you're sleepy. That just doesn't work. Don't stay up and watch *The Late Show with David Letterman* when you know you're going to have to get up in four hours to feed the baby.

Some parents say, "Oh, I just can't miss the late news." What they really mean is that the late news is more important to them than their rest. They don't care that they're tired and unproductive the next day. They also don't care that they don't have the energy to have a tea party or color with their kids for a while. As a parent, you must do what is called being bigger, wiser, and stronger, and that isn't always what's most fun.

Some parents say they don't have enough time during the day to get everything done, so they think that taking a nap is a waste of time. That is exactly why you need everyone's help in cleaning, cooking, and taking care of your kids. Acknowledge that housework will never be completely done, and that someone always will dirty a dish or want to be fed. And don't worry so much that you won't get to everything during the day. There's always tomorrow.

Don't Neglect Your Mate

Pick up any magazine in the grocery store, and you'll find at least one heading that says *How to keep the romance alive* **or** *Take our survey, are you a good kisser?* **or** *Is beer more important to him than you are?* A hidden rule that you as a parent must follow is that you must be good to yourself. If you feel good about who you are, your children will learn to feel good about themselves. Remember, your kids learn by example. If you're happy and laughing and having a grand old time with your partner, your children also have a better chance of becoming happy people.

On top of everything else that you have to consider and work on as a parent, you must also remember that your partner needs love and attention too. Once people have kids, they tend to take their relationships for granted. Relationships tend to fall into the coexisting stage as opposed to one that is still growing and developing.

The most important thing a father can do for his children is to love their mother. — Theodore M. Hesburgh

What you need to do is:

✔ **Go on dates.**

Make it just you two. You don't have to spend money on dinner and a movie. Walk around the mall, go to a free concert in the park, go play tennis, cruise to Tahiti (no wait, that would cost a few bucks). Do something together without the kids. If your lives are so busy that three weeks have gone by and you haven't done anything yet, get a calendar and write it down, schedule it. Make a rule that if it's on the calendar, neither of you can back out. And while you're out, try to avoid the usual conversations about children and work. Instead, talk about your hopes and fears and regrets. You know your partner drinks a double latte with sugar-free vanilla every morning, but do you know his most embarrassing moment or her biggest regret in life?

✔ **Get physical.**

Yes, once upon a time you both used to have sex together — and at the same time. This may be another activity that you'll have to write down on the calendar. I know that sounds really unromantic, but if scheduling sex is the only way you can work it in your schedule, then by all means, schedule it. Flirt with each other all day. Don't forget to hug and give kisses and all the other lovey-dovey stuff you used to do when you were trying to win each other over during your dating days. And if you're really pressed for time, then just touch. Holding hands, kissing, and cuddling on the couch are fun and important.

✔ **E-mail or journal to each other.**

Sending each other notes throughout the day via e-mail can be fun. If you're not a computer junky, then keep a journal where you both can post notes to each other. Include separate wish lists in your messages. Giving someone something that they ask for is great caring behavior: "Please let me sleep in tomorrow morning for 15 minutes." "I'd love it if you brought me home Mint Milano cookies tonight." That way, when you want to do something special for the other person, you'll have a whole list of things they like.

✔ **Create rituals.**

Make dinner together every night. Go for a walk after dinner. Get up early for coffee so you're without kids and interruptions. Make the 25th of every month your official date night.

✔ **Remember the important words.**

Acknowledging that your spouse is special is an imperative. One way you can do this is through the words that you use. Don't ever, and I mean ever, say, "Well I don't need to tell him/her that I love him/her. He/She already knows." That is such bull. If anything, your children need to hear that you love each other. Besides, if you don't profess your love to your mate, how do you know whether you're remembering to tell your children that you love them? Helping your partner feel appreciated and loved is important, but you must first know the terminology he or she needs to hear to feel that way. You can say, "Gee you look hot tonight," thinking that really makes your partner feel great, but in reality, such a comment may offend your partner. Your first step is finding out what your partner likes to hear. Sit down and ask the vital question, "What do you like to hear that makes you feel appreciated or loved?" Don't be surprised when you get a puzzled look for a response. You may even be asked "What did you just ask me?" or, "Don't you know?" You're not asking a typical question, but I'm hoping that it becomes more popular. I love hearing that I'm a good mom, that I look nice, and that I smell good. I also love hearing things like "How can I help you right now?" and "Would you like to have a date?" Just because Dan (that's my husband — and editor) and I are married doesn't mean that I don't like being asked out on a date. And using the word "date" is special for me.

It's healthy for your kids to know that you have a life outside of and away from them and that you're more than just Mom and Dad.

Don't feel guilty about wanting to spend time alone. Your children will discover that you both love each other, want your relationship to grow, and that neither of you takes each other for granted.

Let's Behave, Shall We?

Everything that you and your partner do together sends a message to your children. If you're loving, kind, and fair to each other, that's how they learn to act with their siblings, friends, and in the future, their partners. They will also learn how to deal with conflict and fighting based on how you handle it.

Communicating honestly

Keeping your communication with your partner open and honest, saying that you're tired, unhappy, upset, sleepy, happy, grumpy, dopey, or whatever is okay. Don't feel as if you must try to hide disappointment or anger. Find out how to handle and resolve these feelings. The best part of being honest in communications is discovering that your upsetness or unhappiness is your own. Your partner is vital in helping you resolve your issues by helping you to talk out what and why something bothers you.

Avoid the temptation to blame your partner for your feelings. If you're mad, then those feelings are your own, and your partner isn't to be blamed for them. Your partner may have done something that triggered your anger, but it still is your anger and your problem. Rather than point fingers and say "you did this," look back at yourself and try to figure out why their actions made you mad.

Fun things to do with your mate

Here are some fun things to do with your mate if you're struggling with creative ideas to keep that flame burning:

- Take bubble baths together with lighted candles. You can share a bottle of Diet Coke. (Okay, wine may be a little more romantic, but don't get drunk in the tub.)

- Write each other love notes and hide them in places the other is sure to find them.

- Go out with another couple. Having other adult company is fun. All that you'll end up doing is, of course, talking about your kids.

- Don't forget how much fun staying at home can be. Order takeout food, light candles, listen to music, and cuddle on the couch (maybe even a little smooching would be nice).

- Send the kids to the neighbors and give each other massages.

- Go to bed early and try to remember what you did to make those kids in the first place.

How you handle your feelings shows your kids how they handle their feelings. More important, they need to know how to behave when they have the same kind of feelings and how to make themselves feel better.

Alexander and the Terrible, Horrible, No Good, Very Bad Day by Judith Viorst (Macmillan Publishing) is a good book to read to your kids about having bad days. After all, we all have them.

Arguing in front of your kids is all right as long as you keep it a clean and honest fight. No throwing things, no cursing, no yelling, no sarcasm, and no low punches (bringing up situations or events that don't belong in this argument, but may belong in some other one). From the example you set, your kids learn that you may not agree with someone, but that doesn't mean that you don't love that person. Going through life thinking that every time you had an argument with someone the relationship was over would be awful. The key to arguing is enabling your children to see that, one, it's okay to have disagreements, and two, you've both come to a happy conclusion and that you've kissed and made up.

One of the best things you can do for your relationship is to stop pointing fingers at people when you're upset and angry. Look at yourself to find out why something made you mad. If your partner drinks from the milk carton, and you get angry, then it's your problem that you got angry. Talk to your partner and allow him to help you figure out why this bothers you. And if your partner is truly listening, he won't drink from the carton again.

What counts in making a happy marriage is not so much how compatible you are, but how you deal with incompatibility. — George Levinger

Children-based arguments

Keep arguments or disagreements about your children private. Even though it's okay for them to know that you have disagreements, they don't need to hear the back-and-forth arguments that their parents have about them. They'll use this information against you both later on (that is, of course, if they're old enough to understand what you're saying).

Whenever you find yourself heading into a child-based argument, call for a timeout, which means that you pick a time to start the conversation again when you can be alone with your partner.

Parents rely so much on their mates that when a relationship isn't going so well, any breakdown falls over into the relationships they have with their children.

Surviving Single Parenting

I'm going to step out on a limb and risk offending those who have chosen to be single parents or those who are thinking they can do this on their own. If you can avoid single parenting, then please do. Regardless of what job you're trying to do, having help makes things easier, and this is especially true with parenting. God created us so that it takes a man and woman to make a baby. Parenting is designed to have a man and woman take care of the child. Women help children develop communication and nurturing skills, and fathers help kids develop social and interactive play skills.

The bad part of single parenting is that you don't have anyone to help you. Doing it on your own means that you don't have that backup person to help you parent when you're ill or tired from a long day at work. You must do all the disciplining, punishing, cleaning, cooking, washing . . . and the list goes on.

The good news is that not all single-parent families have bad experiences or negative results. To make single parenting successful for you, consider the sections that follow.

Accepting your responsibility

People who tend to be successful with single parenting have a tendency to openly accept their responsibilities and challenges. They neither minimize nor exaggerate any of the problems, but rather they seek solutions on how to work with their situation.

Being committed to a family environment

Family environments are important for the growth of healthy children. Make this your first priority, which means that you must think of the needs of your child first.

Using good management skills

You must be able to manage your family by being organized and work with many schedules so that nothing gets lost and you don't become overwhelmed with responsibilities.

"My co-parent has serious issues" — Dr. Tim

Don't get me wrong: I love my wife, and we enjoy many rich experiences as co-parents. But the mother of my children sometimes does some really bone-headed things! Of course, I immediately give her the advice and wisdom that can only come from a seasoned clinical child psychologist. But does she listen? No! In fact, she's downright rude: "I bet you don't talk to your clients that way!" And she has no clue about logical reasoning: "I am not wrong. I don't know why I'm not wrong, but I am not wrong." What do you say to that?

On the other hand, you also need to know that I sometimes am utterly amazed by this woman (and not just during lapses in my pomposity). Her manner, her instincts, and her vision as a parent — though different from my own — are priceless gifts that she continually shares with our children and with me.

As parents, how can we appreciate the gifts of our partners — before we strangle them out of frustration! Better communication skills? Maybe. Better scheduling? Definitely. Let me explain.

When our three children were all under the age of 5 (and we were making the proverbial shift from man-to-man to zone coverage), we went out every Friday night. We knew that on this one night someone else — a trusted baby sitter — would bathe them and put them to bed. This was a night when we had the energy and time and desire to be with each other. This was a night when we didn't feel exhausted and frustrated by things we hadn't finish or discussed.

So, what did we do on these Friday nights? First, let me tell you what we did *not* do (or only rarely did). We did not go out with other couples. We did not go to the movies. And we did not go to many parties. We wanted to enjoy *our* time together, and we needed to reconnect as a couple, to huddle as a team, and to make plans for the coming week. This usually meant long, slow dinners at a place known more for its quiet atmosphere and understanding servers than for its fine cuisine.

Imagine what happens when co-parents don't have time to huddle. They try to squeeze in a micro-discussion here or there, which often results in only one person being heard (if that) and little being resolved when they have a difference of opinion. And what happens if the issues become emotionally charged? (For example, "When are you going to make that kid mind you?" or "You have no idea how much I do for these kids?" or "You spent how much?") The pattern that typically emerges is what marital therapists call *demand-withdraw:* One partner makes a demand, and the other withdraws — emotionally, mentally, and sometimes physically. For years, marital therapists thought the main problem with demand-withdraw was a deficit in communication skills. However, they're now finding that training these couples to communicate better often means more clearly articulated resentment!

Be realistic about circumstances that enable the two of you to listen to each other, to show a fondness for each other, and to plan together. If you're realistic about those circumstances, then you'll probably discover that team building won't happen unless it's scheduled.

Find the thing that makes parenting the hardest for you and deal with it. The lack of help and support may be that one thing, so work to solve that problem:

✔ Enroll your children in Big Brothers/Big Sisters.

✔ Ask your family (if available) to spend time with your kids.

✔ Find a play group for your children. They'll get to interact with other children, and you'll get to interact with other parents.

✔ Join organizations that encourage family togetherness. Examples are family sports (a Gymboree class for toddlers, snow skiing for older kids), religious groups, volunteer programs (feeding the homeless), and so on.

If you have plenty of support, but you don't seem to have the time you want to spend with your children, try:

✔ Hiring someone to help with housework once a week, once a month, or whatever you can afford.

✔ Teaching your children to help with housework and cooking. Kids are great at ripping lettuce apart.

✔ Creating an exchange program with friends in which everyone takes a turn cooking dinner (or cleaning for the others) one day a week.

✔ Going home from work when it's time. The pressure to do well at work is even stronger when you know that you don't have another income to fall back on. But you still have a responsibility to your kids to go home and be with them.

Being a single parent is a choice for many people. For others, it isn't a choice, but rather it's something they have to deal with. Whatever your situation, remember your first priority is your children. Good luck.

Chapter 3

Being a Consistent Parent

*T*he *Parenting Game* is played on a huge game board. But it has no squares! Your kids can just run wherever they want. In fact, that's the rule they play by: Run amok. Your job as parent is steering them, guiding them as if little squares existed for them to move across. When you start doing that stuff, you'd better keep it up. That's called being consistent.

Consistency requires hard work. Kids will power-up the charm to get you to break. They'll smile. They'll cry. They'll toss tantrums like the pizza man flipping a pie. As long as you don't waver, the result will be well-behaved children, not brats. (All of your kids' future teachers will appreciate that fact. So will your neighbors, family, and friends.) Basically, anyone who meets your kids will be pretty grateful to you.

Ground Rules for Consistency

Before you can practice your never-ending goal of being a consistent parent, you must set the rules and boundaries for yourself. Yourself? Yes, never mind the kids! They have their own kid-like rules and behave like kids no matter what. Sure, they can be trained, and they eventually understand how to function in society. Rushing them isn't part of your job. No, the rules and boundaries that you set are for you. You're the one who needs to be the consistent parent. Your kids already know how to be consistent; they're kids!

So when you set rules and boundaries, start with yourself by:

- Understanding your child's behavior so you know what they can and cannot deal with.

- Providing a reliable yet real boundary.

- Setting rules for your child while accepting that they are, in fact, children.

- Providing consistency by ensuring that your rules are realistic for your child.

Now you're ready to set the customary limits, like:

- Where your children are allowed to play.

- What kind of behavior is allowed with a big understanding that kids like to play like kids. They don't play like adults (meaning orderly and quietly).

- What your children can play with.

You get the idea. After you've set these rules (and you've made sure they're realistic), you consistently enforce them.

Consistency requires you to be as ignorant today as you were a year ago.
— Bernard Berenson

Where Your Child Is Allowed to Play

Babies' play areas are limited. So decide carefully where that is. You can't allow your children to play in the bathroom one day, and then decide the next day that it's too dangerous to be in there (which it is).

As your children grow older, you can start slowly expanding their territory. This territory depends largely on your house, yard, and neighborhood. If you live in the heart of New York City, your child's territory is different from children who live out in the sticks of Northern Idaho.

You must also keep in mind some basic understandings of child play. Children play like children. They explore, they get loud, and they aren't born understanding boundaries as in where to go or what is okay to play with and what isn't. Therefore,

- You need to keep an eye on them, ensuring that they don't get hurt or wander off.

- You're an idiot if you take them to a fancy restaurant and expect them to "behave." In other words, don't put them in an environment where their natural behavior isn't allowed.

> ✔ You need to provide a safe environment for them. Electrical sockets are closed, hot curling irons are out of the way, fireplaces are blocked off, small LEGO toys are put away so babies don't eat them. This list goes on and is covered more in Chapter 20.

What kind of behavior is allowed

Behavior that you need to keep an eye on is anything harmful to others, like hitting and throwing toys. The same goes for any behavior that is harmful to your children. For example, temper tantrums, believe it or not, aren't always bad. Temper tantrums are a true release of frustrations and anger, and I'm guessing, they feel pretty good to your child. Just don't ever give in to a temper tantrum, or you'll end up encouraging your child to continue with this unacceptable behavior until old age sets in. If you ignore tantrums, children eventually get to the point where they don't want to put that much energy into them, and they stop. No, tantrums are fine unless your child starts banging his head against the floor. (That's an activity that needs to be stopped.)

Don't sabotage your child by putting him in an environment where he can't act the way he's supposed to. Fancy restaurants, weddings and funerals, live theater, and movies are a few places where the environment is typically quiet. Children aren't quiet, and getting them to be quiet takes a lot of practice.

What your children can play with

Everything your children see is a potential toy — buttons, coins, balloons, and candy. You name it, and it has toy potential. Now, out of the things just mentioned, which ones do you think are dangerous for small children to play with? All of them. Babies and toddlers have an annoying habit of putting everything in their mouths, regardless of the taste, because that's their way of exploring. Buttons, coins, balloons, and candy are things babies typically choke on.

Similarly, you don't allow playing with the stereo one day, and then get mad the next day when you catch a child resetting your treble and bass knobs or your teen keeps changing channels with the remote control. You don't stop emphasizing a behavior one day, and then turning your back on it the next day, acting like you don't see it. You should always handle these situations so that children know what they can do and what they can't do.

Be critical in your decisions about what your children can play with. For more information about safety and house rules, see to Chapter 20.

Consistency Is the Art of Being an Unbending Jerk

Nobody suspects that gravity is evil. It's just there. (It's constant. It never gives up.) And it proves that to you all the time. Drop that brick on your toe, and, well, it's gravity again telling you to be more careful next time. Fall out of a window? Hey, gravity pulls you down every time. Gravity won't kill you; it's the sudden stop that does.

As parents, you must be as consistent as gravity. Never yield. This policy is tough, and I'm sure gravity has a hard time of it, too. But gravity is always there, giving its gentle pull to keep us all on the ground.

Then again, don't be a jerk and set unrealistic expectations for your child. It's easier to be consistent when you've set rules and guidelines that are simple and make sense. Don't put temptation in front of your children, like an open electrical socket, and expect them to follow the rules of not sticking a toy in it. They're naturally being themselves when wanting to stick things in holes. Face it, it's fun!

If you've never been hated by your child, you've never been a parent.
— Bette Davis

Make your words the law

Gravity is a law, but it carries no punishment for lawbreakers because everyone obeys (although floating off into the vacuum of space is very threatening). So gravity's reward for being consistent is that no one breaks its law. The other positive aspects are that we don't float off into space, and things tend to stay in our pockets.

As a parent, however, if you practice being consistent, consistency will be its own reward. Two simple rules to follow are

✔ **Think before you say something.**

Being consistent is hard when you say something goofy or something that you don't mean. As long as you've taken the time to consider your words, you need only to avoid the major weapon your child has to battle your consistency. And that is *persistence*. Children can be persistent with their whining and their demands. It's what they do. Just don't let it get to you so much that you end up saying something you can't follow through with. Remember, you still must be consistent and follow through with what you say.

Yes, thinking before you dish out some pleasant threat is hard while you're stuck in traffic with a car full of wild and untamed children. Screaming, after all, is just so much easier. But, if that sounds like a situation you've been in, or will be in, check out Chapter 5, "The Art of Keeping Your Cool."

Maintaining consistency also applies to your general nature. Most people have mood swings. You know, off days where nothing seems to go right. As adults, we usually let other people's moody days roll off our backs. Kids, however, take your bad moods personally. Living with a schizophrenic can't be fun, so don't make your kids feel like they're living with one.

✔ **Make your rules realistic.**

You can't be consistent on a rule that is set before it was really thought through — or on a rule that you would like to set but that just doesn't jibe with having kids around.

For example, you may want to establish the rule that all toys are kept in your children's rooms. But reality sets in, and you realize that such a rule is impossible to enforce, because your kids spend all their free time in the family room. So, rethink your rule. Maybe it would be better that all toys are to be picked up before anyone goes to bed. (That may be a more realistic rule, anyway.)

Stick to your words or suffer the sad consequences

When you make the rules, make them stick. An hour's punishment is an hour long. That's 60 minutes, or 3,600 seconds (and a whole bunch of nanoseconds). The instant you give in, the punishment becomes less effective and your kids have won. So, when you make a rule, make it stick.

"Johnny, why don't you tell the parents what their kids have won?"

"Well, Jack, for the rest of their lives, the kids will be little jerks! Brats! That's right, they know the unbreakable laws of their parents can be broken. And if it can be done once, it can be done again. And if it can be done at home, it can be done at school, at work, for the rest of their lives! That's the grand prize for playing and losing the consistency round of *The Parenting Game*!"

This really isn't about parents winning and kids losing. No! It's about setting guidelines for your kids so they are safe. And it's about teaching them that they can trust what you say. Kids want and need stability and consistency. Therefore, be consistent. Let your word be the law: Think before you make the law. Make the law realistic. Then stick to it, even at the price of being a creep. Remember, no one has been a parent who hasn't felt a child's hate (at least for a little while).

When your kids know that you're not going to stick to your word, you've become part of a parent death wish. Your children will be running your life (which is more painful than bikini waxing). That's the definition of a spoiled child — not one who has too many toys. So, when you make a rule, make it stick.

Please don't raise your kids to be brats. America will thank you for it.

Cuteness and Persistence: The Art of Breaking Your Consistency

Thrusting your jaw forward is easy. Just point your chin to the sun and announce to the heavens that you'll be consistent from this point forward. And you probably mean it. But you should count on confronting two formidable weapons in a child's arsenal against you: cuteness and persistence. A third maneuver that your child will use is pointing out your flaws when you set unrealistic expectations. Ooooohh.

Don't discount these weapons. They're mighty nuclear missiles compared to your vow with your Creator to be consistent. History has shown that kids not only use these weapons, but also adapt their weapons to deal with new situations. So you must strengthen your resolve.

"I'm too precious for your feeble attempt at consistency"

The first several months of your children's lives you spend telling them how utterly cute they are. They're angels. They're cuddly. They're aware of this, and store that knowledge for use in the future, when they can also use their countenances to pour on the charm. "Watch me light up Mommy like a Christmas tree." This is a learned behavior taught by us as parents, and children can put it to good use.

When the time comes to be firm and consistent, think before you speak. You say what you mean. (It's the law, right?) But then comes the charmer. Out pops the boo-boo lip. Eyes swell with tears. Emotional pain contorts the face. "How could you do such a thing to me when I live to love you?"

This is emotional warfare! It has a purpose, primarily to make you give in and part from being consistent.

A consistent disciplinarian — Dr. Tim

How do you know whether you're being consistent in discipline? That can be a tough question because of the different kinds of consistency that exist.

One kind of consistency involves disciplining in the same way as that of a co-parent, which is consistency *between parents*. For example, do two parents have similar strategies for handling children's misbehavior?

A second kind of consistency involves using the same disciplinary approach each time children misbehave, which is consistency *over time*. For example, do parents discipline the same way on Tuesday that they do on Friday?

A third kind of consistency involves using the same disciplinary approach for each instance of a particular misbehavior, which is consistency *across behavior*. For example, do parents respond the same way each time their child hits someone?

Can you guess which kind of consistency is most important? I'll give you a hint: It is the kind that is easiest to implement.

If you guessed consistency across behavior, you guessed correctly. At its core, discipline teaches right from wrong, what is moral and immoral. Parents may differ from each other in their styles of discipline, and they may not be entirely consistent in how they respond day in and day out — these inconsistencies are understandable and rather minor — but when parents are not consistent in disciplining their children for serious misbehavior, the costs can be great.

Inconsistency creeps into discipline because parents inadvertently pursue "lessons" that are unimportant or unclear. For example, some parents use discipline to "teach" children what behaviors are allowed when parents are in a good mood and what behaviors are allowed when parents are in a bad mood.

In my clinical work, I ask parents to make a short list of misbehaviors (five or fewer) that can serve as a disciplinary guide. I discourage them from including catchall behaviors like "disobedient" or "disrespectful." I ask them to imagine taking disciplinary action *each and every time* their child commits one of the misbehaviors on their lists. If they say it isn't possible, I have them shorten the list. Through this exercise, parents learn that focusing their energy on a small set of misbehaviors is the most feasible and helpful kind of consistent discipline.

This declaration of emotional war is the point where you can't give in. Don't give in! No matter what!

Remember, *you* thought of the law first. You set out to be consistent, so keep with it. Don't change your mind.

The most amazing part of this emotional turmoil is that your kids don't really know they're doing this. The turmoil is all yours. Kids just are being true to themselves. They know what they want, and in their world, they truly think they deserve it. Kids are honest and brilliant and haven't been made to understand that crying because you didn't get a third cookie is unacceptable.

Goofy rules set by anal-retentive parents

Goofy rules sometimes slip out of our mouths before we think things through. And before reality has set in, we add some ludicrous consequences that we couldn't possibly enforce.

- ✔ Candy will be eaten neatly, or you'll never eat candy again.

- ✔ There will be no drooling on the furniture, or you won't be allowed to sit on the furniture.

- ✔ Poopy diapers are not allowed to overflow, or I won't change your diaper — ever!

- ✔ Children will always be in bed and asleep by 7 p.m. or no more TV.

- ✔ Children will clean all the food off their plates or no dessert.

Your kids rely on you to be consistent. Don't let them down even though sticking to your guns can appear like just the opposite. If you give in, not only do you lose, but so does the charmer.

Loving a child doesn't mean giving in to all his whims; to love him is to bring out the best in him, to teach him to love what is difficult. — Nadia Boulanger

"Give me persistence, and I'll carve Mount Rushmore with a spoon"

Inconsistent parents are the perfect foil. You tell your child that if he chooses to throw food across the table then he won't get any dessert. He chooses poorly and throws the food anyway. Okay, no dessert. That's final. None.

Then the imp decides to clean his room or do some other chore you've been nagging him for and — lo — a sweet-faced angel asks you for dessert. Don't waver! Your answer is still "No." Your child made the choice to throw the food (or whatever the choice was). It was his choice so now the consequences of that choice must be allowed to happen.

Persistence is the art of doing something again and again, maybe with subtle changes between repetitions, but nevertheless, again and again. Ever wonder why kids continue to ask, again and again, even after you say "No?" Because they perceive some remote chance that you'll change your mind. Why? Because, maybe, just perhaps, at some time in the past, you changed your mind. That's the payoff of persistent effort.

You must be constant! Don't let persistence wear you thin, because when you break down, everyone loses. You lose because the kids know how to get to you, and they lose because they need your constancy to keep them from developing brathood.

Give yourself more resolve to handle these situations wisely by:

- ✒ Thinking before you talk.
- ✒ Giving your child a choice: "Stop this behavior or this will happen."
- ✒ Reminding your child that he had a choice, but by not stopping, he chose, instead, to accept the punishment.

Your kids will continue testing you, but they won't spend as much time doing it when they realize that you don't go back on your word or succumb to whining and temper tantrums. After all, why bother when it doesn't work?

Building Walls around Your Children

Building walls for your children is important. I'm not talking about walls like Edgar Allan Poe's in *The Cask of Amontillado*. No one who loves their children would do that — build brick walls around them in their basement. (Poe was sick!) Instead, these walls are mental barriers erected to keep your kids safe and you sane.

You build the walls by setting rules. The rules are designed to keep your children safe and happy. For example, you set rules against climbing on things and throwing, and rules on how to behave around Grandma, how to act in the store, and how to treat siblings. These rules form walls around your children. But your kids will constantly push against the walls. They'll always test you, and they do this for two reasons:

- ✒ **They need to know where the walls are.**

  This knowledge makes them feel secure. Therefore, you must erect the walls and keep your kids within them if you want secure kids.

- ✒ **They push because they need to grow.**

  Your children can't always have the rule not to play outside unsupervised. Eventually they outgrow that rule — the same way they outgrow rules on naptimes and what they're allowed to play with.

Eventually you move the walls outward. But don't lower the walls — kids need them there. Instead, move them out, setting a later bedtime and changing the off-limits rules. And be consistent about it. Maybe even announce a change and say why: "You've done such a good job of turning off the TV after watching it, we think you're old enough and responsible enough to use the VCR by yourself now."

Moving walls outward is a delicate process that can cause stress with younger siblings. Changing the bedtime schedule, for example, is best done in private so that other children don't moan and complain, "That's not fair!"

Never interpret your kids' pushing against the walls as a reason for taking the walls down. Kids push, but they rely on your consistency. You must be consistent and keep those walls up for them to be secure, happy people. They get some sadistic pleasure in testing you, but they really do like for you to set their boundaries and have you enforce them.

As your children grow older and become more responsible, the more you can let the walls out and enable them to do more things. But even then, they'll still push.

Chapter 4

Following Through

- -

In This Chapter

▶ Learning about follow-through

▶ Making your life easier by following through

▶ Being careful what you say

▶ Discovering the importance of timeliness

- -

"**I**'m going to give you to the count of three, and then you'll really be in trouble."

"Don't make me have to come after you."

"If you do that one more time, you'll be sorry."

Do these statements sound familiar? Maybe your parents didn't use any of them on you, but you've heard them. These are threats of sorts. They're meant to *scare* kids into proper behavior. Do they work? Not really. They may work temporarily, but not overall.

As an adult, if you had someone as big and tall as you are to your kids threaten you like this, wouldn't you listen? Then what is it that kids know that we don't? Could it be that they've heard these threats before and realize that nothing's going to happen? That's why this chapter is about *follow-through,* which is related in a weird way to *consistency.*

Follow Through with What?

Follow-through has three parts:

✔ Think of the situation before you act and talk.

✔ When you tell your children you're going to do something, be it good or bad, you do it.

✔ When you punish or discipline your children, you follow through with the discipline, and then you follow up with your child to ensure that she understands why she was disciplined.

Are any of these situations worth getting in a tizzy about? No, not really. Kids make sense. Take the time to find out what their sense is.

Think of the situation before you act and talk

This is also known as picking your fights. Children, in their world, make sense. They know why they do things and why it makes sense to do them. They don't always have the verbal skills to explain this to you, but they do make sense.

Before you go barking orders and dealing out punishments, try finding out why your child is doing what she is doing, and ultimately, you are responsible for her doing it. For example, your child is playing with the apples in the grocery store. This isn't her fault, really. It's yours. You probably put the cart too close to the apples in the first place. Your child's job is to explore, so she's not at fault for doing what children do.

Say you're walking into the living room and your child has all the cushions and pillows off the couch. Before you go ballistic, find out why. She probably has a really good reason. Either a lost toy or the beginning construction stages of a great ship.

"I said I would do it, and I'm going to"

Children need to know that if you say you're going to do something, you do it. That way they can trust what you say — and trust that you're a reliable person. This trust works for good and bad situations.

When you promise to get your children a treat at the store if they clean their rooms, you give them something to work toward. They know you're going to buy them that treat. When, on the other hand, you tell your children that if they start hitting each other, they'll have their toys taken away for the rest of the night, they'll understand you mean that, too.

Promising to do something (whether it be good or bad) and never doing it, makes you look like a flake, even to your kids. Your children need to trust and believe what you say. If they can't trust their parents, they grow up with trust issues the rest of their lives, which spills over into their relationships forever.

"Now, did you learn anything from this?"

Follow-through after punishment and discipline consists of three different but related situations. To be completely effective, you need to follow each of these steps:

1. **When you see your children doing something wrong, give them a choice to stop the action or behavior.**

   Let them know there is a consequence for choosing to continue with the activity. Don't turn your head and pretend you didn't see it.

2. **If your children choose to continue with the activity, you follow up by enforcing the punishment that you told them you would enforce if they continued with the activity.**

3. **You then follow up by making sure that your children understand why they were punished for what they did.**

   Punishment is not effective when your children don't learn anything from it.

Punishing your children without explaining why they're being punished is extremely ineffective. And never assume that what your children have just done is obviously wrong to them. Remember, kids make sense to themselves, and sometimes your rules don't make sense to them. Children often are oblivious to whether they've done anything wrong. That is why you give them a choice for their behavior.

Discipline and punishment must be used as a form of education. You discipline your children so they learn right from wrong. You punish them for the same reason. For more about punishment and discipline, see Chapter 26.

"Parents must get across the idea that 'I love you always, but sometimes I do not love your behavior.'" — Amy Vanderbilt

Are you ready to try follow-through?

You find your son taking the claw end of the hammer and ripping chunks of wood out of your deck. You tell him that if he continues with this behavior, as a punishment, he can't watch television for a week. So ultimately, the choice is his; either tear up the deck and no television or leave the deck alone and have television.

The follow-up action is to forbid him to watch television if he chooses the deck destruction process. If he comes home from school the next day and switches on *Batman*, and you let him watch it, you've failed. You didn't follow through. You're not being reliable. You're flaking out. So now your son thinks that because he basically got away with the hammer deal, maybe he can try the hammer out on your new car. That should be tons of fun.

Your kids are better behaved when they know their choices and they know that when you say you're going to do something, you mean it and actually do it. You don't give false warnings, and you don't make wimpy threats that you know you aren't going to make happen.

Avoid the common blurt, "You know better than that!" Yeah, maybe they do, but how do you know for sure they know better? It may seem to make sense that they would know better, but what's the point of bringing something like this up? Your job is not to shame your child, but to get him to think before he acts.

I've Followed Through, Now My Life Is Easy!

Your life becomes a heavenly bliss when your kids get to the point where they understand when you say you're going to do something, you do it. You don't make threats and you don't give 20 warnings.

You'll stop chasing your kids after the same violations when they know that you follow through with the punishment that you say you're going to give.

Understand that training your kids to follow your direction takes time. It's a learning process for them. It may take several episodes of punishing your children for doing something you've told them not to do before they get the idea that it just isn't worth it. Then again, your children may catch on quickly. A lot has to do with that stubbornness gene that kids tend to inherit from their parents.

Testing you is the job of your children. Don't be surprised when your children try to get away with something. It's just their way of making your life a little more interesting.

Watch Your Mouth!

Too many parents enjoy hearing themselves say things like, "Ginger, if you don't stop kicking the back of my chair, I'm going to rip your legs off." Do you think the parents really mean it? I hope not. So, if you don't believe it, your child won't either. Your child learns to stop believing threats. I'm not saying that you should start ripping your children's legs off, but rather that you should be careful what you're saying. Make sure that you do what you say you're going to do and that you mean what you say. Parents like to hear themselves make goofy threats. It actually sounds kind of funny, and the kids probably laugh at the very thought. But you know they aren't taking you seriously.

Please keep in mind that your kids make sense. It's up to you to find out what their sense is. If your child is kicking your chair, your first job is finding out whether it's because their legs are short and consequently that's where they happen to fall or whether they're simply trying to get your attention. Kids are not evil. They are not out to irritate you. Find out the reasoning behind their actions before you jump into discipline mode.

Timeliness — It's Oh-So-Important

Kids' memories are fairly short, so when you say you're going to do something, you must act quickly on it. Don't put off discipline or punishment for another day. It's okay to allow yourself some time to gather your thoughts, perhaps even to calm down some — and forget about threatening to send your kids to military school (unless, of course, you really, really mean it).

Don't put off punishment. Your kids will have forgotten what happened if it takes a week after they threw the trash off the balcony (and didn't pick it up) before you decide to do something about it.

Unrealistic threats

Blah, blah, blah. Parents, please, think before you talk. If you issue threats like the ones on this list, your kids will quickly learn to ignore you. Not good training, if you ask me.

- If you don't start cleaning your room, you'll be grounded for a year!

- If you don't get your homework done, I'll never let you out of your room!

- I'll beat you to a bloody pulp if you . . . .

- If you don't behave, we'll never take you outside again.

- I'll never buy you another toy for as long as you live if you. . . .

- Eat everything on your plate, or I'll never feed you again.

Threats are hard to follow through with because they're usually unrealistic and impossible to enforce. If you threaten your child that you'll never take him back to a restaurant, that means you'll never get to go back to that restaurant unless you get a babysitter. Is that what you *really* meant to say?

The purpose of follow-through is so that your kids can rely on what you say. They also discover that their actions have consequences. If you threaten to punish them for something, and you don't do it, you may as well not say anything in the first place.

Chapter 5

The Art of Keeping Your Cool

••

••

Patience? Oh yes, I'm very patient. People who take 40 items to the 15-item express line in the grocery store don't bother me. The drive-through guy who always gets my order wrong doesn't ruin my day. I even laugh at rush hour. Ha! It's a joke!

So why does it drive me nuts that my toddler keeps kicking the back of my seat in my car? Why do I drool at the mouth like a mad dog if my kids don't get in the car like I ask? Why do these things bother me?

Finding Your Inner Coolness

At some point in your childless earlier life, you may have had patience. Or, so you thought. But how are you going to act when you find that your 3-year-old daughter has just emptied a whole bottle of perfume all over herself and has smeared lipstick (not the inexpensive Cover Girl kind, but the expensive Borghese kind) completely over her face, your walls, and maybe even the cat who happened to get in her way, all for the sake of being pretty like Mommy? Do you:

1. Lose all the color from your face, whisk your daughter up, and throw her into the bathtub?

2. Say, "Don't you look pretty. How about we get you all cleaned up? The next time you play dress up, why don't you ask me, and I'll help you?"

3. Look at your daughter, heave a sigh, and then turn around and leave?

If you're sitting there scratching your head, the answer is number two.

Number one is for those parents who don't have any patience, failing to see the humor in the situation. Number three is a lost case. These people are obviously at their wit's end and don't even want to deal with the situation. Parents who chose number two are dealing with their daughter in a calm, relaxed way — at the same time getting the point across that their daughter ought not do this again without supervision.

Being impatient means you will eventually do something foolish.
— Old Japanese proverb

Not having patience may stem somewhat from your own upbringing. Your parents may not have had much patience, so you weren't able to learn from them. Although your inner "coolness" is there just waiting to come out, maybe it can't because of things you're overlooking, such as:

- ✔ Your attitude
- ✔ Understanding the reasoning behind the action
- ✔ How you feel
- ✔ Unrealistic expectations
- ✔ Feeling rushed or hurried

Your attitude may need fine-tuning

Having patience begins with your attitude. If you're a perfectionist, now is the time to get over it. Not until your kids are grown and out of the house will everything be sane, clean, and in order (at least not all at the same time). When you can adopt the attitude that it's all going to be okay — and you can deal with it for about 18 years — you're ahead of the game.

Wisdom is learning what to overlook. — Will James

Don't take things too seriously. Allow kids to be kids and do the goofy things that they're supposed to do. That means they're going to make messes, drop and break things, spill, topple, destroy, mutilate . . . you know, be kids. The key here is not to go ballistic when these things happen. If you accept the fact that these things will happen, you won't lose your patience when they do.

Your thought for the day: I'm not going to be in a hurry today. I'm going to remain calm and relaxed. Whatever spills can be cleaned. Whatever breaks can be replaced or glued. I won't take out my anger or frustrations on my kids because I love them.

Making sense of your kids

As I mentioned in Chapter 4, your kids make sense. It's up to you to find out what *their* sense is. Doing so is one way of finding patience. When you look at your kids in a more curious manner, such as, "Wow, that was rather creative. Tell me more about why you colored on the walls," then their actions can be put into a better perspective.

You may even come to the realization that sometimes kids do things just to get *your* attention because *they* aren't getting enough of it in the first place. If that's the case, then it isn't really their fault, is it? Nope. Spend more time with your kids so they don't have to resort to drastic actions just to get your attention.

"Why don't I have more patience?"

You lose your patience because you're too tired and too stressed to find the real meaning behind your child's actions. Many parents also have a building resentment when they feel they're being overworked without any help, and they don't have enough time for themselves.

If you find yourself in this boat, work to change your life so these situations don't happen. Go to bed earlier and turn the television off. Schedule chores so everyone helps. Schedule alone time so you can reconnect with yourself.

Chapter 2 provides you with information about making the most out of having a partner to help you.

Realistic expectations

You may also lose patience because the expectations you have for your kids are unrealistic. You can't expect your 5-year-old to sit quietly through all your favorite parts of *Gone With the Wind*, nor can you expect your 1-year-old to remember to stay out of the toilet paper even though you've told him at least 50 times. He may really love toilet paper, and you may have to tell him another 50 times (along with taking the toilet paper away and moving him out of the room where the toilet paper is).

Then again, maybe that same 5-year-old always sits quietly while watching *Sesame Street*. And maybe you've only had to tell your 2-year-old to leave the litter box alone three times before he got the idea.

Don't expect your kids to listen to you the same way in all situations, and don't expect miracles from them. Parenting is much easier when you stop setting expectations that are too high.

Don't take devilish actions personally. When you tell your toddler not to do something, and he does it anyway, he's not disobeying you to make you mad. He's either young enough that his stubbornness outweighs anything you can possibly say, or he's just testing his boundaries — pushing on the walls (as described in Chapter 3). Or maybe there's a really good reason why he does something, but you've never stopped to figure it out. Realize that this behavior is typical, is to be expected, and shouldn't be taken personally.

Take responsibility

Take responsibility that your toddler got into the litter box because you didn't shut the door. I mean litter is just sand, right? And sand is meant to be played in. Your toddler doesn't know that litter box sand and beach sand are different. You have to show him.

If your child plays in the flour, then you left the flour out. If your child marks on the walls with crayons, then you left him unsupervised or didn't provide him with a coloring book or piece of paper (although, realistically, the idea of coloring on the walls just sounds cool).

I can't stress this enough that kids will get into things and eat and mark and spill and drop. It's what they do. You have to be responsible enough to create an environment where they aren't in constant trouble because you don't put things away.

"I need more time!"

Patience runs short when time runs short. Being late can drive some people insane, and they take everyone to the asylum with them. If you're that way, you can solve the problem by giving yourself plenty of time to do things and to get to places. Do as much advance planning as possible.

Never wait until the last minute to do anything. Always think ahead, planning out your time. Trying to hurry your kids can be disastrous. Whenever you tell them, "We've got to hurry," that phrase alone automatically puts them in a time lock, and they're sure to go even slower (or what may seem to you like they're moving slower).

If you know that your family has something special to do in the morning, do most of the preparations at night so little is left to do by morning. Lay out clean clothes, pack lunches, put bags by the door or already in the car, get up early so that you have time to prepare before you have to help the kids. Being calm and relaxed is easier when you aren't hurried.

Reason to chill — Dr. Tim

During the last decade, a huge, almost tectonic shift has occurred in the field of developmental psychology. At the epicenter of this shift is the question of how parenting influences children's development. For years, we've heard about the nature versus nurture debate, but that debate has had little effect on common-sense notions or psychological theories about parenting. The prevailing assumption, simply put, was that good parenting begat good kids, and bad parenting begat bad kids. This assumption not only made intuitive sense; researchers had proved it! Right? Not exactly.

What researchers had "proved" was that well-adjusted children typically grew up in homes with parents who skillfully blended warm acceptance and firm limits (and that things were not so good in the homes of poorly adjusted children). But this finding needs an explanation, and the idea that parenting has a significant and causal effect on children's development seemed a reasonable one. The problem with this explanation, aside from the fact that it is only one possible explanation, is that it fails to consider how parenting is itself a product of genetic endowment. Thus, it's possible that the causal role of parenting is more illusion than reality and, that

good parenting and good kids are caused by good genes! Indeed, some researchers argue that parenting matters very little, unless it is extreme (for example, abusive).

So the nature versus nurture debate rages on, but with a change. The "nurture" folks now must prove their case. They admit to having greatly overestimated the amount of influence parenting has on children's development, especially when it comes to intellectual ability and academic achievement. They're still betting that parenting matters, but how it matters and where it matters are likely to be more complicated than first thought.

This new way of understanding the role of parenting comes as good news and bad news for parents. The good news is that we don't have to micromanage every aspect of our children's lives. As long as we are "good enough" parents, our children will develop according to their genetic endowment, which we cannot change. The bad news is that no amount of parenting is going to transform our children into Harvard MDs or NBA point guards. So, if your children don't turn out as you'd hoped, blame it on your partner's genes!

Developing Patience in Your Child

No shortcuts exist when it comes to showing your children how to have patience. Throughout their lives, your children will face several times when really important things, like not being able to get a round toy in a square hole, are going to throw them into a fit of screaming rage.

These situations are difficult; because, as a parent, you want them to find out that they have to work things out for themselves. However, you also realize that you don't want them getting so frustrated that they quit playing with the project (or whatever it is) that has made them so upset.

Watch carefully. When your toddler is getting upset and on the verge of picking up a toy and throwing it across the room, come in and calmly help him. Reassure him that you think he's doing a good job, that sometimes people get frustrated, and that being frustrated is okay. You don't want to tell him something isn't worth getting frustrated over. That's invalidating his feelings. He's frustrated and that's his truth.

When your 6-year-old child is getting upset, let him try to work out his frustration. If he comes to you for help, talk him through his problems, yet still let him work on the project so that in the end he is the one to complete it. Lack of patience and frustration is linked heavily to kiddyhood. Your calm and reassuring manner is the best way to teach your child that no matter what happens, things can be solved calmly and with a little bit of patience.

"I Failed!"

Once I saw this mom who was the queen of patience. No matter how goofy her son was, this mom was there, never raising her voice, never seemingly annoyed. She was great! She also had to be that way only 30 minutes a week, because her name happened to be June Cleaver, you know, Beaver's mom on *Leave It to Beaver*. Fictional stories make life seem so perfect and clean. It's not!

Of all wild animals, the boy is the most unmanageable. — Plato

---

Good days to have patience

The ideal situation is to be patient and understanding every day. The real challenge is to be patient when things seem to be really getting out of control, such as the following . . .

✔ When your spouse changes the diarrhea-filled diaper on your white bedspread

✔ When your 2-year-old takes the time and effort to carefully peel an edge off the wallpaper to more easily rip off a big sheet

✔ When your 1-year-old digs in the drawer, finds an old metal cookie cutter, and leaves it on the floor for you to step on while you're barefooted

✔ When someone leaves the bathroom door open and you find your toddler unrolling an entire roll of toilet paper into the toilet

✔ When your toddler takes a pint of ice cream from the grocery bag that was set on the floor and you find it three days later behind the houseplant in the dining room

✔ When everyone under the age of 5 in the house decides what great fun throwing anything and everything down the laundry chute is

✔ When your 6-year-old joins the cat in finding buried treasure in various indoor flowerpots

In real life, you will lose your patience. It's human nature, sort of like getting zits. It happens to everyone. How you handle the situation afterward, however, is what's really important. When you find yourself losing your cool, apologize to your family. Let them know the point that you were trying to make . . . but also that you should have made your point without losing control of your temper. When you let your kids know that you've lost your patience and that you're sorry for doing so, you're also letting them know that sometimes even parents make mistakes — but you're sorry and you'll try hard not to lose your patience again. Getting your point across to your children while at the same time letting them know that parents aren't perfect actually is possible.

One common way that you, as a parent, lose patience is when you see your children involved in something that you think is taking too long. Avoid jumping in and trying to help them if they seem happy to be working on their project at their own speed. By jumping in, you undermine their confidence, and in the end, you do more harm than good.

Don't give your children a chore to do without the understanding that it probably won't get done as quickly as you'd like. That's okay. Let your children accomplish the task in their time. Don't allow *piddling* (the technical term for standing around and not doing anything), but don't jump in and finish the task when they otherwise are doing everything right . . . just a little slowly.

Patience is a skill, a talent, and a blessing. Whatever you want to call it, it's something that will be tested over and over and over again. Take the time to find out your child's reasoning behind everything. Your kids make sense. Remember that. Finding what their sense is is simply brilliant.

Chapter 6

Behavior Management

• •

• •

*B*ehavior is somewhat an obsession for parents and others who try to control it. Everyone has this control issue, so don't pretend to be looking around wondering who I'm talking about.

Parents start trying to control the behavior of their children from an early age. Parents want their baby's crying to stop. Yes, sometimes you know it's a need the child has, and you want to help with that need. Other times you just want the crying to stop.

Then come those *terrible twos*. You know the term, right? Two-year-olds have a bad rap. The age of 2 is the time in their lives when they're trying to exert their independence, and their parents turn around and call them terrible. Two-year-olds aren't bad; their behavior can just irritate control-freak adults.

Children of *any age* can seem difficult when you go about trying to manage behaviors that come naturally to them or when they aren't managed the right way. This chapter is all about knowing:

✔ What to accept from your kids

✔ What it is about your kids that you need to manage

✔ How to manage your kids

Playing the Manipulation Game

Behavior management has two parts. The first actually is manipulating your children's time and behavior so that they don't have the time — or need — to become involved in situations that make us want to label them *terrible*. If you're an oversensitive parent who thinks wanting to *manipulate* your children is just awful, look the word up. It means to guide, direct, or handle.

The second part of behavior management is understanding the behavior. Everything your child does makes sense to her, and in many cases, is just a natural result of her being a child. Your job is finding out what makes sense to your child. You must understand the behavior before you can guide, direct, or handle her.

So the thought of manipulating your children isn't so bad when you realize that all you're doing is guiding or directing the things that they do so they stay out of trouble. The way you guide your children is by:

- ✔ Giving praise
- ✔ Giving plenty of attention
- ✔ Keeping idle hands busy
- ✔ Maintaining a safe and happy home
- ✔ Not forgetting to laugh

But first, you must understand the behaviors of your children.

Train up a child in the way he should go: and when he is old, he will not depart from it. — Proverbs 22:6

Understanding Will Set You Free

We all make sense to ourselves. We know what we're doing and why we're doing it. Adults do a better job of explaining themselves than kids do. Well, some adults do a better job, anyway. But kids typically don't have the resources or experience to say, "So, Mom, you want to know why I colored on the walls. Well, I colored on the walls because you neglected to furnish me with paper, and this wall happens to be at eye level. And, besides, you have that ugly picture hanging there, so I thought I'd add my own masterful interpretation to your décor. Do you have an issue with me coloring on the walls?"

Wouldn't that be an eye opener for your child coming back at you with that lingo? Instead, we parents say, "Why did you write on the walls?" and the kids respond, "I don't know!"

Before you begin the process of becoming upset with a child, stop yourself so that you can find out why your child did what she did. She will have a reason, but helping her to find the right words and thought process takes work. If you work at being a good listener and asking the right questions, you'll find that your child is brilliant and has great reasoning for her actions.

Here's an example of how to question a child without sounding accusatory:

>**Mom:** Wow, look at that artwork on the wall. Tell me why you chose to draw on the wall.

>**Sweet, innocent child:** I thought it would look pretty.

>**Mom:** Tell me more about that.

>**Child:** Well . . . (and so the story goes).

The words, "Tell me more about that," are powerful. This information-gathering technique can do more for you than just about anything else you can say.

Giving Praise

Offer your children *much* praise. Praise means giving hugs, kisses, pats on the back and on the head, and saying things like, "Wow, look what you did" or "That's wonderful" when your children do something good.

When you praise your children, you're giving them positive feedback for what they've just done. They, in turn, will want to do more of the things that make you happy. Kids love to hear how good they are and that you're proud of them or you think they're special. Don't hold out on giving these comments to your kids, because you need to be their best cheerleaders.

When you praise your children for picking up their toys or taking something to the trash, they quickly learn to do those things again to get that same positive attention from you. Say "Thank you" or "Good for you" whenever you can. When your child brings you a dead spider she found on the floor, smile big, give her a hug, and thank her. She needs to know that you appreciate her efforts.

I've heard parents say, "but I don't think a dead spider is a good gift. I'm lying if I tell her I'm happy she brought it to me." Here is where parents need to see the bigger picture. It's often called, *thinking outside of the box*. Being completely honest with an action is brutal and painful. In your head you may think, "Great. A dead spider. And I hate spiders." The bigger picture, and the one you really are praising, is that:

- ✔ Your child thought to do something she deemed as special.
- ✔ Your child made an effort to think of someone other than herself.

Your children's efforts need to be praised.

Praise, however, is like eating M&Ms. If you ate the one-pound bag of M&Ms all in one sitting, several times a day, you'd get sick from too much of a good thing. But, if you spread that bag out over a period of time and just ate one M&M every now and then, you wouldn't get sick. The same thing is true of giving out praise. You don't want to overdo it, because you and your child would *get sick* (sort of). But, if you dole it out like one M&M every little bit, giving praise will just make you feel warm and glowing all over, just like M&Ms do.

Giving your child *unrealistic* praise is a possibility. The solution? Be realistic. When your daughter shows you her finger painting from school, let her know what a great job she did and that you're proud of her. Go a step further and put the finger painting on the wall or the fridge. After that, you don't need to say or do anymore. Don't feel compelled to say her finger painting is the best you've ever seen and that it should be displayed in a museum or framed in gold. Your kids are bright and will recognize insincerity when they hear it.

Giving Plenty of Attention

Kids love attention, and they find ways to attract it anyway they can. When they can't get your attention by doing good things, they do whatever it takes to get your attention. If the only time you acknowledge that your kids are around is when they do something you've been known to react to, they'll continue doing those deeds. I've seen children walk toward a door, all the time watching their parents to see whether they'd chase after them. To a child, negative attention is better than no attention. That is important, so let me say it again: *Children think that negative attention is better than no attention.*

Give a little love to a child, and you get a great deal back. — John Ruskin

Spending time with your kids is the best way to give them your attention. Regardless of whether you stay at home or work outside the home, you *still* can give quality time to your kids. Quality time doesn't mean the entire family sitting for four hours watching TV. It means turning the TV off (Oh Lordy, anything but *that!*) and playing games together, reading books, going for walks, raking the yard — anything!

Giving kids your attention means listening to them when they talk. I don't mean halfway listening and saying "uh huh" like spouses do when their mates are telling the same work story they've heard umpteen times. I mean sitting down, looking children in the eye, and listening — responding to what they say and asking questions. Be interested. Doing so shows that you're paying attention even when your question turns to, "So you say you painted the cat blue? Tell me more about that." And then allow them to answer.

Raising kids is not the time to be selfish with your time. You can be selfish later on when they're grown and having kids of their own.

If you feel guilty about not being able to spend enough time with your kids, resist trying to *buy* their attention. Every weekend doesn't have to include a Disneyland-kind-of-day. This kind of attention-giving has cruelly been labeled the Weekend Father Syndrome by nasty folks, yet it describes something that typically happens.

And you don't have to continually buy them gifts as a means of letting them know you love them. Time. Time is what they want most from you. You can't buy it anywhere, and Kmart doesn't discount it during its Blue Light Specials.

Look at it like this: Right now, you have someone in your life whose only joy is spending time with you. Don't blow it. Don't be a parent who looks back in life and whose only regret is not having spent enough time with the kids. A day will come when your kids are going to have their own sets of friends, their own interests, and their own schedules. If you don't make time for them now, they may not make time for you later.

The only way to effectively manage your children is paying attention to and spending time with them. Nothing should be more important than your kids. You can't make that true by being a weekend parent, by being oblivious to what your kids are up to, or by not making your kids the most important things in your life.

Keeping Idle Hands Busy

Kids will look for something to do if you don't provide some sort of entertainment. Okay, so that doesn't mean you have to put on the Las Vegas showgirl feathers — although your kids probably would enjoy *that*. It also doesn't mean that you have to fall off the scale on the other end, never allowing them time to be quiet and creative with their own play. However, when you don't keep kids busy most of the time, they may choose to color on the wall, string toilet paper all over the bathroom, or pull all the towels out of the cabinet. And I can personally tell you that putting toilet paper back on the roll is really hard!

The key to keeping children busy is scheduling. Your kids, regardless of their ages, are on some type of schedule. And they should be. Schedules are important to kids physically and psychologically. They get up, eat breakfast, eat lunch, and eat dinner. What do they do the rest of the time? Fill up some of the empty spots in their schedules with activities. Have them help you do something around the house or get them involved in a project. Schools manage so many children that way. Their schedules are filled with organized time and then free time. But their days are filled with activities.

If your children are kept busy, they can't get into trouble, but keeping busy doesn't mean that you have to enroll your children into every conceivable activity. It simply means keeping them active enough so that they have neither the time nor the need to look for other activities to prevent boredom from setting in.

The house is clean, school work is done; what can you do with your kids now? How about a special project? Projects can be fun, family rituals, and chores that help keep the house clean and instill responsibility.

If children hired lawyers — Dr. Tim

Imagine, if you will, that you're having problems with your son. He's defiant and disobedient, and you're always on him about one thing or another. Then one day you hear from his attorney: The little so-and-so has filed for divorce! Desperate, you ask your son if he will give you one last chance.

Now imagine that you're seeing a counselor because of problems in your marital relationship. The counselor is sympathetic to your plight and proceeds to show you some basic skills in behavior management: You learn how to reward your spouse for behaving well and how to use time-out for behaving badly. You think, "Finally, techniques that work!"

These vignettes illustrate two extremes in how we can think about relationships. The first approach highlights the importance of accommodating the other person; the second approach recognizes the value of insisting on change in the other's behavior. In the context of these vignettes, seeing how maladaptive it can be to adopt one of these extreme points-of-view is easy.

All close relationships among people in general — including those between parents and children — involve an ongoing tension between changing and accepting each other's behaviors. Some parents are fine with the task of managing their child's behavior, but they forget that the relationship must also be managed. Other parents are "all about" the parent-child relationship; where they struggle is remembering who's in charge. Putting the goal of managing child behavior ahead of the goal of managing the relationship is a mistake for parents. But we nevertheless have a responsibility to protect and discipline our children.

But, what if you're unsure of how to do both? Recent studies of stable, satisfying relationships suggest the following general rule: Aim for about a 4:1 ratio of positive to negative interactions with your child. In other words, for every interaction that is negative ("I don't care if it's the world television premiere of *Death Battle III;* the TV is going off, and we are eating dinner!"), you need to engage in four other exchanges that are emotionally positive (or at least neutral) in tone. For some parents, maintaining this ratio means letting go of some behavior-management goals (for example, how much children eat, what clothes they wear, how they fix their hair, whether they can say "fart"). For other parents, this ratio can be a reminder that the relationship will survive (and may require) the emotional ugliness of an occasional disciplinary conflict.

Here are a few ideas:

- ✔ After breakfast you all go for a walk around the block.

- ✔ Every day after lunch is an hour of free time before naptime.

- ✔ Every birthday or holiday, the kids make personalized cards (this can be for all family and friends).

- ✔ One hour before bedtime, everyone stops and picks up toys, books, shoes, and so on. Then the bedtime ritual begins (see Chapter 16 for more about the sleeping habits of children).

- ✔ Give the kids the chore of putting the silverware away, putting their own laundry in their drawers, and wiping cupboards.

Remember that praising the efforts of your children needs to be done when you're in the room with them. You not only need to monitor their work in this way to show them good work habits, but it also satisfies the requirement of spending time with your children.

Keeping a Safe and Happy Home

A safe home is a happy home. Although this sounds extremely corny, it's true. The more you do to childproof your home, the less time you spend following your kids around putting back porcelain figurines or sweeping houseplant dirt up off the floor. You'll realize having door locks on your cupboards is easier than following your toddler around all day taking canned soup away from her.

Childproof your home the day that you bring your baby home from the hospital. I know this seems way too early. But you don't want to wait until she's sticking a toy into an electrical outlet before you decide to put plastic caps on them. Likewise, you never know when your baby will be able to roll over to the staircase — until one day she does, and you find her practicing a balancing act on the top stair.

Removing glass objects or picture frames that are at baby-grabbing level, locking all cabinets, putting plugs into outlets, blocking stairwells, and a host of other security measures keep your child out of mischief. If it isn't there to break or mutilate, little one won't get into trouble.

Read Chapter 20 for more information about childproofing your home.

Remembering to Laugh

The best way to manage your kids is through humor. Approaching situations with a good attitude and making everyday tasks fun can turn otherwise uncomfortable confrontations into enjoyable situations.

So think of how you say things before you say them. Rather than saying, "Why isn't your room clean?"(which sounds very threatening and demanding), try saying, "You know, I thought you had carpeting in your room. Why don't you pick up your toys so that I can see your floor again?" Remember to add a "Thank you" to the end.

Rather than saying, "Didn't I tell you to make your bed?" try, "Let me time you to see how long it takes you to make your bed."

When you use humor, you still get your point across, but it comes across better than merely demanding things from your kids. No one likes to be barked at every time she's asked to do something. Your kids will be more receptive to your requests when they come across as friendly and nonthreatening.

As a parent, you're guaranteed to develop those unwanted "character" lines from all the laughing your kids induce. Don't stop the laughing just because things don't seem so funny anymore. If your kids have a messy room or forget chores, it doesn't mean that you have to turn into *the Grinch*.

Chores can be fun. Make picking up laundry into a game of toss into the laundry basket. Turn a day of picking up toys into a race to see who can pick up the most toys the quickest.

Part II
Dealing with Babies

The 5th Wave   By Rich Tennant

And now, I'd like to share some of my day with you.

In this part . . .

Babies are an entity unto themselves. Everything about them is unique. They have their own cry, which people recognize as that of a newborn baby. Their poop is even special, especially for newborns. They require special food, clothing, and transportation devices. And nothing turns strangers into friends quicker than a baby. All boundaries are left behind when a cooing ball of pink is sitting somewhere for everyone to see. So, because they're so special and unique, babies deserve to have their own section in this book.

Chapter 7

Holding and Handling the Baby

. . . .

. . . .

A whole chapter on holding a baby? Are you kidding? Nope. This is important stuff. New parents don't understand that babies' shoulders and elbows and necks are vulnerable areas that can easily be injured. Baby heads flop around, and their shoulders can easily be pulled out of their tiny sockets if parents aren't careful.

Is It Possible to Spoil a Baby by Holding Him Too Much?

Do you get spoiled when you feel like someone loves you? No. So the answer is no, you cannot spoil a baby by holding him. That old school of thought was brought on years ago by Dr. Spock (who later rescinded his comment). The only way to spoil a child of any age is to give in to whining and temper tantrums.

So what happens when you hold your baby all the time? You develop great arm and back muscles for one thing. Your baby also gets to feel your warmth and love. Babies may become used to being held and want to be held a lot, but as your children get older, they'll want to go out and explore things around them. So basically, because you won't be tied to a child forever, never think of any excuses not to hold your baby. The reasons why this is true are

- ✔ Babies need to be held, touched, and cuddled. This helps in their development and helps them feel secure.

- ✔ Actually, limiting how much babies are held is unfair. All kids need to be held. (That doesn't mean you have to pick up your 80-pound children.) Even if your kids get too big to hold, nothing should stop you from cuddling with them on the couch while you read a book together.

- ✔ Babies who are held more cry less often.

A wonderful book called *Love you Forever* by Robert Munsch (Firefly Books) — it's my favorite — demonstrates that kids are never too big or too old to be cuddled.

The Joy of Cuddling Newborns and Infants

Newborns and infants simply don't have much muscle control. When you hold them or pick them up, always put an arm or hand behind their necks. Never, ever, pick them up by their arms. You can hurt them by dislocating the joints in their arms.

When holding newborns, you should either cradle them in your arms or hold them up against you, chest-to-chest. Remember to keep a hand on the back of a baby's head, because it'll bobble on over if you're not supporting it.

Don't try the one-handed, cradled-on-the-hip hold with newborns. It works okay with older babies, but newborns are too floppy, and you can't hold them well with just one hand.

And watch out for what I call the *head slam*. As babies are gaining control of their neck muscles, they start looking around and using them. Then, all of a sudden, without warning, the muscles grow tired — and a cute, bobbly head turns into a weapon as it rockets toward you, slamming into your head at a painful velocity. Contact like that hurts you and your baby. Keep a close eye on this flinging head and be prepared to support this same head when it goes out of control.

Lugging Older Babies

As babies get older and their muscles develop, they'll have better control over their heads and they won't bobble around as much. Nevertheless, you need to remember to follow these safety precautions:

✔ Don't throw babies up in the air. It may seem like fun, but there's always that chance you could drop them, or catch them wrong and hurt them.

✔ Don't pull babies by their arms. You can dislocate their shoulders and elbows by doing this. Always pick them up from under the arms or by holding one hand behind their necks and the other arm under their backs.

Comforting Crying Babies

Babies cry. Now you know. Why they cry is always a mystery to us confused and baffled parents. New parents will stand, rock back and forth while holding the baby and ask, "What do I do?" That is a good question. The baby knows there's a problem, and the crying is your indicator. But what to do?

Figure 7-1, The Crying Baby Flowchart, serves as a guide to give you some things to ponder when you think there's a problem but you're at a loss for ideas.

New moms and dads, especially, seem to have more problems with the crying than anyone else. The excitement of a newborn, plus the tiredness (sleep deprivation) of both parents, makes thinking clearly difficult. Just work through the flowchart until something works.

Start at the top of the flowchart and work your way through. Something hopefully will work.

You'll notice that at one point it says that babies just need to cry. This concept is a tough one. But, think of it like this: Newborns sometimes just need to exercise their lungs. Although it doesn't happen too often and it's tough on parents, you may find that nothing in this flowchart ever seems to work. Sorry!

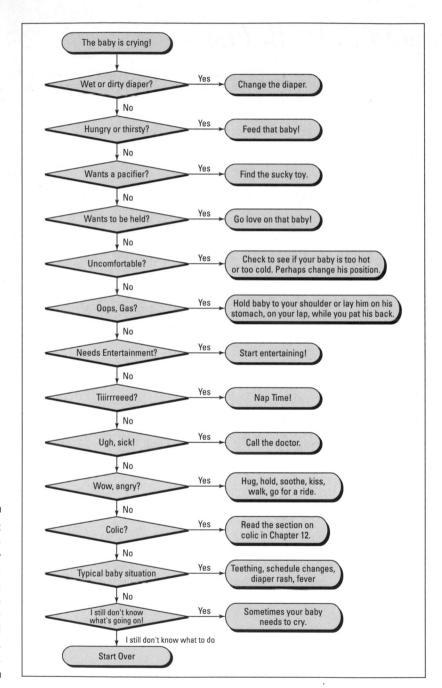

Figure 7-1:
The
Crying Baby
Flowchart.
If you reach
the bottom
and the
baby still
is crying,
start over.

Crying Babies in Public

Babies crying in public sometimes is perfectly acceptable, so ignore those smug looks and disapproving glares. If you're in the grocery store, shopping mall, Denny's Restaurant, then don't fret that your baby is being a baby. It happens. If you can think ahead, try to schedule these activities when your baby isn't hungry or tired. Reality, however, dictates that that won't always happen, and your baby may cry. You may even receive well-meaning comments from people who are uncomfortable that a baby is crying. Personally, I don't like these comments. Your response need be only that, "Yes, babies will be babies," or something like that. And it's the truth. Babies are just being themselves when they cry.

I was in the grocery store the other day, and this new mother looked like she was going to have a heart attack. She was trying to check out, and her newborn was not happy. He was crying and trying to suck on her chin (sign of a newborn wanting to nurse). I felt so sorry for this woman that I finally told her not to worry and that no one cared that the baby was crying. It's what babies do. The look of relief on her face was wonderful.

In certain situations, having a crying baby is not acceptable, and you may be asked to leave. This is a touchy subject for some parents, so hear me out.

Live theater, movie theaters, upscale restaurants, weddings, and funerals are some of the places where crying babies must be removed. My belief is that babies shouldn't even be taken to places like those, where the normal environment is quiet and that's what is expected. Babies aren't quiet, and they really shouldn't be expected to be. So please don't even put your baby in these situations.

Chapter 8

Breast-feeding versus Bottle-feeding

*B*reast-feeding is a huge topic in the parenting world. Many misconceptions exist about breast-feeding and bottle-feeding, which actually are your only two choices at the beginning. Mixed in with the misconceptions are also a lot of mixed emotions about breast-feeding and bottle-feeding. Parents want to do the right thing, but what *is* the right thing?

I have to say that I've never seen so many mothers so adamant about this subject. What is right? Why does breast-feeding seem so easy for everyone else? Why is formula pushed upon me if I'm not supposed to use it? They're all good questions and all discussed in this chapter.

Breast-feeding as a Total Commitment by Mother and Father

Breast milk is the perfect food for your baby. It contains proteins and vitamins that help your baby's immune system, thus giving your baby a better chance of growing up healthy and strong.

But breast-feeding isn't always easy. Seldom does a mother begin nursing her baby without any pain or discomfort, and rarely does the baby latch on and nurse without any problems. Breast-feeding your child takes work and dedication.

Both Mom and Dad need to be involved with the decision to make breast-feeding work. Yes, Dad must be helpful and supportive too, because while the baby is breast-feeding, Mom is completely out of the picture for anything else. Dad must help any siblings, answer the phone, fix dinner, and whatever is required. Breast-feeding comes first.

Here are some things you can do to ensure that you start your breast-feeding experience off on the right foot.

- Try breast-feeding right after your baby is born.
- Have the baby sleep in your room so that you can breast-feed when your baby is hungry.
- Let the hospital nursing staff know you want to breast-feed and that they shouldn't give bottles of formula to your baby (unless your pediatrician decides that a formula supplement is needed).
- Get help from the hospital staff, so you're sure that you're breast-feeding the right way and that your baby is latching on correctly. Most hospitals have lactation consultants for you to work with.
- Avoid supplementing with formula until after your baby is 3 to 4 weeks old (unless your pediatrician recommends formula supplements).
- Avoid using a pacifier before your baby is 3 to 4 weeks old.
- Don't smoke or drink beverages with caffeine in them.
- Eat! You should be eating a well-balanced diet of 2,000 to 2,700 calories per day.
- Drink! Drink lots of liquids like water and juice every day. Stay away from coffee and alcohol. Limit soda pop.

Breast-feeding Pros, Cons, Myths, and Truths

Once you make people aware that you're going to have a baby, they start shooting the questions at you. "So, do you want a boy or a girl?" (as if you can put in a request and get what you want). "What are you going to name it?" "Are you going to breast-feed?"

If you're planning to breast-feed, the only honest answer is, "I plan to try." If the thought of breast-feeding turns you off, your answer is simply, "No, I think not."

But before you say no, think hard about your decision. Yes, breast-feeding is difficult, especially when you're planning to return to work soon. And it's a commitment in terms of time, because no one else can do it for you. But the benefits of breast-feeding far outweigh the hardships. You'll reap the benefits of having a strong, healthy baby the rest of your life. Breast milk has antibodies, and it may help reduce illnesses and susceptibility to allergies.

Should I breast-feed?

"Should I breast-feed?" is a question every new mother asks herself. It isn't always an easy decision, especially when every person you've ever met gives you advice on the subject. The changing times — and people from those times — provide different perspectives on breast-feeding. There was a time when the only way to feed a baby was to breast-feed. Then doctors came along and decided that mothers couldn't handle such an important job: Many doctors concluded that even though breast-feeding is quite natural, mothers should use formula to feed their infants. Breast-feeding was discouraged, and only outcasts would do such a dastardly deed. Now general opinion, based on thorough research, is that breast-feeding is the best thing for your baby. Some people have gone off the far end of the spectrum and think that everyone should and can breast-feed, and they're unsympathetic with those who choose not to breast-feed.

The most important opinion is yours, so to help you along with your decision, I've listed the pros and cons of breast-feeding.

Pros

- ✔ Breast milk is the best food for your baby. The vitamins and minerals in breast milk can't be duplicated.

- ✔ Babies who are breast-fed are less likely to suffer from ear infections, colic, constipation, asthma, allergies, or upper respiratory infections.

- ✔ Breast-feeding can be a great, quiet, bonding time for you and your baby.

- ✔ Breast milk doesn't take any preparation time — quick and easy access.

- ✔ You don't have to wash and sterilize bottles or nipples (and wouldn't *that* be painful?).

- ✔ Nighttime feedings are a breeze. Simply bring your baby to bed with you, lie down, and nurse. This is especially nice during those cold winter nights.

✔ Breast-feeding forces you to sit down and rest. You can't breast-feed and work at the same time. It's a nice break.

✔ If you must be away from your baby during feeding times, you can use a breast pump to *express* milk for later use. That way you're not always tied down to a nursing baby. You can get away for short periods of time.

✔ Breast-feeding helps your body return to normal quicker following your pregnancy by burning more calories — almost 500 calories each day. It helps shrink the uterus back to normal size.

✔ Breast-fed babies are more likely to accept a wider variety of foods when they grow older. Breast milk has different flavors (not like chocolate, vanilla, or strawberry — but *subtle* differences based on what you eat). Experiencing different tastes at an early age leads babies to be more open to other tastes.

✔ It's cheap! Breast-feeding saves money. No extra food to buy.

Cons

✔ Breast-feeding can be uncomfortable. For some, it hurts like heck. When you first start to breast-feed, your nipples can get sore and, for some mothers, they crack and bleed.

✔ Your breasts become engorged (filled with too much milk) if you don't nurse on schedule. That is painful. Engorgement also occurs the first few days of your milk coming in.

✔ Using a breast pump may make you feel like a dairy cow.

✔ For many mothers, their breasts leak and cause embarrassing wet spots on their blouses. They look like they leaned up against a wet window.

✔ You may suffer from a breast infection, which is painful.

✔ Using a breast pump takes some time (anywhere from 10 to 30 minutes). Unless you have some breast milk already frozen, you must plan ahead to leave your nursing baby.

Breast-feeding myths and truths

Like most activities that have been around for a gazillion years, breast-feeding is filled with myths and old wives' tales. Allow me to shed some light on a few of the more popular ones:

Myth: Everyone is capable of breast-feeding.

Truth: This is the number-one myth that leaves mothers feeling frustrated and inadequate. Not everyone can breast-feed. But the reason they can't breast-feed is because the baby isn't latched on well enough. When you don't find the proper way to get your child to breast-feed, it won't work.

Myth: Breast-feeding is a natural event, and you and your baby will fall into the breast-feeding ritual as if you've been doing it for years.

Truth: It takes a while for you and your baby to establish a pattern and both become comfortable with breast-feeding. For many mothers, it takes anywhere from a few days to a few weeks to get the process down.

Myth: Doing nipple exercises helps to make your nipples not so tender, and breast-feeding will be less uncomfortable.

Truth: No matter what you do to prepare, nothing is going to prepare your nipples enough for the pain that comes when your baby isn't latched on correctly. For the first few days, soreness is pretty common, but if the pain is excessive, you have a problem. Check with your doctor or lactation consultant.

Myth: As long as you breast-feed, you can't get pregnant.

Truth: Allow me to introduce my third son, Jonah, to you. He's only 11 months younger than my second son, Simon. *Ahem.*

Parents who have children 11 months apart laugh hysterically at this myth. Although you delay your menstrual cycle (for about six months) while you breast-feed, you still ovulate and can get pregnant unless you use a contraceptive. Abstinence is the best kind of contraceptive, but not as much fun.

Myth: The only way to bond with your baby is by breast-feeding.

Truth: You have several ways to bond with your baby, and breast-feeding is only one of them. Bottle-fed babies are just as capable of cuddling up with their parents and bonding. The breast-fed babies don't have this bonding thing cornered.

Myth: Women with small breasts produce less milk than women with large breasts.

Truth: Not true at all.

Breast-feeding Guidelines

Don't assume that just because you naturally produce breast milk you will, without a doubt, know how to nurse your newborn. It doesn't work that way. For many mothers, breast-feeding takes time and practice before everything goes along smoothly. Then there are those mothers who grab their babies while on the birthing table, hold their newborns to their breast, and never have to think twice about nursing their children.

Keep these thoughts in mind when you're nursing your child:

✔ **Breast-feed your baby immediately after birth.**

This first breast-feeding time may take up to an hour, but it's the first step in a healthy baby/mom relationship.

✔ **Don't get nervous or upset if your baby doesn't latch on to your breast the first, second, or even third time.**

But do get help right away. Learning how this should be done is critical to a good breast-feeding experience.

You and your baby are new at breast-feeding, and becoming accomplished at it may take coordination, time, and practice between you two. The older your child gets, and the more practice you have, the easier breast-feeding will be. Sometimes newborns seem too darn small and floppy to try to hold and feed at the same time. Just keep trying and get some help.

✔ **Don't impose any restrictions on the length or frequency of breast-feeding.**

If a baby is nursing well and getting the milk, she won't be on the breast for hours at a time. If your baby is staying attached for a long time, she's probably not latched on well and not getting the milk. Not being latched on is kind of like trying to suck from a bottle with a nipple that has only one tiny hole. Babies will also use their mother as a pacifier or they may be feeding for a growth spurt.

✔ **Don't assume that just because you've successfully nursed one child, the second child or the third one is going to be just as easy.**

Remember, babies are different people, and each starts as a beginner at nursing. They aren't able to get any good advice from their siblings.

✔ **Don't feel pressured to succeed the first time you try to breast-feed.**

You'll probably have a nurse, husband, or a roomful of spectators anxiously waiting to see your performance. Try not to get nervous or flustered. But if you do, just ask your visitors to leave.

✔ **Don't be surprised if you tend to sweat a lot during your first tries at breast-feeding.**

This state is a combination of your body going back to normal with hormonal changes, calories that are burned, nervousness from breast-feeding for the first time, and the let-down process your body goes through when it's time to nurse.

✔ **Get comfortable when it's time to nurse.**

You'll be nursing quite a bit, so find a comfortable chair, couch, or bed, use pillows to prop yourself up, put pillows underneath the arm you're using to support your baby's head, lean back, and relax.

✔ **Have your supplies ready.**

New mothers are busy, busy, busy. So take the time while you're nursing to have a large glass of water and a snack. Look at it as sharing lunch with your baby.

✔ **Don't forget the football hold.**

If you're having problems nursing your baby with the cradle hold (baby's belly against your belly), try the football hold. You hold your baby like you would a football, tucked under your arm: Your baby's belly is against your side.

✔ **Take care of yourself.**

Nursing is not the time to go on a diet to shed those extra pounds. You have the rest of your life to diet. You need to be eating and drinking from 2,000 to 2,700 calories per day. Simple food is the best, so have plenty of fruit around for you to grab, keep bowls of nuts and raisins out, and keep a sports water bottle filled with water for you. Don't fill it up with soda pop. Your body needs pure, healthy water.

✔ **Watch what you put in your mouth.**

Many things can be transferred to your breast milk: alcohol, medications, illegal drugs, and even some spicy foods. Always consult with your doctor before you take any medications.

✔ **Drink lots of water.**

You're producing milk — a liquid. The more water you drink, the more liquid you'll produce. You should drink at least eight 8-ounce glasses of water per day.

✔ **Follow the basic rules of breast-feeding.**

Hold your breast with your thumb and forefinger behind the areola (the brown area around your nipple), make sure your baby's mouth is wide open like a little bird's, and quickly put the nipple in her mouth before she shuts it. Holding your baby tummy-to-tummy will ensure that she doesn't pull your breast or break away from it.

If you want to breast-feed but are having trouble getting started, consider using a breast pump and then finger-feeding your child (see below). The pump keeps your flow of breast milk going, and you'll still be able to feed your baby. But, more important, finger-feeding also buys you some time so that you can continue working with your baby to get her to breast-feed without the fear of her going hungry.

Some hospitals have breast-feeding classes or lactation consultants to educate mothers about breast-feeding. They cover basic breast-feeding techniques, suggestions about how to reduce sore nipples, and plenty of other helpful information. You can also contact childbirth educators (like Lamaze instructors), midwives, or the La Leche League. For more information on the La Leche League, go to its Web site, www.lalecheleague.org.

Finger-feeding

I discovered finger-feeding with my second child. Poor Simon just couldn't seem to latch on, and I was always in tears. The helpful lactation consultant at the hospital set me up with a breast pump, and together, we got through this fork in the road.

Finger-feeding is a method of feeding that enables you to feed your baby breast milk without using a bottle and nipple, which, if used in the first few weeks of nursing, can hinder a successful breast-feeding experience. I've since learned that finger-feeding also is a method of helping to train your baby to take the breast. Whenever your baby refuses to take the breast for whatever reason or doesn't seem to be able to latch on well, try the finger-feeding method before going to a bottle.

You can also use the finger-feeding method when your nipples are too sore to breast-feed. You can give your sore nipples a break by feeding your baby this way for a couple of days.

Finger-feeding works because it is similar to breast-feeding. Using your finger to feed forces the baby to keep her tongue down and forward over the gums, her mouth wide open — so use a larger finger — and the jaw forward. The motion of the tongue and jaw is similar to what the baby does while feeding at the breast.

Finger-feeding method

Wash your hands and make sure that your fingernails are cut short and that you and your baby are comfortable. Get into your feeding position. You have to make sure to keep your finger *flat* in the baby's mouth, so be positioned so you can do this comfortably.

You need a finger-feeding kit, made up of a feeding tube (#5F, 36-inches long), and a feeding bottle with expressed breast milk, sugar water, or, if necessary, formula, depending on the circumstances. The feeding tube is passed through the enlarged nipple hole into the fluid. Your local hospital should be able to supply you with these things.

Line up the tube so that it sits on the soft part of the finger you're going to use (your index finger is a good one to try). The end of the tube should line up *no further* than the end of your finger. Gripping the tube between your thumb and middle finger and then positioning your index finger under the tube is the easiest method. If you have a difficult time holding this, you can always tape the tube to your finger with bandage tape.

Is my baby getting enough breast milk? — Dr. Mary Jo

Knowing whether your newborn is getting enough milk is difficult. Because the most accurate measure is the baby's weight, pediatricians recommend weighing your baby at 3 to 4 days of life. Usually your milk will be coming in around this time. Your baby will have lost some weight, but she should begin to stabilize. After the 14th day (or two weeks), her weight should be back up to birth weight. For the first few months, feeding needs to be on a supply-and-demand basis until your baby gets on a schedule, which will be around age 4 to 5 months. The more you nurse, the more milk you produce. During the scheduled well-child checks throughout the first 18 months of life, your baby's weight will continue to be monitored. Infants usually double their birth weight by 6 months and triple their birth weight by a year of life. All this growth in weight shows that, yes, your baby is getting enough breastmilk.

Insert your finger with the tube in your baby's mouth so that the soft part of your finger remains upward. Keep your finger as flat as possible. Usually the baby will begin sucking on the finger, and allow the finger to enter quite far.

Pull down the baby's chin, if his lower lip is sucked in.

If feeding is slow, you may want to raise the bottle above the baby's head.

Keep your finger straight, flattening the baby's tongue. Try not to point your finger up. Keeping it flat forces the baby's tongue down, working her lower jaw forward.

Finger-feeding isn't easy at first, so have someone help you. And make sure that you check in with your pediatrician frequently, so your baby can be weighed. Weighing your baby determines whether she's getting enough to eat.

Working through the soreness

You can do some things to help get over sore nipples from breast-feeding. Most women will breast-feed longer when there's a way to *endure* the pain of sore nipples. The first preventative step is making sure your baby latches on properly.

✔ Don't pull your baby away from your breast without *unlatching* her first. Do this by sticking your finger in the corner of your baby's mouth to break the suction.

- *Air-dry* your nipples for ten minutes after feedings and after washing.

- Wear a loose-fitting cotton bra.

- Don't use soap on your nipples because it can dry your skin. Water is all that you need to clean your nipples.

- Break open a vitamin E capsule and rub the oil on your nipples. Lanolin can help, too. Remember to wash your nipples before breast-feeding. You don't want your baby eating the vitamin E.

- Limit feeding time on the sore nipples. Many babies like to nurse and doze off to sleep with the nipple still in their mouths. Once your baby has stopped eating, take her off the breast.

- Express a little milk (allowing a little milk to come out by using a pump or even your fingers) before breast-feeding to stimulate the let-down process of the milk.

- Massage your breast while you're feeding.

- Put warm washcloths on your breasts and nipples before breast-feeding. This action also helps with the let-down process of the milk.

- Use a breast pump on occasion to give your nipples a rest.

Breast-feeding Away from Home — and Away from Baby

You're in luck when you're breast-feeding, and you and your baby are going on an outing. When your baby gets hungry, just plop down where you are and start feeding.

Don't be embarrassed about breast-feeding in public. Be as discreet as you need to be, but remember that this is your baby's food — and your baby deserves to eat now. Look at it like this. If you were hungry and had a candy bar in your bag, you wouldn't feel like you needed to go and hide to eat it. Well, when you breast-feed, you're carrying your baby's lunch in a unique way.

If you're on the modest side and prefer to breast-feed in private, most restrooms have couches or chairs so you can breast-feed your baby.

If your feelings about publicly nursing your child are somewhere in between the plopping-down-anywhere or sitting-in-a-restroom scenarios, you can always use a blanket to cover yourself and the baby so that you can nurse in public. Use a lightweight blanket, or just wear a shirt that can be unbuttoned or easily lifted up. Between your body heat and the heat your baby generates simply from the eating process, you'll need to wear something light so neither of you becomes overheated.

Taking a trip without your breast-feeding baby is possible, but it takes advanced planning and some extra breast pumping on your part.

Figure out how many feedings you'll miss; then give yourself plenty of time to pump extra breast milk and freeze it for later use. When you're away from your baby, your babysitter can thaw and use the expressed breast milk. The milk should be thawed in the refrigerator and used within 24 hours.

While you're gone, continue using a breast pump during your regular feeding times. If you don't, your breasts will become engorged (filled to capacity), and you may stop producing milk.

Warm thawed breast milk by placing the bottle in a pan of warm water, or holding it under hot running water for a few minutes. Test the milk on your inner arm. It should feel just a tad warmer than lukewarm. Never warm milk in the microwave.

To give a breast-feeding Mom a treat, have her express extra breast milk and let her sleep while you take the 2 a.m. feeding.

The Truth of All Truths about Breast-feeding

Some women have it in their heads that if they don't, won't, or can't breast-feed, they won't bond with their babies and somehow will be a failure. I don't know when mothers were brainwashed into thinking that way.

Some women have gotten to the point where they've unintentionally starved their newborns because everyone else insisted that they should be able to breast-feed — but they couldn't. Remember all too many things can happen to prevent an easy breast-feeding experience. You may not have enough breast milk, the baby's mouth may not be able to suck properly, you may have plugged milk ducts, or the baby just may not want to breast-feed for some unknown reason. The list of possibilities is long, but the breast-feeding experts usually insist on trying every known contraption or strategy for getting that newborn to breast-feed.

My advice is to do the best thing for your baby. Without question, breast milk is the best food for your baby, but the most important issue here is that your baby is fed. If you can't breast-feed, use a breast pump so that your baby still has the benefit of getting that breast milk. This practice also keeps your breast milk flowing so that you can continue trying to breast-feed your baby. Medela, Inc., makes a great electric breast pump, although you may feel like you're a cow in a dairy farm.

Breast pumps that you buy at the store usually don't work as well as those that you can rent from a drugstore or pharmacy. Ask your doctor or pediatrician to recommend a breast pump. The nursery in the hospital where you deliver may also be able to give you information about breast pumps. You may find that you have to experiment with a few breast pumps. Electric and manual pumps are available. Some women love the electric pumps because they don't take any effort and are quicker. Other women find them quite uncomfortable.

The bottom line is that your child must eat.

To Wean or Not to Wean (That Is the Question!)

You won't want to breast-feed your 5-year-old, so at some time you're going to have to wean your child from breast-feeding. Some kids wean themselves.

The decision to wean is difficult for many mothers. After all, breast-feeding is a special time that only you and your baby have together. No one else can share in the act, and for most mothers, nothing is more relaxing or fulfilling.

However, because of busy schedules, going back to work, or simply being tired of having leaky breasts and wearing big blouses, the decision to wean your baby from breast-feeding may not be difficult at all.

The easiest and least painful way to wean your baby is slowly, over a period of time. Some mothers actually have been told that the best way to wean a baby is cold turkey. Just stop breast-feeding. An immediate and honest reaction is: "Well, won't that hurt? I mean, my breasts will get engorged." The response: "You'll experience some tenderness. Take Tylenol and put cold packs on your breasts; after three or four days, you should be fine."

Weaning cold turkey has to be the worst advice ever given in the history of advice giving. Mothers usually try this for about a day. By the end of that day their blouses are soaked with breast milk, and their breasts feel like they're going to explode. Smart moms are the ones who grab their babies and say, "Eat, *please!*"

There's a better way. Start weaning your baby by replacing one feeding at a time with formula (or baby food if your baby is old enough to start eating solids) and give yourself plenty of time for your milk supply to start reducing.

After anywhere from a few days to a week of replacing one feeding, replace another. Do this again and again until finally all feedings are replaced. This process takes more time, but it isn't as painful. Anything without pain is best.

The babies of some mothers start weaning themselves once they're started on solids. If that happens, don't feel rejected. Once your baby gets to taste the wonderful world of real food, milk may simply not be enough.

- Statistically, half of all women stop breast-feeding during the first four months. Why? They cite many reasons, but the saddest I've ever heard is that some mothers feel they're looked down upon for breast-feeding an older child.

- Many women wean their babies when they start teething. When those little teeth start coming in, babies may take the opportunity to use your breast as a teething ring. Unfortunately, you can't do much to ease the discomfort. You can unlatch your child every time you feel biting, and eventually your baby may get the idea. However, repeatedly latching and unlatching your baby can make your nipples sore.

- Don't let anyone's opinion about breast-feeding influence you. If you want to breast-feed your kids until they go off to college, so be it. The American Academy of Pediatrics encourages mothers to nurse at least one year. In many cultures around the world, mothers nurse their children for three to four years.

- You may want to wean your older baby onto a cup rather than a bottle. This transition may be easier in the long run. You won't have to go through the same thing all over again, weaning your child off the bottle.

- If your child weans quickly, you may suffer some *discomfort* (another word for *excruciating pain*). Use a breast pump and express just enough milk to ease the pain. Eventually, you'll stop producing as much milk as before.

- Other ways to help with the pain of engorgement are wearing a good, supportive bra to hold those puppies up (don't even think about going braless) or applying ice packs on or chilled cabbage leaves inside your bra (Kathy Lee Gifford claims to have done the latter when her children were babies).

Keep a close eye on your kids as they make the transition from breast milk to formula (or cow's milk if they're older than 1 year). Bad reactions to the change include having diarrhea, developing a rash, spitting up or vomiting, getting a stuffy or runny nose, or wheezing or coughing.

Bottles for Babies

Bottles are another confusing area for parents. The truth? There isn't a great deal of difference between any of them. The only real difference is the type of bottle in which you put plastic liners and squeeze out excess air. Other bottles come in different shapes and sizes; some are plain, and some have cute little pictures on them. Some are angled for babies to get their milk without getting a lot of air. Honestly, they're all about the same.

Some babies, however, are particular about the type of nipple you use. You may end up trying a few different kinds if your baby turns a pug nose up at a particular nipple. Most babies won't give it much thought. They'll get used to whatever you stick in their mouths.

Bottle-feeding guidelines

You have just as much of an opportunity for a strong, healthy, loving baby who is bottle-fed as you do for one who is breast-fed. Don't feel guilty if you choose to bottle-feed your baby. Or, if you're in that group of people who have no choice about it, accept the fact that bottle-feeding your baby is the only way to go. Just be happy that you have a baby to feed.

Here are some guidelines to help make your bottle-feeding experience as wonderful as it can be:

✔ **Expect to feed your newborn anywhere between 2 or 3 ounces of formula at each feeding.**

As your baby grows bigger, finishes all the milk, and seems hungry at shorter intervals, increase the formula. You'll eventually find yourself increasing the formula but feeding your baby less frequently.

✔ **Hold your baby during feedings.**

Take the opportunity to hold, cuddle, and sneak in those kisses while your baby is eating. Never prop the bottle up to feed your baby. This is extremely unsafe. Your baby can choke and be unable to push the bottle away. Holding your baby during feeding also helps prevent ear infections. Babies who lie down with bottles are more likely to have the formula get into the eustachian tube, which is the tube that connects the eardrum to the throat. This feeding habit can cause ear infections. When your baby is old enough to hold the bottle, allow her to do so. That is the first step to independent feeding.

✔ **Heat the formula by placing the bottle in a pan of hot water or holding it under hot running water. Never microwave a bottle!**

The formula should feel a little warm when you dribble the milk on your inner wrist. If it feels hot on your wrist, it's too hot for your baby. Remember, you also heat bottled breast milk this way.

✔ **Don't change formulas.**

Babies have delicate systems. Changing formulas can cause gas pains. When you find a formula your baby likes, stick to it. If for some reason you want to change formulas, ask your doctor for a recommendation. Not all formulas are the same.

✔ **Thoroughly clean bottles and nipples.**

The recommended way to clean your bottles and nipples is to wash them with soap and water, place them in a pan of water, and boil for five minutes. This process gets rid of any germs that simple washing misses.

✔ **Burp your baby halfway through feeding.**

Feed your baby half the bottle and then burp her before you continue with the rest. This practice not only helps your baby feel better (because gas doesn't build up), but it also reduces the chance of your baby burping up the food.

✔ **Don't *handle* your baby right after feeding.**

Allow your baby some time to lie in your arms after feeding and before you hoist the little one up to burp (this advice also applies to babies who are breast-fed). Giving your baby those few extra minutes allows the food to settle — and thus decreases the potential for food to come spewing out.

Heating formula in the microwave isn't a good idea. Microwaves heat food unevenly, and that causes hot spots in the milk. These hot spots can burn your baby. Microwaves also can cause the plastic sack-type bottles to burst. That isn't a good idea, either.

Bottle-feeding away from home

At some point in time, you're going to have to travel with your baby. Traveling may mean going only to the grocery store. But you'll nevertheless look like one of those parents who totes around a 50-pound bag full of goodies for the little tyke.

That's okay. At least you're prepared. Remember these things when you get ready to go on your outing:

> ✔ **Prepared formula (the liquid kind, not powder) must always be refrigerated.**
>
>   If you can't — or don't want — to keep a cooler with you, use the powdered formula.
>
> ✔ **Put the powdered formula into the bottle and take a bottle of water with you.**
>
>   When your baby is hungry, just add water and shake the bottle.

You can take along the ready-to-feed formula in the cans, but I don't recommend it. Not only do you need a way to open the can, but you'll also have to throw away the unused milk if you're unable to use it immediately (or store it in a refrigerator or cooler). I just wouldn't mess with it.

Chapter 9

The Diaper Thing

*P*ee-pee, poo-poo, go potty, tinkle, go #1, go #2, make a BM, caca. Yep, this is a messy chapter. But get used to these kinds of words now because your children will use them. And the more you use them, the more comfortable you'll become with this whole topic.

I remember a time when a messy diaper could trigger my gag reflex faster than just about anything. Not any more. Nope, the whole poop and pee conversation is just normal, because quite honestly, it is a part of life, and we all do it.

Talking the Messy Language of Poop

Your family doctor is interested in your kids' poop, as in how many times a day kids go poop and pee — and what it looks like. These are common questions for about the first year and whenever your child is sick. The poop and pee measurements have a direct relationship to how well your kids' elimination system is working, which is a reflection of their general health.

As parents, you'll become familiar with what's normal for your kids and what isn't. You'll learn to recognize what looks like diarrhea and what may be common. The important thing is that you keep track of these things: Whether drastic changes occur in the number of poops per day, or whether your children stop peeing as much. There are situations that can indicate to you and the doctor that something may be wrong.

Newborn poop

For the first two or three days, newborns pass *meconium,* which looks like sticky, greenish-black tar. This is the stuff that was in their intestines while they were in the womb. The poop then changes in color and consistency, depending on whether they're breast-fed or formula-fed. You can expect your babies to poop anywhere from one to several times per day. Just like adults, every baby is different, and so are their pee and poop schedules.

Formula-fed poop

Formula-fed babies poop Dijon-mustard-looking poop that is sticky and smells really bad. After they're about 2 months old, formula-fed babies may poop as often as five times a day. And the smell never gets any better.

Breast-fed babies

Breast-fed babies produce less-stinky poops than formula-fed babies. The poop is somewhat yellow and may even have small, seed-like particles in it. Because breast milk tends to be more easily digested, it doesn't leave much solid waste.

You can expect as few as two bowel movements a week after about 2 months of age. That is when mother's production of colostrum tapers off. *Colostrum,* some physicians say, acts somewhat as a natural laxative.

Call your doctor if your baby hasn't pooped in more than three days. Also call the doctor if the poop turns black, white, gray, or if there's blood in it.

Creating a diaper-changing station

Change your baby's diaper in a safe, sturdy place. Never just plop your baby down on any old counter, thinking that the change will take place quickly and that everything will be fine. In fact, I recommend creating a permanent diaper-changing area equipped with everything you need close at hand.

Diaper changing tables are okay, but many of them wobble, and you don't have access to a sink. If you don't want to pay the money to buy a changing table, use your bathroom counter (if it's long enough). Set up the bathroom counter by removing all your makeup, cologne, or whatever may be in the way and putting it somewhere else. You don't want anything close at hand that your little one can grab and pop into an eager mouth.

Put a clean towel down to serve as a cushion, and set aside one of the drawers that's close at hand for all your diaper-changing paraphernalia: diapers, butt-wipes, ointment, and so on. Be sure to include gadgets and toys to keep your baby's mind off the actual diaper-changing process. Mobiles are great to hang over your changing station.

Everything you need to change a diaper must be within reach so that you can keep one hand on your baby while the other hand is groping for what it needs.

This bathroom sink setup is a great alternative to changing tables. You have at least one wall to keep things secure so that baby doesn't fall off, and you have a sink in which to wash bottoms that are truly messy from those explosive poops — when those tiny little baby wipes just won't do the job.

- ✔ If you want to be really careful, you can buy straps and side bars to turn your bathroom counter into a changing table.
- ✔ Never turn your back on a child when he's on a changing table. Always leave one hand on a child who's on the changing table.

Changing a Diaper Step-by-Step

Changing a diaper well is an art form, a delicate procedure that deals with sensitive body parts, and a messy procedure that requires special tools and equipment and the mobility of a master acrobatics instructor.

Changing soiled diapers on a wee l'il baby

I know many people who may think this section silly. Everyone's changed a diaper, right? Well, no, that isn't true. And those who have changed a diaper can't always claim victory over the diaper. I've seen some real nightmare situations because people were arrogant and thought they knew what they were doing.

I've also seen many sore baby bottoms because the baby wasn't cleaned properly, and the poor baby suffered.

1. **Open and unfold the** *new* **diaper.**

    Lay baby wearing used diaper on top of new diaper and hand the baby a toy or move the mobile hanging above your head (this is the distraction so baby won't try to escape).

2. **Unfasten used diaper.**

    If you're changing a boy baby, open the diaper just a little bit at first because air tends to make junior want to go right then and there.

Otherwise, with the angle of the baby lying down, you may get sprayed in the face. Alternately, you can also open the diaper and lie a wash cloth or cloth diaper across the baby's penis as a type of shield.

3. **Gather baby's feet with one hand and lift with the other.**

   Remove the dirty diaper, wad it up, and — if it was his or her turn to do this — toss it at your spouse.

4. **Clean the baby bottom.**

   After the baby bottom is clean, lower the baby onto the clean diaper.

5. **Fasten diaper on baby.**

   Say something cute, such as "Oogie booga do boo." Baby will smile and prepare to soil diaper again.

6. **Wash hands thoroughly.**

   You don't want to spread hidden poop or germs around.

Newborns experience an insecure feeling when their diapers are changed. That is why they appear cranky, cry, and reach their arms out to the side. Help them feel a little more secure by keeping either one of your hands or a blanket or towel on their stomachs for as long as possible. This pressure helps calm them.

When changing your little girl's diaper, wipe her bottom from front to back. Doing so helps avoid any kind of bladder or urinary tract infections from the bacteria being spread.

The battle: No way are you changing my diaper!

You can handle those difficult diaper changes by keeping a stash of toys or interesting objects close at hand so that when you lay your little poopy bottom down for a diaper change you'll have something to keep those idle hands busy. You can also hang a mobile over the table for your baby to "ooh" and "ahh" at.

Periodically change the stash of toys that you keep hidden for only diaper-changing time. You don't want to find out that your child suddenly becomes bored with a toy when you're in the middle of changing a full diaper.

✔ Another way to keep babies preoccupied is for you to lean over them, look them in the eye, and sing or talk to them. It's a great time for you two to have a quiet moment and to talk over life's major issues.

✔ Doing the occasional *tummy tzerbert* also preoccupies babies. Tzerbert technique: Place your lips on baby's tummy and blow out to make a *bpbpbpb* sound. Babies go nuts over this.

When your baby wakes up in the middle of the night, wait to change the diaper until he's half through with the feeding (either half the bottle, or done with one breast if breast-feeding). That way you'll satisfy your baby's hunger right away, and you won't have to wake him up to change a diaper after the little one has dozed back to sleep.

Dealing with Diaper Rash (Or the Itchy Bottom)

Diaper rash occurs because of two reasons:

- ✔ Dirty diapers are left on too long
- ✔ Gastrointestinal problems

Your baby's dirty diaper needs to be changed immediately. The combination of the moisture from the diaper and the lack of air to dry it out causes rashes and chafing. Just because you have a diaper on your child that is advertised to hold 20 gallons of fluid and can block more liquid than the Hoover Dam, doesn't mean you have to test it out for yourself.

A rash also can develop because of poop that's acidic — because of a stomach virus, teething, or something your child ate that was too strong for his system (such as citrus foods for babies younger than 1 year old). In any case, this kind of poop can instantly cause a rash that may resemble little blisters.

The best way to take care of diaper rash is *not* to use baby wipes, but, instead, washing the little bottom off in a sink with warm, soapy water (baby wipes are soapy cloths that may irritate the rash). Pat the bottom dry and apply a zinc-oxide ointment. If the rash lasts more than three days, contact your doctor, who'll likely prescribe an industrial-strength ointment that clears it up pronto.

Rashes occur a lot in the groin (top of the legs area). This area tends to be overlooked. Don't forget to pull this skin back between the folds of his legs to wash and dry it well.

Exposing rash-prone areas to the air for a while helps prevent diaper rash or clear up rashes that already have started. After changing the diaper, washing off the area, and patting it dry, allow your baby to crawl or walk around without the diaper for some time. Don't put diaper rash ointment on a baby who's walking around bottomless (the ointment will get everywhere!). Allow the bottomless look only if it's warm out and there's no chance for baby to become chilled. Keep a close eye out though; your baby may take the opportunity to water the carpet for you . . . if you know what I mean.

Taking diaper rash to the doctor — Dr. Mary Jo

Diaper rashes are almost impossible to avoid. Most zinc-oxide ointments clear up mild cases of diaper rash in a day or two. But when the rash lasts longer than a week, or if it becomes blistery, or starts bleeding and peeling, take your child to your doctor. Diaper rashes often are complicated by yeast infections, and special medication is needed.

I've heard new parents say, "I change his diaper all the time. I don't know why he got diaper rash." Yep, that makes sense. Diaper rash can be caused by a variety of reasons. The following table has a list of situations that may cause a rash and their solutions.

Diaper Rash	
Situation	*Solution*
Allergy to the type of diaper you're using	Change diaper brands.
Allergy to the type of baby wipe you're using	Change baby-wipe brands or just use soap and water. Try the unscented wipes.
Detergent used for cloth diapers is too strong	Change detergent.
Leaving a wet or dirty diaper on too long	Check your child's diaper often.
Hot weather	Your baby sweating, combined with the pee or poop, along with the diaper bottom being warm, dark, and wet, begs for diaper rash to occur. This is a good time to go diaperless.
Constant diarrhea	Diarrhea can be caused from teething, a stomach virus, tension, drinking too much juice, a food allergy, or eating something that is too strong for a child's system. Look at your child's diet, health, and mouth.
Food sensitivity	Change formulas, or take your child off the solid food recently started. Diaper rash can be a sign of your child reacting to a new food.

The Great Diaper Mystery

The freckle-faced kid at the checkout counter asks, "Paper or plastic?" You seem to loose at either choice: Do you want to use paper and kill a tree to take home your groceries, or do you want to use plastic and fill up landfills?

Another major life puzzle you'll face as a new parent is cloth versus disposable diapers. People can become fanatical about the subject, and boxes of literature have been produced arguing the pros and cons of both.

My advice: Use cloth or disposable and don't feel bad about your choice. It's a diaper. It collects poop and pee. Nothing more. The choice of what diaper to use seems to be a hot topic among parents. Some may look at this as wasted energy.

Disposable diapers

Good luck when you start hunting for disposable diapers. The shelves are plum full of different brands, sizes, shapes — even those intended for girls, those for boys. It's amazing. Here are some pros and cons for using disposable diapers:

Pros

- Disposables are easy; you just throw them away.
- Traveling is easier with disposables.
- Disposables are great for kids who have diarrhea because these diapers don't leak.

Cons

- Disposables don't disintegrate — so they fill up landfills more.
- Disposables can be expensive.
- Using disposables may increase the time it takes to potty train your child because the little one can't feel it when he's wet.

Cloth diapers

I remember my aunt Margie telling stories about how she used to hang diapers out to dry when there was snow piled up to her knees. Can you imagine how cold those diapers were when she took them down? I often wondered whether she let them warm up before using them on my cousins. Oh well, cloth diapers have some advantages as well as some disadvantages.

Pros

- ✔ Cloth is more natural.

- ✔ Cloth diapers now come with Velcro straps, so you don't have to worry about safety pins.

- ✔ If you don't like washing diapers, you can use a diaper service that will pick up, wash, and deliver diapers to you on a weekly or biweekly basis (provided you don't live too far out in the hills).

- ✔ Washing your own diapers is less expensive than using a service. Cloth diapers, regardless of whether you use a service or wash them yourself, are less expensive than disposables.

- ✔ Cloth diapers make great burp rags (placed on your shoulder so the liquid burps don't get on you). When your kids grow out of them, they make great dusting rags.

Cons

- ✔ Cloth diapers use water and electricity to wash.

- ✔ Cloth diapers must be rinsed out in the toilet, and you have to deal with the mess and the smell.

- ✔ Cloth diapers leak more than disposables (even with the plastic outer pants).

- ✔ Cloth diapers are not good for travel because you have to carry the used diapers with you.

The problems with both disposable and cloth diapers are that both can cause diaper rash equally, and both smell really bad after they've been used.

The diaper solution

One possible solution to the diaper dilemma is using a combination of cloth and disposable. Yes, that's allowed! Use cloth diapers at home and then use disposable diapers for trips, outings to the store, when your child has diarrhea, and possibly even for nap and bedtime.

If you decide to go with the cloth diapers, use a diaper service for the first couple of months after you have your new baby. You're going to be too tired and busy with your newborn to take the time to wash out diapers. You'll be surprised by how much poop and pee a little newborn can produce.

Chapter 10

Just for Babies: Sleeping, Bathing

In This Chapter

▶ Drifting off to dreamland

▶ Keeping your baby clean

Ahh, sleep. Don't you just love a nap on a cold winter day, wrapped up in a blanket, next to a fire? Or lying in a hammock under a tree on a warm summer day? Yeah, naps are great. Then why do kids fight sleeping so much? What's the problem? Sleep is good.

Parents have wrestled with their kids' sleeping problems for eons and still haven't found any easy answers, like pressing the "Sleep" button. I think they may be looking for simple solutions where there aren't any, but getting your kids to fall asleep isn't as difficult as parents tend to make it.

Rock-a-bye Baby: Getting Your Infant to Sleep

If only all kids would sleep as easily and soundly as a newborn, our lives as parents would be near perfect. Of course, keeping them asleep for any amount of time is the trick.

Developing a sleeping routine for babies varies from child to child. The child's temperament and her family's lifestyle determine how she sleeps. Coming up with a sleeping schedule always is a challenge. Be open to different approaches to getting babies to sleep, bearing in mind that not all methods will work with your baby.

Baby sleep facts

Here are some particulars about infant sleeping that can help you better understand how your baby sleeps, thus demystifying this whole sleeping issue.

Babies have shorter and lighter sleep cycles than adults. That is why they usually wake up two or three times a night from birth to 6 months. As they grow older, they'll wake up once or twice a night from 6 months to 1 year; and then they may awaken once a night when they reach 1 to 2 years of age.

Babies' sleep habits typically are developed by their individual temperaments rather than your abilities to get your baby to sleep. It isn't your fault that your baby wakes up, but your before-bedtime rituals have something to do with how easily your child goes to bed. Even when you're dead tired and need to sleep, you can't force your baby to go to sleep. You can, however, create a safe environment that enables your baby to fall asleep easily. Doing so is the best way to establish long-term healthy sleep habits.

Helping your baby sleep

Creating a safe and comfortable environment for your child makes falling asleep an easier process. Some things that you can do to help your baby fall asleep include:

- Holding your baby often during the day. Babies love to be held close, such as in a baby sling.

- Keeping your baby on as much of a regular schedule as possible, such as regular feeding times and bedtimes. You also need to consider how late naps may keep babies up later at night.

- Establishing a relaxed, quiet routine leading up to bedtime, such as a warm bath or massage, singing, or reading a book. Rock your baby. Nurse the baby at the breast or with a bottle. Any active play primes your baby, making it easier and more likely that she will stay awake.

- Waiting until your baby has entered a deep sleep (you'll notice the limp limbs and a motionless face) before moving your baby to a cradle or bed. However, when babies turn 5 to 6 months old, start putting babies to bed when they are sleepy (as opposed to being asleep). That helps your baby to associate the crib with the time to go to sleep.

- Wrapping newborn babies with the blanket like they do in hospitals. Newborns prefer to be *swaddled* in this way. Older babies, however, usually prefer loose covers.

✔ Playing a soothing sound, such as a recording of a mother's heartbeat, sounds of a water fall, ocean sounds, or soft background noise like a fan or dishwasher.

Why babies wake up at night

Babies change dramatically during their first year. These changes can and do affect their sleep. Here are some things that may affect how your baby sleeps.

✔ Pain or discomfort related to teething, dirty diapers, hunger, too hot or too cold temperatures, or irritating sleepwear (watch for elastic).

✔ Medical problems such as a stuffy nose from colds, fever, or the common ear infection (which is the fluid getting trapped in the eustachian tube and causing an infection).

✔ Stressful events such as when routines are not kept and schedules change.

Rituals

Whatever ritual or habit you start with your newborn to get her to sleep is the same ritual or habit she'll come to expect as she gets older. So start your child's lifetime sleeping habits off right. Lay your baby down in her bed when it's time for her to sleep — meaning after your child has eaten and when you see her going into that deep sleep stage. When your child gets older, she'll understand that lying in her bed means sleep time.

The older your children get, the less they'll sleep, and the more their personalities will come out. Then they start exerting their will — and everything is messy from then on. Be grateful for your newborn — she typically doesn't need help falling asleep.

Bedtime

Babies actually adapt to schedules rather nicely. Always allow room for changes in these schedules. As they grow, their naps grow shorter, and they sleep longer during the night. Basically, as much as parents hate it, they grow up. They're heading for that day when they won't need naps.

Getting your older kids to bed is easier when they have a set schedule. These schedules slowly change over time, so you must be aware of and sensitive to these changes as they happen.

Establish a bedtime for your kids. Remember, this is your *kids'* bedtime. It's the time when they act like they need to go to bed. It isn't the time when *you* would like for them to go to bed. Those are usually two different times. Your child's bedtime also isn't the time that *you* think she ought to go to bed, simply because that's when *you* went to bed when *you* were a kid. Your children have their own clocks to go by. And, when you have more than one child, be aware that each of your children may have an individual bedtime, depending on his or her age.

You have to be observant of your children to determine what their needs are. Pay attention to how long their naps are and how long they sleep through the night. When you're aware of your child's sleeping patterns, predicting when she needs to go to bed becomes easier.

When you find that your children don't want to go to bed until midnight, you can adjust their schedules. Cut their naps shorter, or get them up in the morning instead of allowing them sleep in. Or, you may have to do a combination of both. Adjusting their sleeping habits keeps them more in line with what is reasonable.

SIDS

SIDS (sidz) *abbrev.* SUDDEN INFANT DEATH SYNDROME: the sudden death of an infant who has had no serious illnesses and no apparent cause of death. *(SIDS also is also known as crib death, because it occurs when the baby is sleeping.)*

The National Vital Statistics Report cites this bit of scary information: SIDS remains the leading cause of death in the United States among infants between 1 month and 1 year of age. If that isn't scary enough, here's another bit of information: *The cause of SIDS remains unknown.*

Even though the cause of SIDS is unknown, the facts that research has shown are that:

- ✔ Babies from newborns up until 1 year of age are the target victims for SIDS. Most deaths occur by the end of the sixth month, with the greatest number taking place between 2 and 4 months of age.
- ✔ SIDS occurs in all types of families and is largely indifferent to race or economic standing.
- ✔ SIDS occurs mostly among males, those babies born with low birth weights, and premature babies.

✔ Babies are three times more likely to die of SIDS if:

• Their mother smoked during and after pregnancy.

• The mother is younger than 20 years old.

• Prenatal care is poor.

• The mother experiences a low weight gain.

• The mother is anemic.

• Illegal drugs were used during pregnancy.

• There was a history of sexually transmitted disease.

Putting your baby to bed properly is critical. Follow these guidelines:

✔ Lay babies on their backs or sides when they sleep. Do not lay them on their stomachs.

✔ Don't put extra bedding in the crib such as lambskins, pillows, or thick comforters. Babies can become overheated or caught up in bedding and suffocate. Keep bedding simple. All you need is a sheet, bumper pads, and a thin cotton blanket.

✔ Don't overdress babies. Keep the pajamas simple and without a lot of layers. You don't want your baby to become overheated.

Rolling up a couple of blankets or towels into long wiener shapes and putting one behind and one in front of your baby (see Figure 10-1) helps keep her propped on her side and prevents her from falling either backward or forward.

Figure 10-1:
Two towels or small blankets rolled as props to keep a baby on her side for sleep.

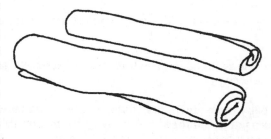

Bathing Babies

Giving babies a bath three or four times a day isn't necessary, even though it may look like they need one after every meal. Parents tend to want to give a lot of baths either because freshly washed kids smell so darn good or they just feel that awful pressure of having a fresh and pretty baby.

Bathing newborns

Newborns don't even get a real bath until their umbilical cord stubs fall off. Until that happens, sponge them off with a washcloth and thereafter give them a bath every other day. Use a cloth to wash their faces, hands, bottoms, and necks on the days they don't get a full bath (their necks are where the drooling milk goes to hide so that it can start to really smell bad at a later time). You may also just want to wash and dry one body part at a time so that babies don't get cold from the evaporation and heat loss.

Newborns typically don't like baths. Being stripped naked and put into water makes them uncomfortable. To help them feel a little more secure, try

- Keeping your body as close to your baby as possible. That is why a new-born tub in a kitchen sink comes in handy. The bath is at your level so you don't have to be a contortionist to stay close to your baby.

- Keeping a warm washcloth on your baby's stomach. Doing so makes babies feel like they have something on and aren't naked to the world.

- Keeping the room in which you're bathing your baby warm. Babies chill easily.

- Talking to your baby in a soft, comforting manner. Your voice calms a nervous baby.

It usually doesn't take a long time for a newborn to get used to — and eventually like — bathtime.

When you give your baby too many baths, her soft baby skin that we all wish we could still have turns dry. And then your baby will develop dry patches of skin.

Don't give babies a bath — especially newborns — right after they eat. Movement in the bath can cause babies to spit up. And never leave a baby alone in a bathtub — even one of those little yellow plastic tubs that sit in your sink.

Bathing infants

Infants (baby between the ages of 3 months to 1 year) need a bath once a day (or at least every other day if that's all you can manage). Don't spare that washcloth on face and hands during the day, too — after meals, for example. They'll fight you on the face washing, but remember, you're the boss, so get it done.

You should always have one hand on your baby when she bathes. She'll squirm and topple over easily, and if you pour water over her face she'll stiffen her little body and fall backward. If you aren't holding her well, she'll bonk her head.

Baby stores sell some wondrous things that are supposed to help hold up your baby while you bathe her. Save your money. Just do a good job supporting her with your arms and hands and only fill the tub with an inch or two of water.

Caring for a baby's penis

A baby boy's circumcised penis requires special care until the circumcision has healed. Follow your doctor's instructions, which usually include placing a petroleum-jelly gauze on the tip of the penis and replacing it when you change diapers. The petroleum jelly prevents the tip of the penis from sticking to the diaper. After it heals, you can stop using the petroleum jelly. If a plastic bell was used to circumcise your baby, you can expect it to fall off on its own in seven to ten days.

Because there are now different kinds of devices used for the circumcising process, please get specific instructions from your doctor about proper care.

A circumcised penis will be red and may develop a yellowish tissue as it heals. Call your doctor if your baby has fever or has pus draining from the circumcision site.

If your baby is not circumcised, then no special care is required. You may occasionally notice whitish lumps of matter called *smegma* coming from underneath your child's foreskin. This is normal and is just the shedding of old skin cells that work their way out from under the foreskin.

Also remember that you do not want to force back the foreskin in an uncircumcised infant.

Chapter 11

Doing Your Part for the Economy: Food, Clothes, and Gear for Babies

In This Chapter

▶ Finding those dining and fashion essentials

▶ Stuffing your duffel bag

▶ Choosing the right car seat

*T*ools, stuff, gadgets, things, doohickeys — having a baby is no cheap endeavor. But the first bit of good news is that you don't need everything all at once, so save taking out a second mortgage for a later time (like when your kids go to college or when they start T-ball). The second bit of good news is that you really don't need everything that you see advertised on TV or in those parenting magazines. Nope, you just need the basics. And some cute stuffed animals!

Manufacturers are so worried about getting sued that they take care to send safe products to market. But if you are concerned about a particular baby product, you can go to the Web site called Children's Safety Zone that has current product-recall information. It can be found at www.sosnet.com/safety/recall.html.

However, you need to ask whether a particular product is the most convenient and whether it will hold together. That is where research comes in. Friends are truly the best source for this information because only an experienced mother can tell you that when you buy a stroller, for example, look for one that has storage capacity and can be broken down with one hand. If you have a toddler in addition to a baby, get a double stroller so both kids can ride together. See? Great advice!

This chapter has more great advice for you. Enjoy!

Food Supplies (Or Bottles and Nipples)

Although you may be planning to breast-feed (see Chapter 8), you still need bottles for giving your baby water during those times after breast-feeding or whenever just a swig is needed to wet your baby's whistle. Bottles also are needed for those times when you decide to go out and leave the baby with grandma for the night. You'll, no doubt, need to do that at some time just for your own sanity's sake.

A moderate selection of different types of bottles and nipples is available, so, as is true of many baby products, choosing can be a bit confusing. The three main types of nipples are standard, standard premature, and orthodontic-type nipples. Most babies do well with standard nipples, but try the others if your baby is having problems.

As far as bottles go, watch out for:

✔ Bottles (or anything) made of glass. They break easily, and your child will throw his bottle at some point in time!

✔ Bottles with the plastic liners. These bottles are supposed to reduce the amount of air that your baby gets, thus reducing the amount of spit up. Research, however, hasn't been conducted that proves this belief to be true. Besides, plastic liners sometimes leak. And if you're an environmentalist, need I say anything more about the waste of plastic liners? Waste! Waste! Waste!

Clothing Supplies

Your baby's primary item of clothing is the diaper — although it's actually more of a collection tool than an article of clothing. Your only choices for diapers are cloth and disposable. See Chapter 9 for more about "The Diaper Thing." It contains information that helps with your diaper dilemma, and it helps you take care of your baby's number one task and product.

You can be a little more creative with other clothes for baby. Even so, don't trust anyone who tells you that you need *this* many shirts, *that* many nighties, and so on. The rule is that however much you have is however much you'll need. Yet, it is true that the more you have, the less often you have to do laundry. However, when your baby is growing at a fast rate, you may have too many clothes and end up not using them. Only *you* can decide how much of everything you need.

Buy clothing that is flame retardant (if you can find it — pajamas typically are flame retardant). The label on the clothing, or the packaging, will mention whether the clothes are flame retardant.

Avoid clothes with drawstrings in them. The drawstrings have been known to get caught in a variety of things — like slides, elevators, escalators — and can cause your child to get hurt.

An easy way to shop for children's clothing is through catalogs. You don't even have to leave the house! Right in the comfort of your own home, you can sit and order clothes without having to drag your kids all over the place. One of my favorites is Hanna Andersson (800-222-0544). The clothes may seem a little pricey, but they won't fall apart, and you'll end up using them longer than a lot of other clothes simply because of the way they're made. They last forever! You can also order online at www.hannaandersson.com.

Bathroom Equipment

No, don't go buying pint-sized porcelain toilets for your precious little poop-maker. At least, not at first.

Actually, baby's first bathroom equipment will probably be a bathtub, specifically one of those small plastic bathtubs that have a sponge lining. These tubs are great for newborns. They're sturdy, they keep the baby at your level so you're not leaning over, and they make bathing in the sink safe and easy. Granted, this special tub is not a must-have item. It's still possible to bathe baby in a sink. However, the plastic tublet is inexpensive, washable, and portable.

Another bathroom item you'll eventually get for babies is a potty. That's their own, wee toilet, upon which they'll hopefully one day — and with much glee — take their first real poop.

Infant Seats

No, babies aren't yearning for an 18-foot-long, L-shaped sofa/recliner with built-in popcorn tray, but they still need a few core items — maybe not tiny furniture, but some special things — that are just their size, such as an infant seat.

Infant seats are those little chairs that you plop your baby in while you're trying to get things done around the house. They're light enough that you can take them to any room that you and baby are going. Some seats are adjustable so that your baby can be sitting up, or lying back; some bounce with your baby, and some even have covers to block the sun.

Changing Tables

Changing tables are tables for changing diapers and clothing. They're like backless bookcases with a small holding pen for baby on top. On shelves below the changing area, you store diapers and other changing paraphernalia.

Fortunately, changing tables are getting bigger and better and cooler than ever. They used to be wobbly, flimsy stands that swayed back and forth when you put your baby on top. Now they're sturdy, truly handy, and look like a piece of furniture that you wouldn't mind keeping. There are even tables called 3-in-1 cradle/changing tables. They start as a cradle and then swing into position to become a changing table. Nifty!

Changing tables obviously need to be large enough to hold your baby. They also need a strap to hold down a baby who gets to that squirmy stage. If you're using a changing table that doesn't have a safety strap, you can buy straps and put them on yourself. Voilà! Other nice amenities are drawers or shelves for storing diapers, wipes, and the other goodies that you need.

If you have a house that has more than one level, and you don't feel like walking up and down stairs to change diapers (or have the energy), use one of your bathrooms as a changing station. Use a bathroom counter that is long and wide enough to lay your baby on. Clear away everything from the counter, put a towel down for your baby to lie on, and place all your supplies in the drawer under the counter. This way you have access to a sink for washing away *really* poopy diapers.

Never, ever walk away from a baby on a changing table. Never leave and never take your hand off your child.

Bedding and Stuff

Baby's biggest piece of furniture probably will be a crib. But before a crib, you may want to consider a bassinet, which can be much more handy than a crib, especially for a newborn.

Bassinets are small, compact, and easy to move around — just like your baby. You can easily take this bed anywhere baby goes. But if you don't like the idea of spending from $50 to $200 on something that you'll probably use for only a short period of time, forget it. Use a crib, instead.

Anymore, cribs are fairly easy to pick. Crib manufacturers must abide by federal regulations, so their products are safe for your baby. Your only decision is finding one that *matches* your nursery theme.

If you're unhappy with the selection of cribs at your local stores, get on the Internet and type `baby bedding` in one of the search engines. Oh my, the selection!

You'll also need receiving blankets and heavier-weight blankets. Receiving blankets are lightweight and used for keeping your baby wrapped in as you both just hang out. Warmer blankets wrap around a sleeping baby. Never use heavy comforters. Your baby could get caught up in them and suffocate.

Bumper pads are *side blankets* that should fit all the way around the crib and either tie or snap together. These fasteners should be attached on the *outside* of the crib so that your baby can't play with them. If the ties are excessively long, tie them where you want them, and then cut off the extra string. This way baby won't be tempted to pull on the ties and, of course, eventually want to stick them in his mouth.

Never buy an antique crib. Although antique cribs are beautiful, they are not safe. Crib slats should be no more than 2⅜ inches apart, and the mattress must fit so snugly that you can't wedge more than two fingers between it and the crib. If the slats are too far apart, a baby can get caught between the crib slats and strangle himself.

A Night Light

Night lights are for more than scaring away the Closet Monster. Positioning night lights wherever you might walk in the middle of the night is nice. Turning on a bright bathroom light at 2 o'clock in the morning is an awful experience for you and your baby. I suggest that you buy light-sensitive night lights that automatically turn on when it gets darker, and then shut off when it gets light. The last thing you want to do is stumble around in the dark trying to find the night light to turn on because you forgot to do it before you went to bed.

When the Little One Goes a-Travelin'

We are a mobile society. We love to travel and go. Soon your child will be going with you to the grocery store, to grandma's, to the park, and maybe elsewhere — providing you're bold enough to take a baby on a trip, supplied with all the right equipment of course!

Important baby bag contents

As your baby grows older, you'll find that you have less to carry with you. And, if your trips are short, you don't necessarily have to load up with everything. But here is a list of things you don't want to be caught without.

- Diapers
- Burp-up towel
- Change of clothing
- Water
- Bib
- Baby wipes
- Changing cushion
- Pacifier
- Bottles
- Doctor's phone number
- Diaper-rash ointment and baby Tylenol
- Food/spoon/snack
- Blanket
- Nipples
- Insurance and allergy information

The all-important-wouldn't-leave-home-without-it diaper bag

Mary Poppins had quite a bag. It was a good size, held everything, and it didn't make one of her arms longer than the other. If only they made such a bag. (Who can forget Julie Andrews pulling all that wonderful stuff out of her bag in Disney's *Mary Poppins*? Little Michael Banks even looked under the table to make sure it wasn't trick photography. Amazing.)

Hip parents of today use oversized travel bags or large purses in place of traditional diaper bags.

Big travel bags or even backpacks are a great idea. They're bigger so they can be used as a purse in addition to having the diapers, wipes, clothes, blankets, and the kitchen sink — which you now must carry with you whenever you go anywhere.

The only things that regular diaper bags have that these oversized bags don't are those special slots to put bottles in so that the bottles don't tip and leak all over the bottom of the bag. (Of course, there *are* bottle lids and caps you can use so that stuff doesn't happen.)

Car seat

You must have a car seat. It's the law. It doesn't matter whether you never plan on taking your baby anywhere, hospitals won't let you leave with your new baby unless and until you have a car seat.

Many brands of car seats are out there — with subtle differences between them in design and fashion. The most popular type of car seat is the one where the seat detaches from the base, and you can carry your baby and the seat all in one. Or you can even find one kind that enables you not only to carry the seat but also to attach it to a stroller. You don't have to wake up a baby to get him out of the car, or unwrap a baby in cold weather. Just unlatch the seat and go.

Go to www.nhtsa.dot.gov/people/injury/childps/recall/canister.htm to find out the latest child-seat-safety recall listing. This is a current list of manufacturers' child seat recalls.

Detachable car seats (where you carry the baby and the seat) are not good for older, heavier babies. For them, you'll have to invest in a larger seat — or just buy the detachable kind that goes with a stroller. In addition:

✓ Don't use a car seat that has been involved in a car accident.

✓ Don't use an infant seat (like those from swings) as a car seat.

✓ Strap the car seat down with the car's seat belts.

  Make use of that special doohickey that you need to lash attach the over-the-neck seat belt to the lap belt. Attach this to the side of the car seat opposite from where you buckle the belt. Doing so keeps the seat from tipping over when you round a corner (and with the way you drive . . .).

✓ Strap your child down with the car seat's restraining belt.

✓ Never put a baby in the front seat where there is an airbag.

✓ Infants are safest when they ride facing the rear of the car (see Figure 11-1). In fact, your baby should ride facing the rear until he's about 1 year of age or at least 20 pounds.

If the idea of buying more than one kind of car seat doesn't appeal to you, look for one that you can use until your child reaches 40 pounds or 40 inches in height. The law requires that your child remain in a car seat until he reaches one of those dimensions or until he's 4 years old. In fact, most states' written driver's tests use the 40 pounds/4-year-old limitation as a question. Don't miss that one!

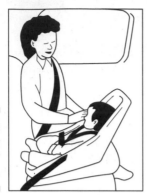

Figure 11-1:
Rear-facing
car seat for
an infant.

Some car seats are even known as car beds, and they're really good for pre-mature babies (babies born earlier than 37 weeks).

If you have a big baby or towering toddler, consider getting one of those lap-restraint types of car seats. Commonly called toddler seats, these abbreviated car seats are ideal for kids who are too big for traditionally sized car seats.

If you're concerned that you may not be using or installing your car seat the right way, you can go to www.carseat.org. This is the SafetyBeltSafe USA Web site, which has some great information for you.

"If you loved me, you'd wear our baby around your neck"

Baby slings make you look like you're recovering from surgery that attached your baby to your hip, chest, or back. Still, people who've had such surgery tend to compensate for their wobbliness by using free arms — and are otherwise unencumbered. For this reason, baby slings can be extremely handy.

Personally, I love baby slings. I also think babies love them, too. Having your baby physically close to you is a nice idea. Your baby will love the closeness and, in return, will fuss less often while riding in it.

Keep the following stuff about baby slings in mind:

 ✔ Getting the hang of baby slings is hard, but they're good for newborns up to toddlers. Learning how to arrange your baby in the baby sling may take a little time and practice, but after you get used to a sling, it's great.

 ✔ Babies like being all scrunched up, and that is how they usually ride in a sling. However, don't let them stay that way too long, or they'll become uncomfortable.

✔ Front packs are great for newborns, but bad for older babies and toddlers (see Figure 11-2 for front packs and backpacks). Without any support for your back, the heavier your baby gets, the harder your baby is to carry.

✔ Backpacks offer fairly good back support, so you can carry your kids in them as they grow heavier. However, backpacks are *not* good for newborns, because they don't have the body weight to hold themselves up, and the backpacks don't offer the support needed for a baby's head and neck. A newborn in a backpack would just crumple down into a little ball. You don't want that to happen.

✔ Backpacks also offer open invitations for hair pulling.

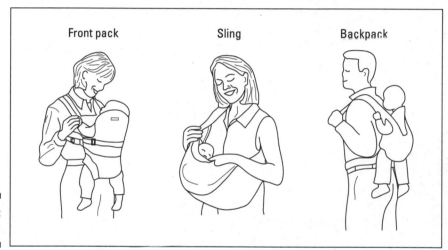

Figure 11-2:
Hands free!

Goodies Your Child Will Eventually Need

As babies gets bigger, their needs change. Along with those changes come some new equipment you'll need to consider buying. Again, most of these are common, baby-associated items. The following sections offer some pointers on what to get and what to avoid for the slightly bigger baby.

New tools for chow time

The day soon will come when your beautiful little baby will be sitting in a highchair throwing spaghetti all over himself, you, and your kitchen. So, of course, you want to have a chair that gives your child the optimal amount of throwing power.

Highchairs

Important highchair details include:

- ✔ **Crotch strap**

  Having a belt for the waist isn't enough. If the belt is too loose, your child can slide under it just enough to get caught and possibly get hurt. The crotch strap is attached to the waist belt but doesn't allow your baby to slip much.

- ✔ **One-handed tray latching**

  These latches usually are in the front, underneath the tray. Many a day you'll hold your baby with one hand and try to get the tyke in the highchair with the other. It's so much easier when you only have to use one hand to unlatch the tray. (Two-handed latches are common in restaurants.)

- ✔ **Adjustable seat**

  The chair seat should be up-or-down adjustable, so that if you want to include your baby in a family dinner, or if your toddler is getting to the point where he can eat with the family but the dining chair is too big, you can adjust the seat up or down to fit at the table.

Figure 11-3 illustrates a chair with the right fittings.

Don't buy an antique highchair. If you like the antique look, new products are available that are made to look like antiques. These are fine. They meet the safety requirements that you want for your baby equipment.

Don't forget to use a plastic mat, scrap carpet, or old, ugly sheet under your high chair if it's sitting on the good carpeting. Nothing stains your carpet quicker than baby food. Strained carrots are the worst.

A simple dining set for baby

By the time your kids turn 1, they'll want to start holding their own cups and feeding themselves. Break out the camera — and consider the following:

- ✔ **Cups with a weighted bottom (a spill-proof cup), two handles, a lid, and a spout**

- ✔ **Plates with separate compartments**

  Such plates are good for toddlers who can be really picky about their food. Sometimes they don't like their foods to touch. (Heck, I know some adults who refuse to eat a sandwich that has been sliced in two by the same knife used to previously slice a sandwich made with mayonnaise.)

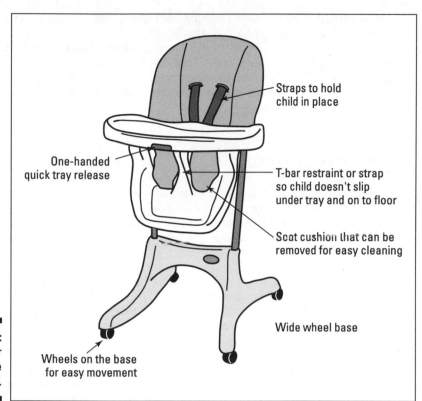

Straps to hold
child in place

One-handed
quick tray release

T-bar restraint or strap
so child doesn't slip
under tray and on to floor

Seat cushion that can be
removed for easy cleaning

Wide wheel base

Figure 11-3:
Highchair
with all the
right stuff.

Wheels on the base
for easy movement

- ✔ **Bowls with suction bottoms**

   This item helps little ones discover how to eat from a bowl without the bowl ending up on the floor.

- ✔ **Toddler-sized fork and spoon**

   These small devices are easier for little hands to operate and to aim for little mouths.

Avoid glass. It breaks. You'll discover soon enough that babies like to throw their plates, bowls, and glasses when they're done with them. It's part of a child's joy of discovering gravity.

The ever-unpopular bib

Invest in bibs so you can save on extra washings. When children turn 1 year old or so, they'll be determined to feed themselves. May I suggest wearing clothing that you don't mind having food flung upon?

Cloth bibs also are good for teething babies. All that drool has to go somewhere, and cloth bibs absorb all the liquid, whereas plastic bibs just let it keep rolling off onto the floor, dog, cat, or whatever happens to be beneath it. Actually, plastic bibs aren't really good for anything. They don't absorb the food or liquid (which is what you want), and when you wash and dry them, they turn hard and crack and then begin smelling bad. YUCK! Just avoid the plastic bibs.

Out and about

Nothing hurts me more than seeing parents dragging their toddler along, pulling a chubby little arm out of its socket. Baby legs are short, and it takes babies many more steps to keep up with your slowest walking pace. And sometimes babies just don't want or know how to walk. In either case, it's time for a stroller.

Two basic types of strollers are available: the umbrella stroller and the super-deluxe limousine type of stroller. The difference (aside from price) is that the umbrella stroller is lightweight and doesn't take up much room. The super strollers, on the other hand, are bigger and take up considerable trunk space.

The choice of which stroller you use is up to you — and baby. Keep in mind that umbrella strollers aren't good for newborns: Babies can't lie down in them, and they offer no support for little bodies. A baby in an umbrella stroller just sits there and sinks down, eventually looking like a little ball of clay before ever so slowly tipping over forward — splat onto the ground.

Super strollers can be used from the day your baby is born all the way up into toddler ages. They're designed for storage of diaper bags and all the goodies that always accompany your kids. These strollers also are great for shopping; You just pile your bags beneath the stroller and take off.

In a stroller, look for:

- **A seat belt with a crotch strap**

  Seat belts aren't always enough. The crotch strap prevents your kid from using the seat belt as a chin strap.

- **A big basket underneath the seat for storage**

  These baskets are great for storing diaper bags, and any extra paraphernalia you manage to need — or pick up — while you're out shopping.

✔ **Wheel locks**

Strollers will roll away when parked on inclines or hills, so the wheel locks are an absolute necessity.

✔ **A wide wheelbase**

The distance between the front and back wheels, and from side-to-side, needs to be wide enough so that when your toddler leans forward, there's no risk of tipping him and the stroller over.

✔ **An adjustable seat**

You must be able to adjust the seat from a lying-down position to a sitting-up position.

Double strollers, which can seat two children, are handy when you have two children who are close in age and size.

A bionic ear for Mommy and Daddy

Those baby monitor listening devices are great to keep in your baby's room while he sleeps. You keep your end with you so that when baby wakes up or makes some unusual noise, you know immediately. That way the poor little tyke doesn't have to sit and scream for 15 minutes before you hear the commotion.

Use the baby monitor only as a signal for when your baby is sleeping. Don't rush to your baby at the first signs of stirring because he may go back to sleep on his own. Be sure that your baby's really awake and ready to be taken from the crib.

Don't use the baby monitor to justify leaving your children alone while they play. You should always supervise young children, especially babies and toddlers.

Just-for-fun Stuff

So many gizmos on the market are designed to make your baby happy that you'll grow dizzy looking at all of them. Meanwhile, your baby becomes happily dizzy from playing on some of these wonderful and often useful toys and contraptions.

Jump for joy in your Jolly Jumper

A Jolly Jumper (see Figure 11-4) is a great baby sitter for your kids (those that aren't any heavier than 25 pounds, anyway). This device hangs in a doorway with a seat attached to it. You place your baby in the seat, and the little one can then jump up and down to his heart's content — and basically be jolly.

If you need a justification for buying a Jolly Jumper, it's great for developing your children's leg muscles and, in general, is great fun for your kids. But on the whole, it's rather unnecessary.

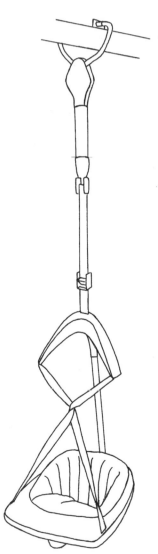

Figure 11-4:
A Jolly
Jumper.

Swinging babies

Swings are a great baby sitter, and your baby will love them. Back-and-forth. Again and again. The swings are good for a short time. But when your baby feels the need to sit up or move around, these things will be history.

Look for the kind of swing that has a detachable chair so you can take it with you around the house. The chair comes in handy when setting baby down. And, if you get this type of swing, remember to stop the swing and remove the chair before removing baby from the swing.

Most swings have a weight limit, which usually is around 25 pounds.

Grind me up some green beans, Mommy

Food processors are nice to have when your baby is making the transition from baby food to regular food. Although they're kind of unnecessary, because you can just as easily smash the food yourself with a fork, food like green beans sometimes just doesn't *smash* real well.

Chapter 12

Infant Health Concerns

· ·

In This Chapter

▶ Going through the first routine checkups

▶ Understanding your main concerns

· ·

Healthy kids mean healthy adults. Your goal is keeping your baby healthy so she grows up to be a healthy big kid, so she's a healthy adult. Now, no one that I know deliberately sets out to keep his or her kids in a sickly state. But, many illnesses that kids go through really baffle parents.

Listed in the sections below are concerns that parents have for their babies and the things you may want to know about these concerns.

Making It Through Your Baby's First Physical Exams

Your baby will go through a series of "well-baby" checkups right after the little tyke is born. Your pediatrician checks weight, growth and development, and the frequency of bowel movements and wet diapers. These factors are important because they let the doctor know whether enough food is going in (food in equals poop and pee out). Doctor visits become less frequent the older the baby gets.

During the first 48 hours of your child's life, the following series of tests will be given.

Apgar test

The Apgar test is a series of measurements of a newborn's vital signs that assess the baby's overall health. It's performed at one minute and at five minutes after birth. Five of your baby's vital signs are scored: heart rate, breathing, muscle tone, reflexes, and color. Each of the five vital signs is given a score between 0 (lowest) and 2 (highest). A total *Apgar score* of 7 to 10 indicates that your newborn is in good condition.

Having successful doctor visits — Dr. Mary Jo

Make your doctor visits as successful as possible by keeping track in writing of what you know your doctor will be asking, such as: How long does your baby sleep at night? How much is your baby eating? How many poopy diapers and wet diapers do you change during the day? What new skills has your baby added to her repertoire? If your baby's been sick, what are the symptoms and how long has she had them? Write down any questions or concerns you may have so that when you're at the doctor's office you don't forget your questions. (And then don't forget the list!) Be sure to bring your child's shot record if your child is receiving immunizations.

Jaundice test

Not all babies need a jaundice test. Your doctor will decide (see "Jaundice" later in this chapter). Blood is drawn from your baby's heel and tested for *bilirubin*, which are the red blood cells processed by the liver.

Hearing test

A hearing test is administered to determine whether intervention is necessary with regard to a baby's hearing, speech, or language to curb related delays in development. Hospitals use either the auditory brainstem response (ABR) test or the otoacoustic emissions test (OAE).

State-mandated screens

The kinds of mandated screening that your baby undergoes vary by state, but they are conducted to check for various diseases and genetic disorders. These tests require a blood sample that is taken from your baby's heel.

Understanding the Things that Parents Worry About

In the remaining sections of this chapter, I discuss concerns that many parents have for their infant.

SIDS

Sudden infant death syndrome (SIDS) is the sudden death of an infant under 1 year of age that remains unexplained after a complete investigation. The cause of SIDS is unknown, but a list of the elements that relate to SIDS is provided in Chapter 10, which covers the topic in greater detail.

Coughing and croup

Kids cough — a lot! Coughing is a symptom that usually accompanies an infection such as a cold. It can also indicate more serious disorders. But, if coughing is in any way related to the lungs, getting your kids to cough to clear them out is good.

However, if your kids are coughing because of a dripping down their throats from a sinus infection or allergies, then no, coughing doesn't help anything. So, know the difference between your coughs. Elevating the head helps with postnasal drip as does frequent suctioning of the nose with a suction bulb. You can keep your child's head elevated by adding a rolled blanket under the crib mattress.

Croup is a dreaded word that parents hate to hear. It's a dreaded word because there is no cure for croup. *Croup* is caused by a variety of viruses but is an infection that commonly occurs in children ages 6 months to 3 years. The virus causes inflammation and infection in the lower throat and swelling and buildup of mucus and secretions that narrow air passages. This narrowing causes the distinctive barking-seal cough. Croup commonly begins in the middle of the night. Your child may have had cold symptoms for a few days already and then wakes up with a loud, dry, barking cough. You can steam up the bathroom (and sit in there with your child) to help her breath easier. Cool night air also tends to help. If neither one of these measures helps and your child is still struggling to breathe, seek medical care immediately.

Ear infections

Ear infections are common in children, especially those younger than 2 years of age. Don't be surprised when you're heading off to the doctor, *yet again,* because of ear infections. Children suffer from two main types of ear infections, outer-ear infections and middle ear infections. Children are more at risk for getting middle ear infections when they're exposed to many other children, when they're frequently around cigarette smoke, when another family member has suffered many ear infections, or when they lay down while drinking a bottle. Ear infections are less common in children who breast-feed.

Preventing ear infections — Dr. Mary Jo

Ear infections are an inflammation within the middle ear cavity. The ear produces fluid to rinse out the middle ear to get rid of any bacteria that sometimes sneak into the ear. This fluid then drains down the eustachian tube, which runs from the middle ear to the back of the throat. This constant rinsing and draining keeps the idle ear clean. If the eustachian tube is blocked, the ear can't drain, and the ear can get infected. The best way to prevent ear infections is keeping your children away from second-hand smoke, not permitting babies to sleep with a bottle, and limiting their exposure to others who have colds. It is also important to keep allergies under control because the presence of chronic allergies can also lead to ear infections.

Outer-ear infections also are known as *swimmers ear,* which usually occurs when your child gets water in her ear, which in turn, may lead to inflammation and infection. This is more common in older children. Any symptoms of earache that your child has will be worse when you move her outer earlobe. She may also have discharge from the ear but probably won't have a fever. These infections usually are treated with antibiotic eardrops.

A middle ear infection typically occurs a week or two after your child has had an upper respiratory tract infection, which can cause inflammation and fluid to build up behind her eardrum. This fluid can then become infected with bacteria, and your child can develop pain in her ear, carry a fever, and become very irritable. You may even catch her tugging at her ears.

Going to the doctor and getting medications are the only things you can do to clear up ear infections.

Jaundice

Jaundice is a yellow coloring of the eyes and skin. This yellow coloring is the result of a buildup of a chemical in the blood called bilirubin. It is a common symptom in newborn babies and isn't usually a sign of serious illness. In very young babies, jaundice is quite common, so your doctor will check for jaundice in the first few well-baby visits. Most often the cause is physiological, meaning it is related to the slow transition of clearing bilirubin via the liver rather than the placenta after the baby is delivered. This type of jaundice usually first appears in the second or third day of life and peaks within the first week of life. The total level of bilirubin seldom reaches an amount worth becoming concerned about or requiring treatment. However, jaundice in babies and children over 1 month old requires a doctor's visit to help determine the cause.

Diarrhea

Diarrhea can cause panic in parents because, if left alone, it can lead to dehydration in children. Diarrhea usually is caused by a stomach virus, especially when it's also associated with vomiting and a low-grade fever. Mentioning any recent travels you've been on to your doctor when your child has diarrhea is important, because many cases of diarrhea are associated with travel. Ever heard of Montezuma's Revenge?

Most cases of diarrhea go away on their own without treatment, except that extra fluids help prevent dehydration. Diarrhea medications should usually be avoided in children unless your pediatrician specifically prescribes them. Also avoid giving too much juice as this can make diarrhea worse.

Blood in diarrheal stools or diarrhea for longer than 14 days should prompt a visit to your doctor.

Fever

Much to the surprise of many parents, fever by itself isn't harmful or dangerous. And unless it is very high — more than 106 or 107 degrees F — it is unlikely to cause brain damage or other problems. Parents in the past always were trained — by I don't know who — to believe that if their child had a fever that brain damage will occur. That just isn't true.

A child's temperature can vary during the day, and it can reach 100 degrees F at about 6:00 p.m., and that isn't cause for alarm. But, if you want some guidelines about what is normal and when to worry, call your pediatrician if:

- ✔ Your infant is younger than 3 months of age and has a rectal temperature above 100.4 degrees F.

- ✔ Your infant is 3 months to 6 months old and has a temperature above 101 degrees F.

- ✔ Your infant is older than 6 months and has a temperature of more than 103 degrees F.

Fever: The biggest parental concern — Dr. Mary Jo

Out of all the questions I get, parents seem the most concerned about their child having a fever. Parents are concerned that a high fever will damage their child in some way or cause brain damage. On the contrary, fever is the body's way of trying to fight off an infection. In trying to determine the cause and severity of an illness, the *other* symptoms your child has can be more helpful than the height of the fever. If a child has a high fever (105 to 106 degrees F), she should be evaluated to look for the cause, but the fever itself will not cause damage. This guideline does not apply, however, to infants under 3 months old because even low-grade temps may be a sign of a serious infection.

Runny noses

Is the runny nose a result of teething? Is it a cold? Is it allergies? A runny nose usually is associated with the common cold. Another common cause is allergies, especially when nasal drainage is clear. Persistent runny noses that last for more than 10 to 14 days, can indicate a sinus infection. Sinus infections can be painful, so see your pediatrician immediately. Take notice of the color of the mucus coming from the nose, because your doctor will want to know about it. Signs of a sinus infection include green or yellow mucus coming from the nose, halitosis, and facial swelling.

Thrush

Thrush is a common yeast infection in infants. It causes a white coating inside the mouth that cannot easily be removed and doesn't go away between feedings. Thrush usually does not cause any discomfort or feeding problems, but it can be transferred to nursing mothers, and that can be painful for the mother. Call your doctor to receive a medication to treat it because it probably won't go away on its own.

Vomiting

Vomiting usually is caused by a stomach virus and may also be accompanied by diarrhea. You should contact your pediatrician if you find blood or green bile in the vomit.

Giving small amounts of liquids frequently helps prevent dehydration. If your child is breast-fed, give smaller, more frequent feedings. If your child is bottle-fed, you can try Pedialyte or a similar oral electrolyte solution. Warning signs for dehydration include no tears when your child is crying, dry mucous membranes — such as sticky saliva versus the watery drool that normally comes from your child's mouth — and no urine for 12 hours.

Allergies

Allergic rhinitis, or hay fever, is a common problem in infants and children. The most common symptoms include a stuffy or runny nose with clear drainage, sneezing, itchy eyes and nose, sore throat, throat clearing, and a cough that may be worse at night and in the morning. Symptoms may occur only during certain times of the year — a seasonal allergy. Keeping kids indoors when high levels of pollen from trees or grasses are present can help. Children may also suffer from allergies relating to nasty things such as pets, dust mites, second-hand smoke, and molds. Don't try to guess about allergies. Let your pediatrician know if you are concerned that your child has allergies; treatment is available.

Colds

Here's the bad news: There is no treatment for the common cold. Here's more bad news: Colds spread easily and are probably the most frequent type of infection in children. In fact, eight to ten colds per year can be normal. The symptoms of the common cold include a runny nose — with clear, yellow, or green discharge — a cough, fever, sore throat, and irritability. Colds typically last 10 to 14 days. Because the common cold is caused by viruses, antibiotics are not effective against it, and they won't help you get better any faster.

You can try making your child more comfortable by using a pain or fever reliever and/or moisturizing nose drops, getting plenty of rest, drinking plenty of fluids, and using decongestants and/or cough suppressants, if needed for children older than 6 months old. Most pediatricians don't recommend these medications until children are older than 2 years old, so check with your pediatrician first. You can also use a humidifier, which helps loosen secretions. Use a cool mist in the humidifier to prevent burns.

Teach your kids early to wash their hands frequently (and you, too!), and to sneeze or cough into the bends of their arms, or a tissue, rather than their hands, which is where germs are to begin with. Prevention is the only real deterrent for colds.

Colic

Colic is a term that describes unexplained crying. A colicky baby will usually cry between one to two hours at a time. Colicky babies will draw up their legs and act like they're in a lot of pain. If your child under the age of three months cries but is not hungry, tired, or ill — and then acts fine for awhile — your child probably has colic. But go to your doctor and let an expert decide if it's colic. Your doctor will tell you to try a variety of things, such as changing the baby's formula. Or if you're breastfeeding, you'll be asked to cut out dairy products from your diet. It'll take a while to see if any of these steps helps. Sometimes they may, sometimes they may not.

A colicky baby is a nightmare. There's very little you can do to comfort a baby with colic. Picking a fussy baby up usually stops the fussiness. Picking up a colicky baby doesn't do anything.

Try these ideas for relieving colic. They may or may not work, but at least it'll give you something to do.

- ✔ You can try laying your baby on his stomach on your lap. Place one hand on his back and the other on his bottom, and then bounce your legs lightly. Sometimes you'll get a big burp out of him, or maybe he'll just puke down your leg. If you're really lucky, your baby will fall asleep.

- ✔ Try putting a warm water bottle on your baby's stomach. This may or may not work to comfort your baby, but at least it's worth trying.

- ✔ Give your baby weak mint or diluted chamomile tea. This may help with colic.

- ✔ Give your baby diluted 7-Up (half water/half 7-Up).

- ✔ Leave your baby with a family member or friend for the evening. You need your rest and some quiet time to help rekindle your nerves.

Colic is usually over by three months of age. If your baby continues to have symptoms of colic past this age, consult a doctor.

Cradle cap

Some mothers become hysterical with fear over cradle cap. Babies with cradle cap have greasy, yellow-colored, scaly areas with redness on their scalps. Your baby may also have redness behind her ears or on the creases of her neck. Cradle cap is not itchy and shouldn't cause your baby any discomfort. It improves on its own, but you can use a shampoo such as Selsun Blue and use a soft brush to remove the scales. Gentle scrubbing may be required to help remove the scale.

Chapter 13

Growth and Developmental Stuff

*W*hat is normal? When should you be concerned about things? Has your child reached the normal development milestones for holding a bottle, walking, talking, grabbing, and doing all those wonderful things that parents wait for with bated breath?

This chapter is dedicated to giving you general guidelines about the development of your child. Note that these are *general* stages of development that the average child reaches. Your child may vary somewhat from these descriptions or time guidelines, and that's okay. As always, whenever you're concerned, talk to your pediatrician. More than anything, I hope the information in this chapter serves as a reality check for you when your neighbor brags about his one-year-old daughter quoting Shakespeare and tap dancing.

Newborns

Newborns, in a sense, are like their own separate life-forms. They're so small and helpless, they sleep all the time, and their poop looks kind of different. Here's a person who you've been waiting nine months to meet, and now that he's here, you think, "What do I do now?"

You cherish them; that's what you do. During the first year of life, babies need a warm, loving environment. Hold your baby and respond to his cries. Don't ignore them. These actions are essential in building strong, healthy bonds. Disregard that old wives' tale that holding a baby spoils him. It isn't possible. You can't spoil a baby. Talking to your baby as you go about your day encourages your child's brainpower and begins developing his language skills. And sing! Yes, sing all day long. Babies enjoy having songs sung to them.

How a newborn looks

A newborn's head usually is the largest part of his body and may even seem to be shaped a little bit weird. The bones aren't firmly set and can be somewhat squished from moving through the birthing canal. Don't worry because this appearance doesn't last long.

A newborn's nose often is flat and may be covered with little pimple-like bumps, which are immature oil glands that will go away — so please don't try to wash them off.

The baby's breasts and genitals may look a little swollen, but like everything else, that will change. This swelling is a normal reaction to maternal hormones that the baby receives while in the womb.

Many parents are surprised by newborn skin. It typically isn't the rosy pink you'd expect, but rather is slightly blotchy and may be covered with a pale, cheesy coating. Your baby may also be covered with fine, downy hair that usually disappears within the first few weeks.

What a newborn does

A newborn can do many of the same things you can do: cough, sneeze, yawn, or even hiccup (all of which he can also do before he is born). He cries when he's uncomfortable or even lonely. He grasps and responds when startled. His reflexes include sucking and rooting to look for a nipple. A newborn can see to about 10 inches but doesn't focus very well. Make sure you keep your face close to your newborn.

Your baby is alert immediately after birth. He will probably even look right at you. He communicates his eagerness to feed by moving his hands to his mouth and making small mouth and tongue movements, eye movements (even when his eyes are closed), and body movements.

During the next several months, your baby will go through a series of well-baby checkup visits, and the routine for each visit is pretty much the same. Your baby's height, weight, and head circumference (the distance around the head) will be measured. The head is measured because the circumference of the head is an indirect measure of brain growth. If this growth rate slows, a problem may exist, and your doctor would determine why the head has stopped growing. You'll also be asked about new developments with your child since the last visit. This is a good time to talk about events that may have happened and that you're curious about or to ask any health questions you may have.

Keep a notepad in your child's room so you can write down any questions that you may have about your child's health or development. Get into a habit of taking the notepad with you on doctor visits so you can ask the right questions of your doctor and so you can document the doctor's answers without getting all the way home and wondering, "Now, what did she say?"

Another thing you'll see on your visit to the doctor is a chart where the weight and height will be documented. Your pediatrician will show you where your baby's measurements land on the standard growth curves. My kids were always way above the normal height and weight, and I quickly learned not to be concerned. The growth rate is much more important than what your baby's actual weight or height are at any given moment. That holds true for every checkup.

After a few of these visits, you'll join the ranks of mothers sharing weight and height differences of their children with each other. "My son weighed 24 pounds at 1 year." "My son weighed 24 pounds at 6 months!"

If a baby is premature, his development will be closer to his corrected age. For example, if your child is six weeks premature, subtract six weeks from the chronological age to get a corrected age to compare with growth and development.

Two weeks

By two weeks of age, your baby probably has regained most or all of the weight that he lost in his first week.

In the next few weeks, you can expect your baby to look at your face, startle at the sound of loud noises, lift his head, and begin smiling spontaneously. He may even begin recognizing familiar objects and sounds.

During your two-week visit, your pediatrician will ask the following questions. Don't worry if your baby doesn't seem to be able to do everything on the list. Every baby develops differently. Answers to these questions are guidelines that enable your doctor to monitor the growth and development of your child.

- ✔ Can your baby lift his head for short periods of time?
- ✔ Does your baby move his head from side to side?
- ✔ Is your baby able to focus on items 8 to 12 inches away?
- ✔ Does your baby respond to loud sounds and blink at bright lights?

One month

By the end of one month, a baby typically can lift his head for a short period of time, move his head from side to side, make jerky arm movements, and bring his hands to his face. You'll notice that he prefers looking at your face rather than anything else. He even turns toward your voice and other familiar sounds. He blinks at bright lights and may startle to loud sounds.

Two months

The glorious part of the two-month milestone is that your baby may begin showing signs of sleeping through the night. Hallelujah! In addition, you've probably adjusted to breast-feeding, and you're on a regular schedule.

Your pediatrician will ask you the following question, but again, don't worry if your baby hasn't mastered everything on the list.

- ✔ Does your baby smile?
- ✔ Does your baby coo?
- ✔ Can he repeat sounds like "ah" or "ooh"?
- ✔ Can your baby keep track of objects with his eyes?
- ✔ Is your baby lifting his head up when he is placed on his stomach?

Three months

At three months, your little guy is going to seem really active. He will be able to raise his head and chest when put on his stomach and kick and straighten his legs when on his back, which probably amuses him quite a bit. He can open and shut his hands and push down with his legs when he's placed on a hard surface. Hold on tight when he does, because he can get quite slippery when jumping around. He may even try jumping while on your lap.

You'll also notice that your baby has a great smile, imitates sounds, and recognizes objects and people and his hand-eye coordination is beginning to work to the extent that he can bring his hands together. Time to learn pat-a-cake!

Four months

Your doctor will ask more questions when your baby reaches four months of age. Again, your baby may not be able to do all of these, so don't lie to your doctor or stretch the truth. Many parents feel the need to paint a brighter picture of what's going on instead of being perfectly honest. Remember that you and your parenting skills are not being judged, but rather, these assessments serve as guidelines for your baby's development.

- Can your baby follow moving objects from side to side?
- Does your baby sleep through most of the night (somewhere around six to eight hours at night)?
- Does your baby seem to hear well?
- Is your baby rolling over?
- Is your baby babbling or making noises other than crying?
- Can your baby sit up with support?
- Is your baby exploring objects (and his hands) with his mouth?

Because babies like to explore at this age, keep small objects out of reach, because they're likely to go right into the mouth. You also need to make sure that toys of older children are kept out of your four-month-old's reach — especially anything that has small breakable parts. And, because baby is rolling over, don't leave him unattended on a bed or on a changing table. Babies of this age will roll off!

You'll notice that your baby recognizes a bottle or breast, whichever you use to feed him, but in general, everything he grabs he pops into his mouth. This behavior is an exploration move for your baby, so don't even try to keep it from happening. Just keep small objects away from him.

Five months

The teething process can begin (although you may not see the first tooth until the 12th to 15th month). Oh my gosh! Here come the drool, the low fevers, and the crying. But five months also means that your little guy will be using his hands to grab for objects, and he can see across the room.

Six months

Most parents are pretty comfortable with the new routine and the new family member after six months. You're getting to know each other pretty well, and some major developmental things are happening. A real personality is recognizable, and baby is learning at a fast rate. Here are the questions your doctor will ask. Again, don't fret if your baby isn't there yet. It's okay!

✔ Can your baby roll over and back again?

✔ Can he see small objects?

✔ Can he see across the room?

✔ Does he sit by himself or with minimal support? Does he sit like a tripod with his hand in front of him for support?

✔ Does he reach for objects? Can he hold them?

✔ Can he drink from a cup with help or hold a bottle?

✔ Can he transfer things from hand to hand?

✔ Is he babbling?

Seven months

By age seven months, the whole hand-mouth thing is going strong. Your baby will be able to feed himself finger foods, he can play peek-a-boo (you'll need to show him how) and imitate many sounds, and he has started recognizing emotions based on the tone of your voice.

Eight months

At eight months of age, your baby chews on virtually anything he can get his hands on. He reaches for the spoon that you feed him with, and he even makes you aware of when he's done eating by turning his head away. You can expect your baby to sleep anywhere between 11 and 13 hours at night and take two to three naps during the day. He sits by himself and gets up on his hands and knees.

The eight-month-old is a true babbler and does so enthusiastically. He also enjoys passing the time of day by dropping objects over the edge of the high-chair, so keep those glass objects away.

Nine months

The development leap for the last few months seems huge, and much happened to your little guy in that time. Here are some of the nine-month questions that you can expect to hear from your doctor. Because you know these questions are coming, keep track of the answers so you'll have complete answers when your doctor asks them.

- ✔ Does he reach for objects?
- ✔ Can your baby focus on small objects?
- ✔ Does he use his index finger and thumb to pick up small objects?
- ✔ Can he transfer objects from hand to hand?
- ✔ Does he seem to be able to localize sounds?
- ✔ Can he sit by himself?
- ✔ Is he babbling? He may not be specific, calling a toy dada or the cat mama.

Don't let the sitting independence fool you. Your baby can still loose his balance in a bathtub, so never leave him alone and make sure that you're right there by his side the entire time. Unless your baby is more than 20 pounds, he still needs to be in a rear-facing car seat. And don't forget this one: Now is the time to put gates on the tops and bottoms of stairways, because your baby is becoming mobile and soon will start scooting around.

Ten months

At ten months of age, your baby begins turning into a toddler. He can stand if he holds on to someone or something, and he can pull himself to a standing position.

Eleven months

Eleven months marks the coming of the gentle sounds of "ma ma", "da da", and "no" (in one more month, these words will become more specific and clear). Clapping hands and waving good-bye are typical of an 11-month-old. Expect frequent tumbles and falls as he practices his balancing skills. Babyproof your house *now,* if haven't yet done so. Investing in those soft, cushioned, corner guards for sharp table edges is a good idea. Don't forget that little fingers are able to reach into drawers and cabinets, so make sure that you have locks on them, too. Keep hot or otherwise dangerous objects safely out of reach, away from table and counter edges. Now is also a good time to turn your water heater temperature down to 120 degrees F to help prevent burn injuries. Little ones can grab the hot water knob and severely hurt themselves.

One-Year-Olds

One year is a true milestone for many parents. Tradition is that you don't give your child his first haircut until his first birthday, which is a major photo op for many parents. That first haircut marks the transition from baby to little boy or little girl.

Answers to the following developmental questions are what your doctor is going to want to know.

- Does he pull himself up to stand?
- Can he walk around holding on to furniture?
- Does he wave "bye-bye"?
- Can he say any words? What are they?
- Can he imitate sounds (like animal sounds)?

Because your child probably is rather mobile, make sure that you have those safety locks on all the cabinets and gates at the tops and bottoms of stairways.

One-year-olds are so much fun. They take one to two naps per day, and they typically have tripled their birth weights. Your young lad is probably very active, too. He's probably dancing, walking around holding furniture, pushing and pulling and dumping toys, pulling off hats and socks, and even identifying himself in the mirror. Like I said, one-year-olds are all about fun!

Fifteen Months

The 15-month visit is, in many ways, similar to all the other checkups, but it also marks a few milestones in your child's health. It often marks a time when you can first see the little boy or girl in the baby you've known for the last 15 months, and it frequently is the last time immunizations are given before prekindergarten shots.

Here are the developmental questions you'll be asked:

- Can he perform hand-eye-coordinated tasks like building a tower of blocks?
- Can he walk without help?
- Does he use a spoon?
- Does he understand a one-step command, such as "bring me the box"?
- Have his language skills increased to several words?

Part III

Serving Your Child's Physical Needs

In this part . . .

The chapters in this part are all about the physical needs of your child — mealtime, bathtime, bedtime, and that fun time for all: potty training. Definite "Yes, do this!" and "No! Don't do that!" elements are included in these chapters.

I also wanted to be honest about the struggles that you'll encounter and to empower you with the knowledge that the rough times do pass. Kids eventually sleep through the night — and graduate from potty training school.

Chapter 14

Understanding Food and Nutrition

. . . .

. . . .

ood and nutrition are not the same thing. Food is what you *want* to eat; nutritious food is what you *should* eat. Actually they're both subcategories of things-we-put-in-our-mouths. Although most anything that you put in your mouth can be considered food, it may not be nutritious. As a parent, your role is deciding what's food and what's nutrition — and how much of each your children need.

They All Go Through It

Your children will go through several food stages during their lives. Besides mood swings during puberty, nothing will be more disturbing than the changes that kids go through with their eating habits.

This fluctuation is disturbing to parents because eating changes can be rather dramatic. One day, you think your child has a hollow leg, and she can't seem to get enough to eat. The next day, she may not be interested in food at all.

Trust your children. They know how much they need to eat. When they push the bottle or spoon away, or don't clean their plates, trust that they've had enough to eat. If they keep asking for more food, by all means shovel it in. As long as you're giving them healthy foods, they should be allowed to eat as much as they want. They'll stop when they're finished (or when you run out of food, whichever comes first).

Feeding issues — Dr. Mary Jo

Providing the "what and when," in other words *what* food and *when* it is offered, is the parents' job. Deciding how much they want to eat is the job of your children. Kids won't starve themselves; moreover, they're likely to try new foods when you offer them in a neutral environment. In other words, leaving foods to try rather than badgering or begging your children to try them.

If you give your kids the choice of what they want to eat, make the choices healthy. For example, do you want corn or green beans as your vegetable tonight? When you give children a choice between chocolate or Brussels sprouts, they typically choose the sweeter of the two choices.

Your children are unique. They grow at a different rate than other children. Their eating habits also probably won't match any food chart you've read. Changes in eating habits not only include the amount your children want to eat, but also the times at which they eat. Don't be surprised when they aren't hungry at dinner time, but 30 minutes later, they complain that they're starving. To be really convincing, they may even show you their rib cages for special effects.

Is It Time for Solids Yet? (Babies)

Start your baby on solids anywhere between 4 months and 6 months of age. Your doctor may recommend solids anywhere between these ages, depending on:

- ✔ Whether your baby's birth weight has doubled.
- ✔ Whether your baby stops gaining weight.
- ✔ Whether your baby is gaining too much weight. *Note:* Formula is high in calories and may put excess weight on your baby.
- ✔ Whether your baby wants to eat frequently (more than 40 ounces of formula a day) and doesn't seem satisfied.
- ✔ Whether your baby is interested in the food you're eating.

Your doctor may suggest waiting on solids when your baby is gaining weight at a normal pace or when you have a history of allergies in your family. Starting a baby on solids too soon can cause food allergies later on.

When your baby shows you signs that she's ready to eat the good stuff (solids), proceed slowly and follow the guidelines described in the following sections.

Allergies and food intolerance

True food allergies aren't as common as most people believe and affect only about 2 percent of children. Most younger children outgrow food allergies by the time they are 3 years old.

Meanwhile, you may have to deal with an allergy, or what appears to be one. Symptoms of a food allergy, which can be mild to very severe, include wheezing, difficulty breathing, itchy skin rashes, hives, vomiting, and swelling around the mouth and in the throat. Symptoms usually develop fairly quickly after your child eats the food she is allergic to — often within only minutes. The severity of these symptoms depends on how much of the food your child ingested and the degree to which the allergy affects her.

More common than food allergies are intolerances to certain foods that can cause vomiting, diarrhea, spitting up, and skin rashes. A very common intolerance is to lactose, which means that your child has a reaction to drinking milk or eating milk products. Eggs, soybean products, nuts, and wheat also are common food intolerances.

Avoid foods that cause your child to develop allergy symptoms after being exposed to them. When you aren't sure about your child's reactions to specific foods, try keeping a diary for a few weeks and recording what foods your child has been eating, especially new foods, and when she develops symptoms. Doing so can help you figure out what she's allergic to.

When you determine what your child is allergic to, read food labels carefully. Your child may be allergic to an ingredient in the foods. Also ask restaurant waiters about how foods are prepared so that you can decide whether to order a specific menu item.

Pick a good time

You don't want to try starting to feed your baby this new *gooey-stuff-on-a-spoon thing* when she's too hungry. Feed her a little from the bottle or breast — so that she knows you're not planning on starving her — then proceed with some food.

Pick a good place

Your baby should be sitting upright. That means either in an infant seat or sitting on your lap. Don't lay her down and try to feed her; otherwise, she may spend most of her time gagging and choking. When she's old enough to sit up on her own, you can make that big move to the highchair.

Start off feeding your baby rice cereal

Iron-fortified baby cereal is the best way to start most babies on solid foods. This rice cereal (that *doesn't* mean Rice Krispies) is easier to digest than other cereals. Offer cereal twice a day: at breakfast and then again at dinner. Make the rice cereal thin in the beginning. Your baby must discover how to move the food around in her mouth and then to swallow it down her throat. You'll spend time putting the same spoonful of rice back into her mouth before she gets the idea of how to eat. When you find that more of the food is staying in her mouth — and you're not shoveling the same food in again and again — you can make the cereal thicker. But don't put baby cereal in bottles. Your baby has to learn to *eat* the cereal. She already knows how to drink.

Start off slowly

Your baby's going to think you've lost your mind when you start with the solid food, and she's going to have to get used to the idea that not all food comes in liquid form. Put a small dab of food on the spoon, slowly put it in your baby's mouth, and then watch her make a funny face and spit the food out. Wipe up the food, and try again. Don't give up hope when your baby doesn't seem to like new food. Spitting the food out doesn't necessarily mean she doesn't like it, but rather that she's just reacting to something new in her mouth. When you keep putting the food in, and she makes a horrible face and spits it out, she may not like the food. You may want to keep trying, or you may want to move to a new food.

Introduce new foods

After your baby gets the idea of how to eat (which means you're only shoveling the same bite of food in once or twice), and she doesn't have any allergic reactions to the cereal, slowly start introducing vegetables and fruit into the diet. Give your baby vegetables for a month or so before introducing fruit. If she starts off eating fruit, she may turn her nose up at vegetables. Fruits are naturally sweet and more appealing to your little one than vegetables — which mankind pretty much agrees are bland.

Introduce new foods (including baby cereal) one week at a time. This strategy gives your child's body a chance to react to the food, if it's going to at all.

No Picky Eaters Here! (Toddlers)

Your kids are going to turn their noses up at some of the foods that you offer. Depending on your children (because they're all different), they may refuse everything that you put in front of them, or they may rarely sneer at food. Toddlers are especially good at being picky eaters.

Here are some things you can do to avoid raising a picky eater:

- ✔ Introduce a wide variety of foods.
- ✔ Don't give up on a food after one try.
- ✔ Leave warfare out of mealtime.
- ✔ Don't overwhelm your child with too much food on her plate. A good rule of thumb is to put 1 tablespoon per year of age.

Plenty of neat foods

Giving your kids a wide variety of foods at a young age offers them an opportunity to experiment with food and find more things that they like. It also makes them more open to trying different foods.

Japanese, Thai, Indian, and organic foods have many different textures, colors, and tastes. In addition, they're good sources of vitamins. You may not like *miso* soup, but your 1-year-old may love it. But remember, don't give any of the raw stuff to babies. They only need the cooked stuff.

By the way, we're talking about one-star Thai food here. And with the Japanese and Indian food, avoid the spicy stuff. That green stuff — *wasabe* — is too much for babies. And Indian food needs to be made less spicy. You can accomplish that by ordering the nonspicy food that is available. Indian and Thai restaurants are good about letting you know what spice you're going to be able to handle and when you're going to need a fire extinguisher.

Take more time at the grocery store and actually look at all the different types of food instead of always reaching for your regular items. Take the time to experiment with new flavors or textures. Food can be great fun.

Keep trying

If your kids snub carrots, don't give them a candy bar as a replacement. Just give them another vegetable. Offer them carrots again in a week or so (allowing for an *off* night for carrots). When they still don't like the carrots, wait. Offer the carrots again in another six months. The kids may have a different attitude about them at that time. If six months down the road they still look at the carrots like you set a plate of worms in front of them, try again in another six months. Your job is distinguishing between, "Yuck! These things can't be in the same food chain that humans eat!" and, "I don't think I'm in the mood to eat carrots tonight." The first situation is where you want to reintroduce the food later — as in six months or so. The second is where your child is just being a kid who's trying to exert the decision-making process over *something*. Put the carrots back on your child's plate the next time you choose to fix them. Your little one may have a different attitude the next time around. Sometimes you have to offer foods more than ten times before a child will give the food a try.

Always give your children a choice between two healthy foods. As long as they're getting the nutrients they need, it doesn't really matter whether they grow up liking carrots or not.

And don't let your own prejudices about food stop you from giving those foods to your children. Although you may detest Brussels sprouts, your kids may love them.

Remember, these are small people who you're dealing with. Just like you, they're not going to like everything that you put in front of them. Adults learn to be polite and eat the green glob of *goo* rather than be rude. Kids don't care. If they don't think they're going to like it, they don't mind letting everyone know.

No fighting

Dinner shouldn't be a battle zone pitting you and your children against each other. Neither should a winner and a loser be declared. It's food — not a power struggle of the wills.

As people grow up, their taste buds develop, and food has more of a flavor than when they were younger. To little kids, much of the food they're offered doesn't really have much of a flavor. That's why kids love *sweets* so much. The flavor is strong, and they can taste it. Peas? You may as well give them some wet cardboard to chew on.

Dinner shouldn't be a time of crying and temper tantrums. There are plenty of different kinds of nutritious foods to offer. You don't need to force your 2-year-old to eat something that she obviously doesn't like.

If your kids start throwing temper tantrums and want to eat only sweets for dinner, make them leave the dinner table. They'll eat when they're hungry.

French restaurants do such a wonderful job presenting the meal. You know it's going to be great food simply because it *looks* so good. You could be eating tar, but that's okay, because it's tar that is presented well. If you have a child who tends to reject food, try making the food look fun. Cut sandwiches into shapes, arrange corn in the shape of a heart, or serve it in a plastic toy (washing the toy first, of course). Do whatever you can think of to make meals more fun.

Kids have an interesting way of testing food. Don't be surprised when your kids put the food in their mouths and then take it out. It isn't necessarily a sign that they don't like the food; it may simply mean that they're testing the food for flavor and texture.

No Food Problems Here!

Some children eat just about anything. Part of the reason that they do is, I believe, their nature. The other part of it is that some parents understand that the food shouldn't be an issue, and they don't turn it into an issue. To ensure that your children don't have any food problems, remember that mealtime needs to be a good experience. Allow your children to feed themselves. As soon as they can start popping food in their own mouths, let them have at it. And give your children healthy choices so they can decide what they will eat, so they will at least eat. And remember, choices must be of the same food group: apples or pears, green beans or peas, yogurt or cheese.

Avoid mistakes that many parents make that cause mealtime fights: They allow their children to drink too much before mealtime, so they aren't hungry for the main meal. They force their child to eat when they aren't hungry.

The Balanced Diet Concerns for All Ages

According to nutrition experts, to have a balanced diet, everyone needs to eat

- At least one serving of a vitamin A food, such as apricots, cantaloupe, carrots, spinach, and sweet potatoes, every day.

- At least one serving of a vitamin C food, such as oranges, grapefruit, and tomatoes, every day. This recommendation is only for children over 1 year old.

- At least one serving of a high-fiber food, such as apples, bananas, figs, plums, pears, strawberries, peas, potatoes, and spinach, every day.

- A *cruciferous* vegetable, such as broccoli, cauliflower, Brussels sprouts, and cabbage, several times a week.

Based on this list, how well do you do? You can stop laughing now. I know, accomplishing this balanced diet on a daily basis is hard — especially when your kids go through their growing spurts and don't seem to want to eat anything. You're also supposed to be giving your family five servings of fruits and vegetables a day. Again, that is hard to do. If you can't get all these foods in every day, try looking at your eating schedule in terms of every *48 hours*. Getting these foods in by every two days is better than not getting them in at all.

Working these foods into your family's diet is easier if you do it by substitution: Replace chips, crackers, cookies, and ice cream with fruits and vegetables. It's just as easy to grab a banana as it is a graham cracker.

Your children will learn good eating habits not only from what you feed them, but also by what they observe. You need to have good eating habits, and so do older siblings. If baby sees her older sister eating chocolate pastries for breakfast, she'll want to eat them, too.

Avoid processed foods. They're high in salt, sugars, and fat. These foods hide in cans, bottles, and plastic bags. To be sure, check the labels for sugar, salt, fat content, and the name of any chemical that you don't recognize. Get in the habit of reading labels.

Diets for children

Richard Simmons, Lean Cuisine, Jenny Craig, Weight Watchers, The Diet Zone, and all the other lose-weight-my-way programs are designed for certain people: those who are overweight or those who have eating disorders. None of these programs are for your children.

Unless specified by your doctor, the only "diet" your children need to be on is a normal, healthy, eating-the-right-kind-of-foods diet. Don't count the calories or fat grams for children. Just keep them away from sugars, fast foods (grease), junk foods (crackers, chips, candy), and too much processed meats (like hot dogs and bologna), and they'll be fine. Doing that may sound impossible, but if you make the effort, you'll at least reduce the intake of these foods considerably.

Hot dogs and other lunch meat products contain nitrates. Bad, bad, bad. Nasty nitrates, nasty.

As your children grow, they may seem chunkier at times, and then they'll slim down. Such fluctuations are normal. If you're concerned, however, that your children are too thin or too heavy, talk to your doctor. But don't automatically put your baby on a low-fat or no-fat diet. Babies need fat to develop healthy bodies and brains. Children under 2 years old do not need dietary fat restrictions. They need fat and cholesterol for their brain and nervous system development.

If your children are older than 2 years of age, you can start cutting some of the fat out of their diets. They can be on the same diet as an adult as recommended by the American Heart Association (no more than 20 percent of calories from fat). Remember the food pyramid you learned in school? That's the diet your kids need to follow. But you can also buy low-fat milk or low-fat yogurt, for example. Just don't go on a strict *no-fat* diet with your kids. Get rid of the bad fat, not the good fat. Bad fats are those found in chips. Good fats are those in avocados and olive oil. For lots more choices, take a look at www.americanheart.org.

Don't fall into the trap that captures many people when it comes to fat in their diets. They have the idea that if they buy *no-fat* chips, or *no-fat* ice cream, they're doing fine. Chips and ice cream still are considered junk foods; they don't do anything for your body. Your kids, especially, don't need them.

Many foods that are advertised as low-fat actually are high in sugar, which is of no benefit. Keep your kids on a naturally low-fat diet by giving them plenty of fruits and vegetables. It's the best solution to the diet dilemma.

Snacking

Your children's bodies are unable to consume enough during one meal to last until the next. So let them snack! Work in those fruits and vegetables for snacks. The word *snack* doesn't have to imply junk food.

Plan to feed your children three meals and two or three snacks a day. These snacks are needed to help balance their diets and give them the energy to terrorize their siblings and jump on beds.

Children after the age of 12 months often decide they don't like three meals a day. Some children take only one meal per day and then are happy with several small meals or snacks during the day. Don't worry. This behavior is normal. Just make sure the small meals or snacks are healthy foods.

If you don't like the idea of cooking for a child who just takes two bites and then runs off, give her small portions on the plate and refrigerate the rest (this is where that $300 worth of plastic containers that you bought at a garage sale comes in handy). When the kid's ready to eat again, give her the rest of the meal.

The Basics of Kiddy Food

According to the American Cancer Society, the cancer rate in America children is growing. This increase is partially caused by all the processed meats and sodium nitrates — the stuff meat manufacturers put in lunch meats, hot dogs, and most other processed meats.

More and more, families are spending too much time at fast-food restaurants eating foods that are high in fat. Limit fried burgers, French fries, and buttery popcorn from movie theaters. Start giving out raw fruits and vegetables instead.

If your child tends to have mood swings or gets cranky easily, it may be caused by her blood sugar going up and down. Diet is the reason for this. Eating foods that are high in carbohydrates and sugar is one of the reasons everyone tends to be moody, tired, and easily upset. Foods that are high in carbohydrates and sugar are presweetened cereals, crackers, cookies, cakes, and ice cream (basically all the good stuff that makes life worth living). Reduce the carbohydrates and raise the amount of proteins that your children take in.

Moodiness, crankiness, or hyperactive behavior can also be caused by food allergies. Allergies to food don't necessarily involve breaking out in little red bumps all over one's body. Allergies can also alter behavior. For example, your docile, sweet child may be fine all morning until lunch. And, after your child eats a peanut butter and jelly sandwich, you may find yourself peeling the kid off the wall. This kind of behavior can be a reaction to the bread, the peanut butter, or the jelly. If you suspect that your child is allergic to some sort of food, you can try your own *at-home* test. Take your child off all processed foods, sugars, and anything with food coloring. Your child will then be on a protein, fruit, and vegetable diet. See how your child does. If she doesn't seem to have any problems, slowly start adding foods, one by one, to the diet, observing how she reacts to each change. If this seems like a long process, you may just want to take your child to the doctor and let an expert know of your concerns. The doctor can give your child a series of tests to look for any food allergies.

Kids, like adults, need water. Start them out as babies with a sip of water after they've finished eating. But only a sip. Newborns get most of their water from formula or breast milk. This practice not only helps them get used to drinking water, but it also washes out their mouths — which is the first stage of proper dental care. As your children grow older, have a water bottle around for when they need a quick drink to quench their thirst. Being a kid is hard work.

Babies who are breast-fed or bottle-fed can develop a bacteria in their mouths called *thrush* if their mouths aren't rinsed out after they eat. Thrush looks like white, caked-on milk, and it can be transferred to your breast when you're breast-feeding. That is painful, so be aware.

Food Do's And Don'ts

Kids have their own special needs when it comes to food. If you're not careful, food can be not only a source of nutrition but also a health and safety hazard.

✔ **Feed your baby with a baby-size spoon.**

Preferably the ones that are covered with rubber. You'll have less food coming out because the bite sizes are smaller — like your baby's mouth. The rubber on the spoons prevents your baby's gums from getting hurt.

✔ **Keep food in small, child-sized bites.**

About the size of your thumbnail for your kids. Remember, kids choke easily.

✔ **Peel foods like apples, pears, and plums.**

The skins get stuck in those little swallowing pipes.

✔ **Cut pulpy fruit like oranges and grapefruits into small pieces.**

They are also easy to choke on. And watch your kids carefully. And only give these types of foods to children older than 12 months old.

✔ **Buy baby fruit juices in the baby-food department of your store.**

When you choose to use the canned or frozen juices that the entire family uses, dilute them in half with water. If you give your baby this kind of juice without diluting it, it may cause diarrhea. It's stronger than *baby juice* found in the baby-food section of the grocery store. Also, be sure that it is pasteurized to help avoid illness from things like E. coli.

✔ **Buy only juices that are 100 percent juice.**

Read the labels. There is a difference between fruit juice with 100 per-cent juice and fruit *drink* (which may actually contain no juice at all). Don't buy juice that has added sugar or fructose.

✔ **Keep kids in a highchair or at a table when it's time to eat.**

Running around and trying to eat at the same time increases the risk for choking. Besides, confining your kids to the table or highchair during meals keeps your house cleaner. Nothing is worse than sitting on a chair and finding its arms coated in peanut butter and jelly.

✔ **Keep a stash of raw vegetables in your refrigerator for snacks.**

When your kids start out eating raw peas, carrots, or celery for snacks, they won't know what they're missing. Unless, of course, some neighbor kid corrupts them for you, sneaking them chocolate behind your back. Ummmm, chocolate.

✔ **Limit outings to fast-food restaurants to only very special occasions.**

The hamburgers and French fries sold at fast-food restaurants are high in salt, carbohydrates, and fat. Eaten in moderation, this food is not a problem. But parents, in their hurried lifestyles, tend to grab a quick burger far too often.

✔ **When you want to give your kids sweets, limit the amount they eat.**

Don't give them hard candies (it's the choking thing again) and avoid sweets with caffeine, like chocolate and soft drinks. Sugar isn't what necessarily makes kids hyperactive, it's the caffeine. Giving a kid a caffeinated soft drink is equivalent to an adult drinking four cups of coffee.

✔ **Look for baby food that doesn't have any added sugars or salts.**

Read the labels. Some baby food manufacturers still add sugar. You *don't* want to use these products.

✔ **Always wash fruits and vegetables that you get from the grocery store.**

Grocery store produce is covered with pesticides, which aren't healthy for you or your kids. Whenever it's possible, buy organic fruits and vegetables, which are grown without pesticides. Go to a farmer's market or grow your own (which may be unrealistic for a lot of people, but it's an idea). And remember to wash the organic vegetables, too. Dirt isn't exactly the best thing to consume.

✔ **Don't give your kids citrus fruits or citrus-fruit drinks until after they are 1 year old.**

Citrus is too acidic for their little bodies. Your kids may react with vomiting, nausea, or acidic poops that burn their bottoms.

✔ **Don't feed your child honey until after the age of 1 year.**

Honey contains a bacteria (botulism) that makes babies sick. Read labels, especially those in yogurt. Food manufacturers are now adding honey to their ingredients as a "good" sugar.

✔ **Be careful when using your microwave to warm food.**

Microwaves heat food unevenly and can cause burns in sensitive, little kid mouths. When you use your microwave, stir the food and taste it to make sure that it isn't too hot.

✔ **Don't force your kids to clean their plates when eating.**

Forcing a child to eat everything that is set in front of her is leading her down the road to becoming an overeater.

✔ **Don't add salt, sugar, or artificial sweeteners to your children's food.**

Your children don't need it. All you're doing is seasoning the food to the way you like it. Children are used to the natural taste of foods and don't have the bad habits that we have of overseasoning . . . yet.

The best way to teach your kids how to eat is by example. You should be eating the right way. Your kids deserve to have you around for a long time, so be nice boys and girls and eat more protein and fresh vegetables — and give up the doughnuts. You'll feel better!

Food Safety

Children are among the people most at risk for serious illness from food poisoning. Federal officials say that 5,000 people die in the United States every year because of food poisoning.

Protect your child from food poisoning by following these precautions:

- ✔ Washing all fruits and vegetables before cooking or serving raw.

- ✔ Not giving your child undercooked poultry, meat, fish or eggs.

- ✔ Washing your hands, utensils, and kitchen surfaces after handling uncooked poultry and meat.

- ✔ Not eating rare meat.

- ✔ Promptly refrigerating leftovers.

- ✔ Not leaving foods at room temperature for more than a few hours.

- ✔ Defrosting foods in the refrigerator (rather than leaving them on the counter or in the sink to defrost).

- ✔ Keeping your refrigerator set to at least 40 degrees F and your freezer to 0 degrees F to keep your food properly refrigerated.

- ✔ Never eating raw eggs.

- ✔ Not eating or drinking anything that smells or looks bad.

- ✔ Not guessing about your safety. If you aren't sure whether food is still good, throw it out!

Chapter 15

The Joys and Perils of Bathtime

In This Chapter

▶ Bathing your babies

▶ Making the bath a safe place

▶ Useful supplies to have on hand

▶ Washing and drying those special places

▶ Using lotions, powders, and bubble bath

Something about taking a bath brings delight to a child. Maybe it's because the water is warm, and things are slippery. Or perhaps it's because Mom, Dad, Grandma, or Grandpa is nearby and paying total attention.

Bathtime can be fun and entertaining, but it's also a very serious and important time. Accidents can occur in the tub. Perhaps baby knows that, and that's why he's so charmed with you being there. You provide safety. But the bath also serves a highly useful purpose by helping to promote your baby's health and hygiene. This chapter shows you how to splash around with your tyke in the safest, most effective manner possible.

Do I Really Need a Bath?

Most kids love taking baths. When they reach a certain age (like around 5 years old), you just let them loose in the water. Cleaning themselves may be secondary; the bath is the thing. But no matter what your child's age is, bathing is an important — if not social — event.

Your children lose weight every time they take a bath. — My Mom Shirley

This is what you win when you don't keep 'em clean

Bathing is not only a means of having a cute, sweet-smelling child — or an excuse to play in water — it also helps to keep down diaper rashes and yeast infections. By giving your child a bath, you're washing away germs that fly around, are picked up, wiped up, and smeared on your children. It's yucky stuff. The simple process of washing hands and faces can keep down infections that are easily spread to everyone.

Most infections are spread by the hands, and a smaller percentage are spread by coughs. Here are some of the ways infections can be spread:

✔ Toddlers are especially good at passing along infections, because they have a habit of touching everything and sticking everything into their mouths.

✔ Most cases of diarrhea — and hepatitis — are caused by poop (which is 50 percent bacteria) getting on hands and being spread. Wash those hands after using the bathroom or changing diapers. Watch that your child doesn't reach down and get dirty hands when you change those messy diapers. (Giving your child a toy or towel to play with helps keep little hands busy while you change his diaper.)

✔ Respiratory infections commonly are spread by nose, mouth, and eye discharges (like runny nose, eye infections, and coughing). These discharges are spread by dirty hands.

✔ Contaminated objects, such as hats, combs, and brushes, can spread yucky stuff like ringworm or lice.

✔ Eye infections can occur when your children rub their eyes with hands that are covered with dirt (which can contain more than you'd care to know) or runny-nose stuff.

And there are healthy benefits to a bath as well

Baths are a great way to relieve stuffy noses. Set your child in the bath and pour warm water over his head (a little at a time). Wipe the snot away as it comes out of your child's nose. Make sure that you support your child's back well. When pouring water over a baby's head, he will lean back (trying to get out of the way of the water) and topple over if you don't have a hand behind his back.

A Safe Bath Is a Happy Bath

Baths can be dangerous if you don't prepare properly. When it's time to give your kids a bath, remember that:

- ✔ Safety comes first.
- ✔ Supplies must be close at hand.
- ✔ Holding your baby is important.

Safety first

Bathing your kids is one of the true joys of life. Nothing is more fun than seeing your kids, piled into a tub with as many toys as possible, trying to dodge you as you attempt to wash their hair. But bathing also can be dangerous — and never should be taken lightly. Always be on your toes during bathtime.

Starting the bath carefully

Turn on the cold water first, and then gradually add hot water until the water temperature is where you want it. When you want to turn off the water, turn off the hot water first, and then the cold water.

Checking the water temperature

Bathwater needs to be a little warmer than room temperature. Always test the water before putting your child in the tub. Stick your hand in the water, moving it around the tub and feeling for uneven water temperatures. Water temperatures change and can cause hot spots in bathwater. In addition, either you or your child can accidentally knock one of the faucets, causing the water to become hotter or colder.

The water from your hot water tank should be no hotter than 120 degrees F. If it's too hot, either turn it down yourself or call a plumber and have it changed for an outrageous fee.

Keeping kids seated

As your kids grow older, bathtime play becomes more rigorous — and children get to the point where they want to stand up to grab a toy or just to walk around. Don't let them. Make it a steadfast rule that light play in the tub is fun, but never allow them to stand up or walk around in the tub. Falling and hurting themselves on hard and slick tub surfaces is all too easy. If your bathtub has no nonskid surfaces, invest in one of those ever-so-fashionable bathmats or rubber stencils that stick to the bottom of tubs. You can find some really cute ones that your kids will love to try to peel up.

Watch the mats and stick-ons carefully. When you see that they're beginning to turn black, peel them up, throw them out, and buy some new ones. The black stuff is mold caused by water that's trapped under the rubber.

Keeping water levels low

Kids always want the bathwater so high that they can "swim." It isn't really necessary (and for babies, it's downright dangerous). When the water is too high, babies and toddlers have a hard time keeping anchored down — and they'll float. Yes, float. As they begin to float — because they weigh less than the water — they tend to fall over. See the danger in this? When you fill your tub with high water for your older kids, all they do is kick and splash and make a mess. Be careful with the water level for the little ones.

Never leaving kids alone

It takes only an inch of water in which to drown.

You must keep a constant eye on your kids. Never leave them alone in the bathtub. The comments of parents whose children have drowned are all the same, "I only left him alone for a few minutes." It takes only a minute.

People are programmed to answer bells. When the phone rings, you run to it. If someone rings the doorbell, you run to the door. When it comes to your kids in the bathtub, you can do one of two things. Either ignore the door and the phone, or install an intercom system throughout the house and carry a cordless phone with you wherever you go. Whatever you decide to do, don't ever leave the bathroom with your kids in there alone. Take them with you when you leave.

Don't let them drink the water

I don't know why kids do this, but if you don't watch closely, they'll drink the bathwater. Because kids are infamous for peeing in bathwater, drinking it is anything but a healthy idea.

Before filling a tub with water, you can start the water running, and then set your child in the bathtub (remembering to keep your hand in the water to keep a close track on the water temperature) before you close the drain. This strategy allows them a few minutes to pee in the bath. After they're drained, you can plug the tub's drain. That way your child isn't sitting in a bath full of pee water.

When you let your child sit in a tub with running water, keep one hand in the water flow until the tub is filled. If the temperature of the water changes, you want to be the first one to know.

Supplies at hand

Keep all your bathing supplies close at hand. They should all be within arm's reach. You don't want to leave your kids alone to go hunting for their bath supplies. Before starting the bath, do a quick inventory so that you know everything is right where you need it.

Another possibility is creating a bath basket. Get a large basket and put everything in it that you could possibly need at bathtime. You'll need at least the basics in the following list. That way, when you decide to give an impromptu bath in the kitchen, you can just grab the basket and go.

- Bath soap
- Washcloths
- Lotion
- Petroleum jelly
- A comb or brush
- Baby thermometer

- Shampoo
- Towels
- Powder
- Baking soda
- Diaper-rash ointment
- Liquid acetaminophen

Besides the basics, don't forget the fun bathtime supplies. Great bath toys include plastic cups, boats, rubber animals — even dolls and action figures. Keep toys that are too small, those that require batteries, or those that have sharp points out of the water. You don't want little bottoms sitting on those things.

Whenever you have to give your kids liquid acetaminophen (or any kind of sticky, liquid medication), you may want to do so while they're taking a bath. This stuff usually is very sticky, and — kids being kids — they'll drip it on themselves. But, if they're already in the tub, just hose them off. Instant clean!

Don't Overlook Those Body Parts

Being a baby is the only time when having extra folds of skin is thought to be cute. Those extra folds lose their charm with age.

Because babies have these extra folds, you need to pull them back and wash the skin that's between them. Just because these areas aren't usually seen doesn't mean they don't get dirty. Rashes can develop if you don't regularly clean and dry these areas. Keep in mind that these body parts aren't limited to babies. Your children, regardless of their ages, still have to scrub these areas like they're going into surgery. Babies typically are the ones that have the extra folds — but not always. Look at your Great Grandma Mattie. Now, there's a woman with folds!

Washing the secret hiding places

You wouldn't think washing a baby or small child would need to be so thorough. I mean, it's not like they're out digging ditches or paving roads. How can they get so messy? These little bundles of joy need special care for special places because they, too, have their own lifestyles that require cleaning and upkeep.

- **Neck and under the chin** — Drool sneaks out of the mouth, under the chin, and hides in the folds of the neck. If you just gave your baby a snack, that drool is mixed with all kinds of stuff that you don't want to be hiding in a perfect little neck.

- **Behind the ears** — Food and milk sneak behind the ears and wait to turn sour. Don't even try to guess how it gets there. The fact is that it does, and kids get crusty behind the ears if you don't scrub back there.

- **Feet** — Yes, your kids' feet can smell just as bad as anyone else's in your family. Their little toes like to hang on to the fuzzies that socks leave behind, so don't forget to wash between the toes, too.

- **Penis** — Gently pull back the overlapping skin of the penis and wash with soap and water. Smegma (it's like skin residue) collects around the penis if it isn't washed and rinsed thoroughly. This advice is only for circumcised boys. If your son is uncircumcised, clean around the outer and exposed areas, but don't try to pull back the foreskin of the penis.

- **Vagina** — Open the lips of the vagina and, very carefully, wash the area with soap and water. Remember to wash from front to back so as not to spread germs. Just like little boys, little girls collect smegma, and it needs to be cleaned.

- **Butt** — otherwise known as bottom, tush, and heinie. Even after your baby has been sitting in a tub of water for two hours, if you don't take soap and water and wash the bottom (and the little hole the poop comes from), poop will continue sticking to your baby, and you'll end up wiping it off with one of your pretty towels.

- **Lower back** — When your baby has one of those explosive bowel movements, it sometimes goes up the back (poop, like water, takes the path of least resistance). Although you may do your best to clean that area when you change that diaper, you won't always be able to do a good job. After all, it is kind of hard to get to.

- **Hidden crack areas** — The prime target for diaper rash is the inside cracks of legs near your baby's genitals. This area usually has a lot of fold to it, and it gets wet and warm — the breeding grounds for diaper rash and yeast infections. Pull back these folds and wash the area. Explosive diapers hide extra poop here, too.

Drying the secret hiding places

Thoroughly drying your baby's secret hiding places is just as important as the wash job. When you leave folds of skin wet, rashes and yeast infections develop. That, of course, is not a good thing.

After baths, lift the folds of skin in between the cracks of legs near the genitals, under necks, under arms, behind knees, and around wrists and ankles. Some babies who are extra chunky (umm, like peanut butter) look like they're wearing rubber bands around their wrists and ankles. Those areas are just hiding places for water.

Lotions, Potions, and Powders

The smell of a child can't be duplicated. Depending on when you take a deep, loving whiff, it can be a clean, natural smell — or that of soured milk, strained peas, or an old baseball glove with a hint of peanut butter.

Lathering with lotions

Some parents are obsessed with the lotions and powders designed to make their wee babes smell better, be softer, and look better than they naturally are. Lotions and powders have a purpose, but you should use them sparingly.

Lotions are designed to make baby skin soft. The only time it isn't soft is when you give too many baths, or during the wintertime when heaters take the moisture from the air. When your child's skin feels naturally soft, don't bother with the lotion.

Don't put lotion on your children during hot weather. Lotions clog the pores. This warning is especially important for babies because they don't drip sweat like adults do to cool themselves. They can feel extra hot if you apply lotions.

Read Chapter 18 for more information about children and the heat.

Putzing with powders

Powders are designed to soften and cool the skin and absorb dampness. They're good to use on warm days to help keep your baby cool and prevent heat rash. However, overuse of powders, like anything else, is bad. I've seen parents pour bottles of powder on little bottoms. I'm not sure if they think the power is going to absorb all the pee or what, but it's too much. If you use too much powder, it can absorb urine, and if that isn't washed away thoroughly, it may cause infection.

Powder is good for backs, under arms, behind knees, necks, and stomachs. Use sparingly, and only if the situation calls for it. Before you apply powder to your baby, first sprinkle the powder into your hand, and then apply it to your baby. That way, you won't have powder flying all over the place.

When you powder your baby, it's like love.

Fun with bubbles

Bubble baths are a fun way to make bathtime a little more interesting. However, use bubble baths sparingly and make taking one a special occasion or a fun-time treat or reward. Some kids may be sensitive to bubble baths and develop bladder infections, not to mention the fact that the soap, if used too much, can dry out their delicate skin.

Bathtime pleasures

I hope you have a child who loves to take baths. But heed this warning: Just because your child is in the bathtub doesn't mean that you're not fair game for getting a few suds on you, too. I suggest that you get fully dressed in your *parenting* clothes, which, of course, is anything that you don't mind getting wet. Enjoy your bathtimes, and keep that camera close at hand. You need a great picture to show to your child's first true love!

Chapter 16
Sleep, Glorious Sleep

In This Chapter
▶ Planning for bedtime
▶ Undoing old habits
▶ Troubleshooting bedtime problems
▶ Dealing with kids who wake up at odd hours
▶ Doing naps properly
▶ Sleeping with your children

*T*his chapter is all about sleep. Specifically, it's about your children and how they sleep. For you, I'm afraid, all hope is lost. Remember the night before you went to the hospital to have your first baby? That was the last solid night of sleep you were entitled to! From now on, it's the kids who get to sleep. You can steer them as best you can. You can effectively set bedtime, deal with kids who wake up in the middle of the night, and arrange for naps and such. But for you, your college days of sleeping 20 hours a day are long, long gone! Kiss 'em good-bye as you kiss your child good night!

Strategic Bedtime Plans

The Golden Rule when putting your children to bed, regardless of their ages, is: *They must be sleepy.* Trying to put them to bed when they're not tired is a fruitless effort. Your kids more than likely fight bedtime anyway. (Excluding newborns. They live to sleep.)

Before you actually try to put your children to bed, work up to bedtime. That means helping your kids to feel sleepy. You can accomplish this by following these steps:

1. **Play with your child — a lot of activity.**
2. **Offer your child a snack.**

3. **Give your child a bath.**

4. **Have a quiet time to calm your child down.**

5. **Put your child to bed, turn off the light, and leave.**

A fun book to read to your kids about getting them in bed is *Just Go To Bed* by Mercer Mayer (Western Publishing Company).

Activity time

First, chase your toddler around the house or yard; crawl around the house with the baby. Do things that encourage them to run, crawl, or scoot. This physical activity is not only good for them, but it also makes them more ready for bed. Basically you're trying to wear them out. Plus, I believe you'll find that they enjoy playing with their parents.

Snack time

After you've worn your children down with activity time, they're ready for a snack. Feeding your kids before they go to bed makes them more likely to sleep longer and not wake up in the middle of the night wanting steak and potatoes. Snacking is an optional stage, because some kids won't need a snack before going to bed. That's perfectly okay. Remember that snack time also starts the process of calming your children down.

Good evening snacks are warm bowls of soup or a warm grilled-cheese sandwich. Feeding your children something with *substance* gives them a full, comfy feeling — which of course helps make them feel sleepy. Feed them sweets, however, at your own peril.

Bathtime

Next, give your children a warm bath. No exciting play is allowed during this bath. It should be a calm, relaxing time — so you don't want to start a water fight that'll get them pumped up and ready to go some more. Warm water makes us sleepy, which, again, is the purpose here. See? Warm water = sleepy kids.

Quiet time

After playing, snacking, and bathing comes quiet time. You've worn them out. Now you must let them know that they're really tired and they want to go to bed. During all this nighttime preparation, turn off the television, put on some soothing music (or just have it quiet), and grab a good book to read to your kids. When your kids are old enough to start paying attention to the fact that there's a television, they'll start watching it and becoming involved in what's going on. If there's an action, shoot 'em-up movie or Mutant Power Ninja something or other on, your kids may become excited and want to start play fighting like they are on TV. Again, this kind of activity defeats your purpose of wanting to calm them down for bedtime.

Sit down with your kids and read a story. When they're too young to sit and really listen, just go through the book and point out the pictures, or make up your own stories as you go along. Your toddler will like to point out various things on the pages, like a tree or a dog.

Giving your kids enough time to quiet down is important. The amount of time required depends on your children. For some, It may be only 15 minutes. For others, it may be an hour. That's why the snack time and bathtime also need to be a part of the calming phase for your kids.

Bedtime

After all of your preparation is done, tuck them into bed, kiss them good night, turn on the night light, *and leave.* It's that simple.

You don't think so?

Getting your kids to bed actually should be that easy, although for many parents, it may not be. Sleeping problems begin with the bad habits that you develop with your newborn, bad habits that *you* start. In fact, most sleeping problems develop during the first year of life.

Some sleeping problems occur when parents decide that they don't want to rock their 2-year-old to sleep any more and that same 2-year-old says, "Hey, what do ya think you're doing? Don't you dare think that you're going to get out of doing this anymore. I like it."

Putting your kids to bed because you're exhausted just doesn't work. They are the ones who have to be tired.

For some reason, kids think all sorts of fun happens after we put them to bed, and they want to stay up and participate. You know, after the kids go to sleep, you break out the candy and cookies, run around the house, and jump on the beds — all the fun things that you won't let them do.

After your kids are used to your evening ritual, they'll fall asleep more easily than when they're all wound up and pumped full of sugar with action/adventure shows running through their heads. This ritual needs to be followed every night. Don't feel bad when you find it's too late for the bath or story. You've probably done something else to fill in that time anyway. But try to stick to your schedule as much as possible.

"I've Already Started Something I Shouldn't Have — Now What?"

Famous parenting experts have advised parents on ways to put their children to bed — which include letting them cry, ignoring them, and shutting the bedroom door and holding it closed so that your child can't escape the bedroom. (Honest-to-God, I'm not making this up.) I can't say that I agree with these methods. I don't ever advocate ignoring your children or locking them away.

When your children already are accustomed to being put to sleep by some ritual, you can start making those changes you need to make so that the bedtime ritual isn't such a hassle. Be aware, however, that it's *your* habit that needs to be broken here. Your child is logically expecting you to continue whatever bad bedtime habit you where doing before. In their little world, it is you who's behaving illogically, so they will put up a fight.

If you're trying to get rid of bad bedtime habits, start by explaining what you're going to do. "Daddy needs to be sure that you're in bed by 8 o'clock. I know that Daddy let you stay up later before, but then I noticed that you get really cranky in the morning. So, I'm guessing that you need more sleep."

When they argue, listen to their protestations but continue reinforcing your position: "But what can I do so that you aren't cranky in the morning?" It also helps when you reinforce your position as long before bedtime as possible. Trying to explain your position when your kids are already in bed invites them to talk and become excited, which is counterproductive.

Follow the same rules of preparing your children for bed that are described in the previous section about "Strategic Bedtime Plans." Then, when it's time for them to go to sleep, kiss them good night and leave the room. They may or may not fuss for a while.

After you leave the room, *listen carefully.* Are your children fussing (whining, whimpering), or are they screaming bloody murder? There's a difference. Stay near the door and listen to the fussing. They may stop after a few minutes. *Fussing* means only that your child isn't really happy with the situation but can live with it for a while. *Screaming bloody murder* means you need to go in and help out a little.

Assume for a moment that your child is screaming pretty loudly. Go in and comfort her, and then leave again. (Comforting means laying your child back down, stroking her hair for a few minutes. Don't pick her up, because she'll be *really* mad when you put her down again.) Wait a little longer before you go in the next time. Gradually add to the time that you wait before going back in, and remind your child that she just has to be in bed. If she wants to just lie there, that's fine, but she must be in bed. If she's sleepy, she'll stop fighting it and go to sleep.

You'll probably need to take the time to wean your child from your old sleeping ritual by combining it with leaving while she's still awake. For example, if you've developed the habit of patting your child on the back while she falls asleep, gradually reduce the amount of time that you pat her back. Be prepared to go back into the room and pat some more if she cries, but then leave after a few minutes. Gradually increase the amount of time that you're gone, and decrease the amount of time that you stay in the room. This weaning process won't happen overnight. You've developed a habit that your child likes, and she isn't going to part with it willingly.

Remember, explain bedtime to your children. Let them know that it's coming. Give them warnings — just like they do in football, but more of them: "Thirty minutes to bedtime!" then "15 minutes," then "10 minutes," then "5," then "1," and then do a countdown "10, 9, 8, 7, 6, 5, 4, 3, 2, 1." Kids feel comfortable when they know what to expect. Doing otherwise with them is insane.

Telling them that you *will* come back and check on them later (which you do anyway, right?) is another approach that often helps. Your children find it comforting to know that you're still around, and you still care even after they're asleep.

A different kind of weaning

Parents take the time to wean their children off of breast-feeding, bottle-feeding, and diapers. I think parents can be compassionate enough to wean their children off of any bad sleeping habits that they've started with them. I also don't see the need to set a world record by getting children to sleep on their own within a matter of only a few days. I would prefer to take more time weaning my children from their bedtime ritual. That way they learn to fall asleep on their own instead of sitting in bed crying for 45 minutes while I stand outside their door listening and crying, too.

And what if a child goes to bed just fine, but pops back awake at 3:00 a.m. *every single night?* See the "He's Waking Up, He's Waking Up!" section at the end of this chapter.

When All Else Fails

Putting your children to bed every night and keeping them there isn't always going to go smoothly. If every night seems to be a struggle, review your night-time ritual to see whether you or your children are doing something that makes going to bed even harder. Ask these questions:

✔ **Are they really tired, or do you just think they should go to bed?**

There's a big difference. Maybe it's time to adjust bedtime. You could be putting your kids to bed too early. Remember, all kids are different. There are night-owl kids just like there are night-owl adults.

✔ **Are they getting too many sweets or too much caffeine before bed?**

Think twice about ice cream, cookies, cake, Jell-O, soda, and crackers. Try a bowl of soup rather than of a bowl of ice cream. Or are they eating something they may be allergic to, causing them to be hyperactive?

✔ **Are they getting too much stimulation right before bedtime?**

Whenever you and your kids are roughhousing and then you abruptly stop and say, "Okay, time for bed," they may be too wound up to go to sleep. Television also can be a source of too much stimulation. You need to have a quiet time before bedtime to calm everyone down.

✔ **Is there too much noise outside the bedroom?**

Some kids, regardless of how much you *try* to tiptoe around them, are sensitive to noise.

✔ **Does your child have a fear that she isn't talking about?**

Perhaps you shouldn't have mentioned your fear of the closet monster when you were a kid. That may be your child's biggest fear now.

✔ **How's the room temperature?**

Kids have a harder time going to sleep when they're not comfortable — just like grownups.

He's Waking Up, He's Waking Up!

Many times kids may sound like they're awake when they really aren't fully awake. Don't be tempted to run into their rooms to comfort your children. All you'd really be doing is waking them up. They'll go back to sleep on their own.

Try standing outside the bedroom door or just peeking in. If they're still in bed, all is well. If they're standing in their room crying, that means something different.

When a child actually gets up, walks out of her room and into yours, and then taps you on the shoulder, you know she's definitely awake. Persistence on your part is key here. Don't be tempted to stay up and play (remember, you'd be starting a nasty habit). Take her to go potty, give her a drink, and then escort her back to bed. If she gets right up, take her again. Don't give in no matter how tired you are. She has to learn that 3:00 in the morning is not a time to get up and watch TV. It's a time for sleep.

Although you may have to endure several nights of crying and whining, *you'll* stop soon enough. Remember Chapter 3, "Being a Consistent Parent." This situation is one where you'll have to consistently take your kids to bed. Not to worry, though. They'll eventually grow out of it. I mean, how many 17-year-olds do you know who are still waking up at night wanting their parents to take them potty and get them a drink of water? Here are some other solutions to consider:

- If your child routinely wakes up and just wants something to drink, leave a cup of water by her bed.

- When your children actually wake up, try not to pick them up or have them walk. Doing so gives them the false hope that they get to play for a while — which you know not to be true. And, it wakes them up even more. You don't want your children to go from a drowsy, "I'm thirsty" state to a state of "Now I'm really awake, let's play!" Do you?

- You may need to check a baby's diaper when a little one wakes up for no apparent reason. Try doing so without exposing her entire bottom to chilly night air. That alone can wake your baby up even more.

Naps (Those Things Adults Long For)

Your children will want to nap anywhere from once to several times a day. It really depends on your child. Some kids are nappers, some aren't. Newborns nap all the time. By the time your children reach age 3 or 4, they may be taking only one nap a day or simply lying down with a book to rest. Some kids may want a nap until they're 5 or 6. Some kids start fighting naps at age 2. You'll have to determine what your children need as they grow up.

Schedules

Babies to toddler ages usually will take morning and afternoon naps. The time varies from child to child.

Don't worry about the amount of sleep that your children are getting. They'll sleep as much as they need to. Although, when afternoon naps are getting longer and your children are going to bed later and later at night, you may want to start waking them up earlier from their afternoon naps. You don't want to have to stay up until midnight because your toddler's nap was too long and now she isn't tired.

Try keeping your children on a daily schedule (or routine) for naps. Your children will go down easier knowing that naptime comes after lunch and a story.

No nap!

If your children don't seem to want to take a nap, consider these things:

- ✔ **Did you get them ready for a nap?**

    Getting them ready means calm, quiet activities. Or did you just take them off of the trampoline to put them to bed?

- ✔ **Did you check for dirty diapers?**

- ✔ **Is the room contributing to a nap?**

    Make the room quiet, with neither bright lights nor piles of toys in bed, not too hot or too cold, but just right.

- ✔ **Is it naptime?**

    If it isn't, have your children displayed signs of needing a nap, such as being cranky, rubbing eyes, and whining? Perhaps they became overexcited and are too wound up for a nap. You'll have to take time to wind them back down so they can rest.

- ✔ **Are your children getting too old for naps?**

    Perhaps your children are reaching the age — which varies from child to child — when they won't go to sleep, but they still need to lie down with a book and rest.

You know you've become an adult when you look forward to naps. — Dan Gookin

Sleeping with Children

There's a lot of talk about *family beds.* That is when the parents and children sleep together. Remarks have been made from "Oh, what a great idea" to "That's gross." This section covers the pros and cons of a family bed — and the compromises that can come from both sides of this debate.

Yeah for sleeping together

People who like the idea of sleeping with their kids all agree that it's a great time to bond and spend time with their children. They love the idea of cuddling. Mothers agree that it's easier for breast-feeding, and they're able to have a quicker response to their babies. Some mothers even think that their babies sleep sounder and longer when they can feel their mother close by. Besides, parents have been sleeping with their babies for thousands of years. Some researchers believe that it is unnatural for a birthing mother and child to be separated during sleep because the first nine months of the baby's development was spent attached to her mother.

Boo for sleeping together

People who disagree with the idea of sleeping with their kids think that it's a bad habit to start. They say it allows neither the children nor the parents to sleep well (obviously there are differing opinions here). Kids need to learn independence, and having their own bed is the first step toward that independence. Children and parents sleeping together also makes the *private time* that parents need more difficult to achieve (if you know what I mean — wink, wink).

You also have to be careful not to roll over on a baby or small child or use big pillows and comforters that can smother them.

And then there's always that time when you have to finally end the family bed — or do you have four teenage boys sleeping with you? It's hard to stop something after you've started it. How do you tell your children that now they can no longer sleep with you — and not have them feel rejected?

The compromise

Like most situations in parenting, there's always room for compromise. The family-bed situation doesn't necessarily have to have a strict set of rules that you either follow or you don't. Here are some things to think about:

- ✔ Most women who breast-feed won't have to get up several times in the middle of the night to feed a newborn who is already in their bed. Keeping a baby nearby is handier and quicker for everyone.

- ✔ As your baby starts sleeping more, put her in a bassinet next to the bed so that you can easily grab her without having to go anywhere far. Lay her in bed next to you, nurse, and then put her back in her bed when she's finished. If you doze off, and she ends up staying for a few hours, that's fine. She'll eventually spend most of her time in her own bed. You'll sleep more soundly.

✔ You can always welcome your older kids into your bed for those times when they don't feel well and are having a hard time falling asleep. Let them fall asleep next to you, but then take them to their beds. This strategy is especially helpful for kids who share rooms. If they can't sleep, they may wake the others up.

✔ You can also bring children to bed with you in the morning when they happen to wake up a little too early and you're hoping to con them into just a few more minutes of sleep. Sometimes this works — and sometimes you may all lie in bed and giggle (and get little fingers shoved in your ears and up your noses).

✔ And, of course, everyone is welcome into the bed (including grandmas, grandpas, aunts, and uncles) when it's time to watch *The Emperor's New Groove* or *Shrek* for the 10,000th time.

Chapter 17

Potty Training Perfected

You'd think that kids would *want* to learn how to use the potty. After all, doing it in your drawers can't be comfortable. What about the smell? And lugging all that extra cargo around when the little ones are all so active? Then again, think about how awful it is to get up in the middle of the night to go to the bathroom (the cold draft when you lift up the covers, sitting on the hard, cold toilet seat). Maybe doing it in your pants isn't such a bad idea, after all!

Despite what may seem like their ever-growing size and your waxing loss of patience, your child will eventually want to use the potty. It can never be as soon as you'd like, but it will happen. Just keep in mind that it's *you* who has to be the patient one. This chapter tells you how and why and provides other enlightenment as your child drags his brimming drawers down the butt-wipe paved path to the real toilet.

Waiting for the Right Time

Like everything else that your child discovers, learning to go pee and poop in the potty takes time. It may not happen at 9 months old, or at 12 months, or 16 months, or even older. And your neighbor or relative who boasts about training her kids at 6 months is full of it; see the sidebar "The myth of potty training at an early age."

And potty training is not all that hard. The trick is not to start too early, or have the attitude: "As of today — as God is my witness — my child is going to learn to use the potty." Your child has to be physically and emotionally ready to use the potty. No matter how much *you* want it to happen, using the potty is really up to your child.

Time is the greatest innovator. — Francis Bacon

When to start the potty train

Toddlers learn to use the potty between 2 years and 4 years of age. If that span seems kind of old to you, keep in mind that not until between the ages of 18 months and 24 months do toddlers begin recognizing what it feels like when they have to go pee or poop. Before then, these bodily functions just sort of magically happen. You know, sort of how *"Lucky Charms are magically delicious!"*

Most toddlers provide you with signs about when they're ready to use the potty. I'm not talking about written notices placed strategically around the house saying, "Hey, I'm ready for that potty thing you gave me," but rather nonverbal signs like the following:

- Running to the corner, squatting, making grunting sounds, and maybe even turning red.
- A dry diaper for several hours.
- A dry diaper after naps. Although for some children, this one may not happen until long after they've been potty trained during the day.
- Regular bowel movements.
- Tugging at a diaper when it's dirty, or other indications that your kid knows there is a mess in the diaper. Your child may even tell you that he's dirtied his diaper: "Poop!"
- Letting you know that he *has to go* poop or pee — or that he just went.
- Bringing you a clean diaper.

The myth of potty training at an early age

If you have friends who say they have potty trained their babies at 9 months old, feel free to snicker behind their backs. What has actually happened is the parents themselves have actually been trained. They've learned their babies' habits well enough to know when their children have to go potty. When that time comes, the parents whisk unwitting babies off to the bathroom, plop the victims on the potty — and the children then do the doody.

When you talk to these parents in more depth, you find that their babies have "accidents" all the time. (But these babies don't really have *accidents,* because the poor kids have never really been potty trained.) What has happened is that as their babies grow older, their bodies change. So, just because their kids used to go poop right after lunch, doesn't necessarily mean that they'll go right after lunch for the rest of their lives.

Don't panic or get frustrated if your child never does any of these things. Every child is different and, because of their particular situations, they may never have regular bowel movements, may never let you know when they go poop, or may always seem to be wet.

The education stage

After you start noticing signs that your toddler may be ready to use the potty, start educating him about his body and the potty. You can also get your child used to the idea of going potty. It would be too frustrating for you and your toddler if, all of a sudden, you say, "Okay, today you're going to learn to use the potty. Here it is. Go for it!"

Imitation is a wonderful tool for teaching and learning, so if you're not too modest or shy, let your toddler in the bathroom with you to see what a potty is used for. Tell your child what you're doing. If your toddler has an older sibling, encourage this sibling to help with the teaching process by demonstrating how and for what the potty is used.

After your toddler is potty trained, you must teach your child how to wipe after using the potty — and don't forget the washing-of-the-hands ritual.

Many wonderful books and videos are available to help you with potty training your children. A big time favorite of mine is the video, *Once Upon A Potty* by Alona Frankel and produced by Frappe, Inc. *Once Upon A Potty* is also a book, but the video has this great song that you'll hear over and over and over again (even in your sleep). "Yes I'm going to my potty, potty!"

Sitting on that potty

Sitting on the potty — and using it — is a critical moment that is different for everyone. Pay close attention to your children to see how they react to the whole potty thing. Potties can be cold and hard . . . and can make you feel like you don't have any support down there. So don't be surprised if your kids don't like the feeling. Keep trying every now and then, and they'll get used to it, just like you did.

Here are three different approaches to the actual process of sitting your toddler on the potty (hoping for positive results):

- ✔ Sit your child on the potty at regularly scheduled times when you know the kid tends to go poop and pee.
- ✔ Don't go by any schedule, but watch for signs that your little one may need to go to poop (like when your kid squats, grunts, and turns red).

> ✔ Do a combination of both. You may want to sit your child on the potty first thing in the morning, or after naps. During the rest of the day, watch for signs that your toddler may have to go poop. You can also ask if your child has to go poop or wants to use the potty.

After you've accomplished the *sitting-on-the-potty* process, it's just a matter of consistently placing your child on the potty and encouraging its use. It takes time before your child automatically does it on his own and you can stop asking your child to use the potty.

Step by step one ascends the staircase. — Turkish proverb

Fun you can expect from the potty experience

Training a child to go potty takes time. Even after the first successful "Mommy, I have to go poop," you will encounter some interesting episodes. Here are some things you can expect:

> ✔ Accidents up to ages 4 or 5. For some kids, even up to the age of 10.

> ✔ Accidents or setbacks when schedules or events change in your toddler's life. Overexcitement or being upset about something can cause accidents (sort of like cocker spaniels).

> ✔ Your toddler may not be able to stay dry through the nights, even though the day is without accident. Keep a diaper on your toddler at night, and every couple of months or so try going through a night with underpants. Let your child know that he needs to try going through the night without a diaper.

> ✔ Don't be upset or angry when your little one doesn't make it through the night. Don't make a big production of changing pajamas or bedding. And definitely don't shame your child for having an accident. Be sympathetic to the accident and let your child know that sometimes these things happen. Believe it or not, your child won't wet the bed on purpose. And it has nothing to do with laziness or stubbornness. It's bladder control, pure and simple.

If your toddler is having a hard time staying dry all night, you can try limiting the amount of liquid intake right before bed. Give small sips of water, but don't allow your child to drink extra-large glasses of juice before bedtime. Also, ask your child to try to go potty before going to bed.

Some helpful potty hints to keep in mind

Learning to use the potty is a major event in a toddler's life. It takes maturity, body control, and body awareness. Don't get upset and yell at a child, or, worse yet, don't call him names like *baby* when your child has accidents. You didn't scold your child when he fell learning to walk. You didn't yell when the same child got messy trying to feed himself. And you shouldn't get upset, yell, or shame a child who's learning to use the potty.

- Bedwetting can continue until age 5. A small percentage of kids continue to wet the bed until age 10.

- The Golden Rule in getting your children to bed is that they must be sleepy. The Golden Rule in potty training is that children must be willing and ready to be trained. They have to want to use the potty. If they fight you on the idea, wait and talk to them about it later.

- Let your kids pick out their own training pants. You can let them know that you're going out to pick up big kids' underwear. They may be more aware of their body functions when they know they'll soil Beauty and the Beast when they have an accident.

- Some kids are frightened by the idea that a part of their body (the poop) is going down the toilet. It's their thinking, so it's a legitimate fear.

Remember, you love your children.

Warning: Potty problems

If your child seems to be having problems using the potty, maybe you're trying too hard with your training. Your child won't be in diapers forever. Give this potty thing lots of time and don't pressure your child to do something that he may not be ready for. And don't allow yourself to feel pressure from other parents or family members who think they know what's best for your child. I hate it when that happens!

Part IV
Seeing to Your Child's Health and Safety

The 5th Wave   By Rich Tennant

"DON'T TOUCH ANYTHING. DON'T PICK ANYTHING OFF THE FLOOR AND EAT IT. DON'T PLAY WITH YOUR EARS. DON'T FOOL AROUND WITH BILLY MAGUIRE'S RETAINER. DON'T GRAB ANYONE'S HAIR. DON'T FORGET TO SAY PLEASE AND THANK YOU. DON'T PICK YOUR NOSE, TALK LOUD OR PLAY WITH TOO MANY TOYS. AND HAVE A WONDERFUL TIME."

In this part . . .

The sun, the snow, household cleaners, coffee tables, and hot dogs . . . What do all these things have in common? They can be dangerous to your child. This part covers some of the more common dangers to which your child is exposed and explores how you can make things safer for your child. Being aware of the dangers is your first step in protecting your child. So read on and be aware!

Chapter 18

Health and Hygiene

Good hygiene doesn't always come natural to kids. They'd never volunteer to take a bath and brush their teeth if we didn't tell them to. They'd stay out in the sun until they blistered; they wouldn't put on gloves. Boy, they'd be a mess. So it's up to us parents to keep our kids healthy by helping them avoid the things that make them sick. It requires effort and common sense, both of which seem to be lacking when it comes to a kid's regular mode of operation. This chapter is dedicated to the things that can make your children sick or can put them in danger.

The Nasty Elements (Sun, Heat, and Cold)

The sun, heat, and cold are harmful elements if you don't correctly prepare for them. Your children have very delicate skin, and those elements affect them more than they would you — someone whose skin has aged and been weathered, kind of like a really comfortable saddle. Ahem. But I digress.

Our Mr. Sun

If it's a nice, sunny day, your kids are going to want to be outside. And they should be. The sun is a great source of vitamin D. But like most things in life, the sun is good only in moderation. Take these precautions when your kids are outside:

✔ **Use sunscreen on your children anytime they're going to be in the sun (except for babies younger than 6 months old — they shouldn't be in the sun at all).**

This also means winter sun. Use a sunscreen with SPF 15 or higher, one that says it is waterproof and hypoallergenic, or nonirritating. SPF stands for *sun protection factor.* These types of sunscreens won't have heavy perfumes in them and will be gentler for delicate skin. Besides, you don't want the family dog hovered over your children licking off all the sunscreen because it smells like a coconut pie.

✔ **Apply sunscreen on all body parts that are exposed to the sun.**

This includes ears, behind the ears, noses, backs of hands, and the backs of necks. You'll also want to use a lip balm with sunscreen so that your little ones don't get burned or chapped lips from the sun and wind.

✔ **Lubricate your children with the sunscreen liberally.**

Really smear it on good. But don't apply sunscreen near the eyes — it can be very irritating. Also, don't use sunscreen on babies younger than 6 months old (again — they shouldn't be out in the sun at all).

✔ **Read the directions on your sunscreen.**

You'll find that you'll have to reapply it often. One slathering never is enough.

✔ **Avoid letting your children go out into the sun between the hours of 10:00 a.m. and 3:00 p.m.**

This is the time of day when the sun is the strongest. It's hottest during this time, and the sun can do more damage to the delicate skin of a child. That is especially true for places like Texas where it is 1,000 degrees in the shade and nothing lives under the sun.

✔ **Keep a hat on your child, if she's going to be in the sun.**

A hat not only protects a child's skin from the sun, but it also keeps her head cooler, which, in turn, helps her avoid sunstroke. And a hat can be very fashionable.

The sun will burn a child's skin from reflective surfaces. That means water and snow. And a common mistake made by parents is forgetting that the sun can be more harmful and stronger than they think it is. Nine of ten skin melanomas are linked to severe sunburn during childhood.

It's okay to let a child go all summer without a tan. It's sociably acceptable to be pale. After all, it isn't like your children are in the backyard comparing tan lines.

Dealing with sunburns

Sunburns actually are mild, first-degree burns. When your kids get sunburned, make a compress of equal parts chilled milk and cold water. Apply the compress to lips and eyelids to relieve the swollen, hot feeling. Cooled tea bags placed on the skin also help relieve sunburn. Give acetaminophen or ibuprofen for a few days to help with the pain. Use a moisturizer and a 1 percent hydrocortisone cream three times a day. And don't forget to give your sunburned child plenty of fluids to drink.

It's too darn hot!

Kids will play forever in the sun without complaining. You or I feel that first drop of sweat, and we're running in to air conditioning or off to the shade. But for some reason, kids just don't know temperatures. It may even take them a while to figure out what happened after you slide an ice cube down their shorts. Follow some basic safety rules:

✔ When it's hot outside, keep a close eye on your kids. If they appear too hot (red-faced, sweating, looking pale or faint), bring them in and cool them down.

✔ Don't let your kids stay outside for more than an hour at a time without having them cool down.

✔ Provide your kids with plenty of liquids. Cool water is the best thing you can give them on a hot day.

✔ Babies don't sweat well, so you must take some extra measures to keep them cool. Give them plenty of liquids, and give them lukewarm baths to cool them. Don't put sun lotions on babies, and never put them in the sunlight without a hat — and never for more than a few minutes at a time. Don't forget those nifty parasols that attach to strollers.

Children can suffer from heatstroke just as easily as adults. *Staying in the heat too long causes heatstroke;* the body is unable to cool itself. If you think your child may have heatstroke, call for help immediately, move her to a cool place, and — starting with the head — sponge her down with cool water (not ice water or rubbing alcohol). With heatstroke comes dehydration, so start giving your child cool liquids. Children commonly have strokes when they play outside in the heat for too long and when they're overdressed for the heat.

Dealing with the c-c-cold

The best way to spend winter is inside, nestled in a big, overstuffed chair, sitting by a big roaring fire, and drinking hot peppermint tea with a bag of Oreos on the side. Okay, so that's my opinion. Children think differently. As is true of the heat, children don't seem to mind the cold. And they can become over-exposed to the cold, so:

✔ **Never send your kids outside in the cold without proper clothing.**

That means long underwear, turtlenecks, water-repellent long pants, water-repellent coats and shoes, heavy cotton socks, hats that cover the ears, and mittens that are lined and waterproof (they'll keep your children's hands warmer than gloves).

✔ **Keep children's fingers and toes dry when they play outdoors in cold weather.**

Wet clothing makes skin cold and increases the risk of frostbite. Buy waterproof clothing.

✔ **Make sure boots and other winter shoes are not too tight.**

Tight footwear affects the circulation and can lead to frostbite.

✔ **Limit the time your children spend outdoors.**

When the weather is windy or rainy, when the temperature is below 32 degrees F, or when the wind chill reaches 0 degrees F or below, limit the exposure time.

The cold air of winter can cause children's faces to become chapped. To prevent chapping, apply moisturizing cream to their faces before they go out. If they have a runny nose or are in the drooling stage, put petroleum jelly under their noses and on their chins. Petroleum jelly won't wash off as easily as moisturizing cream.

Looking for signs of frostbite

Listen to your kids whenever they say they're getting cold. Bring them inside and look for these signs of frostbite:

✔ Their skin feels very cold, and they've lost feeling in that area.

✔ Their skin is pale, glossy, and hard.

If you think your child has frostbite, call your doctor immediately. To help with frostbite, give your child warm liquids to drink, and put the child in warm water to start bringing warmth back into the frostbitten area. Be careful of the water, because it will feel warmer than it actually is. You may also try warming your child by wrapping her in blankets or putting the affected area in a warm washcloth or heated towel. *Don't rub the affected area.* Rubbing not only is painful, it can also damage the skin. As your child begins warming up, her skin may feel like it's burning or tingling, and it should start turning red. You can do nothing about the burning feeling.

Sniffles and Sneezes

It's sad, but a time will come when your child gets a cold, and you'll wonder who feels worse — you or your child. You feel bad because there isn't really a whole lot you can do for someone who has a cold. And your child feels bad because that's what colds do to people.

When you notice the sniffles and sneezes coming on, immediately start to work:

✔ **Washing doorknobs and toys that can be handled by other children.**

Germs are transferred mainly by hands, and you don't want anyone else getting sick.

✔ **Washing your and your children's hands every chance that you get.**

You don't want to catch the cold, and you don't want to pass it on to someone else. You also don't want your children rubbing snotty noses, and then rubbing their eyes, spreading germs all over the place. That is how eye colds or eye infections begin.

✔ **Being prepared to give your doctor a detailed description of your children's symptoms.**

Can you describe how your children are acting, eating, and feeling? What their bowel movements are like? If they're pulling at their ears? Coughing and producing anything (and what it looks like)? If their noses are running? And what color (clear or green) the stuff coming out is?

Your baby will feel better when cool. Don't overdress a child hoping to sweat out the cold. It doesn't work. A child also sleeps better when kept a tad cooler, instead of being kept in a warm, stuffy room.

Give your baby frequent warm baths. Pour a cup full of water over her head (while also supporting her back because she may jerk back) and wipe away the phlegm that comes from her nose. Do this a cup at a time, until your baby's nose seems clear. When your child is too young, she can't blow her nose, and kids typically don't like snot-sucking syringes stuck up their noses — which is another a way to clean out the nose. Actually, I don't know anyone who likes to have things stuck up their nose.

I got the fever!

Fevers are a sign that the body has an infection, such as a cold or flu. You can do nothing to make a fever disappear other than healing the body to make the infection go away. Medications such as acetaminophen will reduce the fever, but they won't cure the problem.

Ask your pediatrician about giving your child acetaminophen (like children's Tylenol).

When your child has a fever, she has an infection somewhere. That usually means that your child is contagious. Wash your hands as often as possible until the fever is gone. Germs are passed by the hands, and you don't want whatever is making your child sick to make you sick — and you don't want to pass it on to other family members.

Give your child plenty of water and juice to help your child feel more comfortable and dress your child lightly. You'd make a sick, feverish child feel even more uncomfortable if you overdressed your patient.

Always ask your doctor about brand names, amounts of medicine, and appropriate times to give it *before* ever giving your child any medication. Never, ever give your child aspirin unless your doctor has prescribed it.

Those annoying ear infections

Suffering ear infections and never seeming to be able to get rid of them is a sad fact about many babies and small children. Their ear canals are small, which can trap liquid and lead to an infection.

Your doctor prescribes medication for ear infections that should clear them up within seven to ten days. Always go back to the doctor for the recommended checkup, because these infections aren't always easy to clear up. Lingering infections are common and can cause damage.

Don't take ear infections lightly, because they can lead to other, more harmful problems. Whenever you see your child pulling at an ear, take her to the doctor. Children with ear infections may also be irritable, run a fever, or have other signs of illness.

Recognizing the Signs of Illness

Don't wait to call your doctor when your child acts very ill but has only a low fever. Other signs of illness include:

- Difficulty breathing
- Screaming loud with knees drawn up
- Pulling at ears
- Swollen glands
- Sleeping past feeding times or not eating as much as normal

- Other changes in sleeping schedules or difficulty in waking up from sleep

- Looking pale or gray or with dark circles under the eyes, blue lips, acting limp, and lacking any energy

- Bad breath

- Smelly private parts even after a bath

These all are problem signs. Get your kid to the doctor; don't ever take chances on your child's health.

Be wary of doctors who suggest that you have tubes put in your child's ears, especially when the suggestion comes on the first visit for an ear infection. In some children tubes help decrease infections, but this solution isn't always necessary. Go to a homeopathic doctor or a family practitioner and get a second opinion: They will most likely give you another alternative to tubes.

Preventing the Spread of Germs

Germs *rarely* are spread by flying through the air with the greatest of ease. They're transferred by hands or by some sort of touching. Keeping this in mind, follow these suggestions on how to restrict the spread of germs to a minimum.

- **Don't share towels,** especially if you dry off one child with a runny nose and then use that same towel to dry off your other children. See how this spreading thing works?

- **Don't share cups.** Sure, giving your child a drink from your cup is an easy habit to fall into, but try to avoid this type of sharing as much as possible. You can designate a cup for each family member to use for an entire day. That way you're not using every cup in the house, but you're also not sharing each other's coughs and colds.

- **Don't kiss your pets.** As much as people love their pet cats, dogs, iguanas, or whatever, they need to reserve the affection to petting and giving them proper care. Save the kissing for your family. Pets carry germs around, and you don't want to get anything that they have.

- **Don't sit on a dirty toilet seat.** Toilet seats can be pretty nasty. That's why someone developed those paper butt gaskets you have to sit on in public restrooms — which eventually stick to your rear or get caught in your clothes.

- **Don't eat raw meat or eggs.** As much as I love sushi, this is hard to write. (Of course, I eat only the cooked stuff.) Raw meat and eggs carry bacteria.

- **Don't smoke.** If you smoke, get out of denial and into the real world. Second-hand smoke increases the amount and severity of colds, coughs, ear infections, and respiratory problems in those around you. If you smoke around your kids, they're smoking, too.

✔ **Don't touch your face.** Although it's a hard lesson to try to teach, little hands must be kept off little faces. Consider the following basic math problem:

Touching a runny nose + wiping something out of your eye = eye infection.

✔ **Teach your kids to sneeze or cough in the right place.** The rule is not to cover your face with your hands when you sneeze or cough, but rather to cover your face with the bend of your arm. Sneezing into your hand and then grabbing the door handle means your giving your germs to the door handle. Sneeze into your arm instead.

✔ **Do wash your hands.** And everyone else's hands, too. Wash them after using the bathroom, after changing a diaper, after you sneeze or cough, before and after handling food, before you eat, after working in dirt, and after cleaning. Wash your children's hands before and after they eat, after they go potty, if they grab themselves during a diaper change, after they play with friends, when they get home from school or day care, and whenever you see them wiping or rubbing their eyes or nose. Basically, you spend all day washing hands.

✔ **Do disinfect your house often.** Disinfecting your home is a lifelong process for you. Wash everything, including doorknobs, anything and everything in your kitchen, and anything to do with your children — like toys and diaper changing stuff. (Just give up and by some stock in Lysol right now.)

Train up a child in the way he should go: and when he is old, he will not depart from it. — Proverbs 22:6

Is Your Medicine Chest Okee Dokee?

You don't want to have a sick child on your hands, glance in your medicine chest, and find bare shelves. Prepare for the worst beforehand. When your children do catch colds, flu — or, for that matter, use their heads to stop the floor — be prepared to take care of things. Look for the checklist of medicine chest essentials below in Appendix E, too. You can cut it out and take it with you to the store so you don't forget anything.

✔ **Thermometer**

Out of all the different types of thermometers, those that you stick in the armpit and those stuck in the ear (and these are two different kinds) are fairly accurate, easy to use, and my favorites. Figure 18-1 is an oral thermometer with a digital readout.

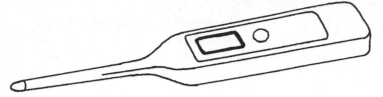

Figure 18-1:
Oral thermometer with a digital readout.

✔ **Suction syringe**

These devices (see Figure 18-2) are used to clean baby's tiny little nostrils, nostrils that tend to fill up with snot and can make gross sucking noises that don't seem to bother baby — but bother you a lot. The best syringes are the ones they give you after you've had your baby in the hospital. The syringes sold on the market aren't nearly as effective.

To make the syringe more effective, carefully place it in one nostril and close the other nostril with your finger. This is sort of like when you blow your nose and you close off one side. Things come out easier. Wash the bulb with warm soapy water after each use to kill germs.

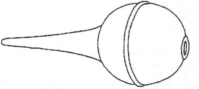

Figure 18-2:
Suction syringe.

✔ **Eyedropper**

Children occasionally get eye infections along with a cold. They rub their faces and smear germs all over, including into their eyes. Eyedroppers (see Figure 18-3) are good for dropping mild salt water into a child's eye to help clear up the infection.

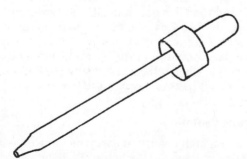

Figure 18-3:
Eyedropper.

✔ **Medicine dispenser**

You'll need something to give out medicine. Drug stores usually have a dispenser that looks like a large eyedropper with measurements on the side (see Figure 18-4). Remember to clean the medicine dispenser after every use.

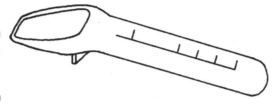

Figure 18-4:
Medicine
dispenser.

✔ **Children's or infants' pain reliever**

Use only acetaminophen (Tylenol is one brand) or ibuprofen when your doctor recommends it. Keep in mind that this medicine should be used sparingly, and only when your children have considerable discomfort from a cold or flu. Tylenol, or any medicines of the same nature, won't cure colds or the flu. Their only purpose is to hide the symptoms of an infection and make your children feel better.

✔ **Ice packs**

Gravity and your children will become well acquainted. The end result will be several bumps on the head and a few bloody lips. Those are the times when you need your ice pack. You can buy ice packs that look like bunnies that you keep in your freezer, or you can make one by putting ice and cold water in a baggy and wrapping it in a washcloth. Never put ice directly on child's skin. Not only does it hurt when you do this, you can also damage the skin.

If your child gets a deep cut, put an ice pack on the cut and go to the doctor. Doctors are better equipped for this kind of injury.

✔ **Adhesive bandages**

If your child falls and skins a knee, the best thing to do is to wash the cut with soap and water and then leave it alone. It's better for cuts to be open to the air. But sometimes kids won't leave a cut alone. They're too interested in it and want to touch it and mess with it. That's when you'll need an adhesive bandage (Band-Aid is one brand), simply to keep their hands off of the injury. Put the bandage on loosely so that the cut still can get some air — then sit back and watch the fun as your child tries to pick off the bandage.

✔ **Electrolyte replacement solution**

A baby with diarrhea or a high fever, can easily become dehydrated and in need of an electrolyte replacement solution (Pedialyte is one such solution, specifically intended for use with babies). Using such solutions is one of the best ways to prevent dehydration, whereas water and juice don't always help. In fact, if you give your child too much juice when she is sick, that alone can cause diarrhea. Ask your doctor about these solutions and about when and how much should be given.

✔ **Diaper-rash ointment**

The diaper-rash ointment needs to contain zinc oxide.

✔ **Petroleum jelly**

Petroleum jelly is for chapped lips or faces, to put under runny noses so your kids' faces don't get sore from wiping their noses, to prevent diaper rash, and for those ever-so-popular rectal thermometers.

✔ **Lip balm**

Whenever your children catch a cold, their lips are likely to become chapped, because they're breathing through their mouths. If lips become too chapped, they'll crack and bleed, so keep those tender little lips nice and lubed.

✔ **Anti-itch lotion**

This lotion is for when your children become the main course for hungry mosquitoes. It's also good for rashes, insect bites, and poison ivy.

✔ **Syrup of Ipecac**

You give this syrup when your children swallow something poisonous. *Give this to your child only if you have been instructed to do so by your doctor or the Poison Control Center.*

✔ **Flashlight or penlight**

These items are for looking down sore throats as well as removing splinters.

✔ **Pad of paper and pen**

Use this stuff to write down symptoms of illnesses, questions that you have for your doctor, and times and amounts of medicines you've given your children. This information helps your doctor and homeopathic doctor when you call them.

✔ **Moisturizing soap and lotion**

Lotion is especially needed during the winter months when skin tends to dry out. Don't use lotions on children too often during the summer, because it only makes them feel hot.

✔ **Tweezers**

A definite must for pulling out splinters.

✔ **Cool-mist humidifier or vaporizer**

This type of vaporizer (even if you *can't* fit it in your medicine chest) is great for when your children have colds. The cool, moist air is easier to breath than dry, warm air. It also loosens the mucus in their noses. You must clean the humidifier daily so that it doesn't get moldy.

✔ **Scissors**

For cutting bandages, gauze, or tape to size.

Medicine is not an exact science — heck, it's an *art*. Usually, more than one way of solving a problem exists. Use your gut instinct. When your doctor prescribes a medicine or does something that doesn't sound right to you, don't hesitate to question what's going on. Remember, you've hired this doctor and you have the right to know what is going on.

Healthy Habits

Developing healthy habits for your family keeps them safe and free from illness. Practice the following actions and turn them into habits that stay with your children the rest of their lives:

✔ Practicing proper nutrition by eating three meals a day and two snacks, limiting high-sugar and high-fat foods and pushing fruits, vegetables, meats and dairy products.

✔ Getting regular exercise for everyone in the family.

✔ Going to bed! Getting enough sleep.

✔ Visiting your doctor for regular well-child exams and keeping up to date on all of the recommended vaccines.

✔ Having emergency phone numbers by your phone.

✔ Learning to pay positive attention to your child.

✔ Turning off the television and reading a book or playing a game.

✔ Being smart with your food. Washing fruits and vegetables, and not eating undercooked meats or poultry.

✔ Teaching the dangers of drugs, tobacco, and alcohol.

Chapter 19

Going to the Doctor

1 hate going to the doctor. I hate waiting in the lobby just so I can go into a very small room that's either too hot or too cold. Once there, I'm greeted with magazines that are older than me and I have to wait some more. Then, just when I've almost forgotten why I even came, the doctor arrives, asking, "So, how are you today?" Is this the time when the doctor really wants to know, or is this the time when I politely say, "Fine" all the while thinking, "Of course I'm fine. I just like to come see you so that you can stick that piece of wood down my throat and make me gag."

That is a really *bad attitude,* and it shouldn't be passed on to kids. Showing children that doctors (or other medical professionals) are for helping is up to the parents. And, no matter how much they poke, prod, and stick, doctors *are trying* to make you feel better.

Finding the Right Doctor

Before your baby arrives, you need to be interviewing and researching doctors and their staffs. You can choose either a family practitioner or a pediatrician. Pediatricians are medical professionals specializing in children's medicine.

A doctor is going to examine your baby the day you deliver. It's therefore best if you can select your doctor before this first checkup, so that he gets to know you and your baby and can continue on with your child's care.

The best way to find a doctor is by referral from a friend, a relative, or your obstetrician. Start asking around *before* your delivery date. You want to have plenty of time to do your research.

When someone refers a doctor to you, ask these questions:

- ✔ What do you like about this doctor?
- ✔ What do you dislike about this doctor?
- ✔ Does this doctor seem open to your questions?
- ✔ Is this doctor kind and gentle to your children?
- ✔ Do your children like this doctor?
- ✔ Does this doctor take the time to listen to your concerns and discuss problems with you?
- ✔ Does this doctor have experience with mothers who have successfully breast-fed?
- ✔ Does this doctor share your points of view on nutrition, starting babies on solids, weaning, and so on?

If you don't know of anyone from whom you can get a referral, get out the phone book. Start with those doctors who are located closest to you. The less travel time the better.

Call and do some research over the telephone first. You want to spend a few minutes talking to the receptionist or nursing staff, because you'll also be working with them. If they seem unfriendly or uncooperative, take that into consideration. Do you want to hear that kind of attitude over the phone every time you call them?

You can use the Internet to find the names of physicians who are certified by the American Board of Pediatrics. Go to www.abp.org and click on "Certified Pediatricians."

Plenty of questions to pose

Here are some questions you can ask the doctor's office staff:

- ✔ **What are your open hours?**

    Does the doctor have extended hours so that you can catch him in the evening after work or on Saturdays for minor emergencies? Kids can be pretty inconsiderate at times, getting sick on weekends and holidays. And there's the curse of the *midnight boogers*, which may require some late-night professional nose cleaning.

Midnight boogers are when your baby gets a stuffy nose and has difficulty breathing (because babies insist on breathing through their noses, even when they're stuffy). Cleaning out the nose is the only way to help their breathing.

✔ **How do you handle follow-up visits?**

Kids come down with a variety of illnesses, such as ear infections, that require follow-up visits to make sure they're getting well. Find out what the procedures are for follow-up visits and whether you're required to pay full price for follow-up visits.

✔ **Do you have bench checks?**

Look for a doctor who has what some refer to as *bench checks*. Bench checks don't require an appointment. You come in when your child is finished with the recommended dose of medicine, and the doctor quickly checks out the medical problem to see whether it has improved. Typically these bench checks are less expensive than normal checkups. Doctors do this to encourage parents to bring their kids back without having to worry about paying full price — which, as you soon will find out, can be quite pricey.

✔ **Is there a payment plan?**

Do you have to pay first, or will they bill your insurance company for you?

✔ **What do I do in case of an emergency?**

Is the doctor on-call at night in case of an emergency?

✔ **Do you have additional doctors?**

Does this doctor share office space with other doctors? If so, do you have the choice of seeing only one doctor, or do they do a rotation with the patients? If your child is rotated among other doctors, developing a doctor-patient relationship is more difficult. On the other hand, with more than one doctor, chances are good that you'll be able to come in to see someone at the last minute. And, if there is more than one doctor, don't forget to ask whether the staff likes the other doctor(s)?

✔ **Do you have backup doctors?**

It's unrealistic to think that a doctor can be on-call 24 hours a day, seven days a week. The doctor needs rest, too. So, it's important that the doctor has a backup doctor in case of emergencies, and it would also be nice for you and your child to be able to meet this backup doctor. If you ever do need a backup doctor, it would be nice to visit someone with a familiar face.

✔ **How is your waiting room arranged?**

Some doctors' offices are large enough to have an area for healthy kids who are there for general checkups (or just tagging along with Mom or Dad), and then another special place for sick kids. Kids spread germs mainly by their hands. Toys found around the doctors' offices are coughed on, sneezed on, and spit up on. If your kids are healthy now, they won't be after playing with those toys. It's nice to find a place that either separates the healthy and ill children, or has separate hours for the healthy children so they aren't around the ill children.

A family is a unit composed not only of children but also of men, women, an occasional animal, and the common cold. — Ogden Nash

The ask-the-doctor interview

When you've found a doctor's office whose staff has answered the questions to your satisfaction (and they were nice doing it), make an appointment to meet with the doctor. Let the receptionist know that this meeting is just for you to meet the doctor and to ask some questions. Again, you want someone who is open and willing to be interviewed. If the receptionist says something to the effect that the doctor doesn't do this (but the receptionist is happy to answer the questions!), continue your search. You want someone who is going to respect your need to do research.

Once you meet with the doctor, you may want to bypass the questions about education and passing the medical board. After all, if the doctor graduated from Upper Thoracic State Medical College, would that mean anything to you?

You want to ask questions about the things that concern you or about the doctor's thoughts on treating kids and dealing with illnesses. If you're a new mother, you can find out how your potential doctor feels about breast-feeding, nutrition, and so on. If you're determined to breast-feed, you want to have a doctor who is 100 percent dedicated to supporting you as you breast-feed, not one who is constantly pushing formula coupons at you.

Be perceptive to how the doctor handles your questions. Does the doctor take time to listen to you? Does the doctor seem understanding? These practices are important to your patient-doctor relationship. You don't want someone who doesn't seem to ever have time for you, or doesn't listen to you.

You want a doctor whose goal is not only to make your kids feel better, but also to educate you to continue the doctoring role at home. You want a doctor who's willing to share information about your child's symptoms, illnesses, and any preventive care that you can do. Once you learn more about how to help your children, you'll be able to do more for your children at home and (it is hoped) see less of the doctor. But, remember:

- ✔ Not everything can be perfect. You may find a doctor who has a marvelous personality but isn't thorough. Personally, I'd rather have a doctor who is thorough — yet has the personality of a vending machine.

- ✔ Don't forget your gut! You may find a doctor who seems to have all the right answers, the staff is nice, the facility is clean and close by — but you just don't feel right about the situation. Don't stop looking. You have to like and get along with your doctor, as do your children. If something about a doctor bugs you, don't feel bad about continuing your search.

Call your local state medical board to find out whether any doctor you're considering has been accused of or disciplined for any offenses.

The Child/Doctor Relationship

Your child looks to you to observe how you behave in situations. So setting a good example is up to you when you take your child to the doctor. The example you want to set is that you think the doctor is a good person even though he or she may do things that hurt or are uncomfortable such as shots, sticking cold things on your chest, flashing lights in your eyes, probing in ears. Your child needs to know it's all for a good purpose.

Keep these rules in mind when going to the doctor:

- **Be happy and relaxed.** If you're relaxed and comfortable, your child will be more relaxed.

- **Greet the doctor cheerfully.** That lets your child know that the doctor is a person you like and are happy to see.

- **Use the doctor's name.** People seem more like friends when you address them by name. This practice also teaches your child the name of the doctor.

- **Thank the doctor after the examination.** This strategy again reinforces to your child the fact that the doctor is someone who is here to help.

- **Don't use going to the doctor as a threat against your child.** Avoid saying, "If you aren't good, I'll take you to the doctor for a shot." The next time your child has to go to the doctor, the kid's going to feel in trouble for something and be worried the whole time about getting a shot.

- **Don't tell your child that something is going to hurt, or that it won't hurt if you really know that it will.** The best thing to do is keep quiet and let your child decide whether it hurts.

When to Go to the Doctor

The first few months of your new baby's life, you're going to feel that you're living at the doctor's office. Don't worry! The older your child grows, the less you'll have to go in for shots and *well-child exams* (these are general checkups to make sure your child is developing well). Table 19-1 gives you an idea of when you'll be toting your little one off to the doctor, and for what reasons.

This schedule is current as of the writing of this book. Please, if your doctor tells you there are more shots, go by what he says. Immunizations change every so often, so I can't guarantee this will be accurate by the time you take your child to the doctor.

Table 19-1	Immunization/Age Chart	
Age	**Immunizations**	**Age Ranges**
Birth	HepB #1	Birth – 2 months
2 months	DTaP #1	
	Hib #1	
	IPV #1	
	HepB #2	1 – 4 months
	Prevnar #1	
4 months	DTaP #2	
	Hib #2	
	IPV #2	
	Prevnar #2	
6 months	DTaP #3	
	Hib #3	
	IPV #3	6 – 18 months
	HepB #3	6 – 18 months
	Prevnar #3	
12 months	Hib #4	12 – 15 months
	MMR #1	12 – 15 months
	Varicella	12 – 18 months
	Prevnar #4	12 – 15 months
15 months	DTaP #4	15 – 18 months
2 years	HepA (HepA #2 booster in 6 months)	

Age	Immunizations	Age Ranges
4 years	DTaP #5	4 – 6 years
	IPV #4	4 – 6 years
	MMR #2	4 – 6 years
11 – 12 years	Td	11 – 16 years

This shot schedule isn't chiseled in stone. Some doctors give you an option for giving your child shots at different times. Here are some guidelines:

✔ Your doctor may want to see your newborn more often than this chart shows, depending on your child's health and his weight gain for the first month.

✔ Don't overlook those times when your child gets sick. And never take cranky behavior, low fevers, or any other unusual behavior too lightly, because it may mean that an illness is developing or an infection is brewing somewhere.

When to Change Pediatricians

You don't have to keep a doctor who makes you or your child feel uncomfortable. Nope, a doctor is not only someone you hire but also someone you can fire when he isn't meeting your needs. Whenever you only have a few complaints, talk to your doctor and tell him about your concerns. Tell him you'd prefer that your calls are answered more promptly and then ask whether that is possible. Or you can say that you don't feel like he takes your concerns seriously. Honest, open communication is important with your doctor.

An effective doctor's appointment — Dr. Mary Jo

Parents generally have many questions for their doctors, but their minds go blank when they reach the doctor's office. Write down the questions and concerns that you have about your child before the appointment. Bring this list with you and then write down the answers. Be sure to makes notes about symptoms your child may be having. Your doctor will want to know how long your child sleeps at night, his eating habits, how long he's had the symptoms, whether your child has a runny nose, what the stuff coming from the nose looks like, and how the cough sounds (dry or wet sound). Eventually, you'll learn all the things your doctor looks at, and then you can keep track of these things.

Here are some situations that may prompt you to want to look for another pediatrician:

- ✔ **You can't get an appointment within a reasonable amount of time.** What's the point of having a doctor if you can't get in to see him or her? And what is *reasonable* time? You should be able to see your doctor either the same day or early the following day. If the waiting time is beyond that, find another pediatrician.

- ✔ **You don't feel like your concerns are taken seriously.** Yes, doctors hear the same sniffle, sneeze, and cough concerns all day long. But that is no reason for your doctor to make light of the situation.

- ✔ **The doctor doesn't alert you to potential medical or immunization side effects.** Knowledge is comforting. Knowing that your child may have a fever or a sore leg after an immunization is helpful. You need to know this kind of information, and your doctor needs to share what you can expect from medications or shots of any kind.

- ✔ **You can't understand your doctor.** Doctors have their own lingo, but that doesn't mean you or I understand it. Your doctor needs to speak to you in a language and style that you understand.

- ✔ **Your doctor isn't nice to your child.** No one wants to be treated like a number rather than a real person with real problems. And yes, doctors are busy. However, your child deserves a doctor who acts like he is truly concerned about your child's health and well being.

Don't Forget the Pharmacy

Almost as important as the doctor is the location of the pharmacy that you'll be using. Keep these things in mind:

- ✔ **Location:** A pharmacy in the same building as your doctor's office is ideal. Anything that doesn't require taking kids in and out of car seats works great including a drive-through pharmacy.

- ✔ **Hours open:** Ideally, a 24-hour pharmacy is best. You can expect your teething toddler to wake up screaming at 2:00 a.m. (it happens) . . . when you're out of liquid Children's Tylenol or Orajel (the goopy medication you rub on your baby's gums to help numb them).

- ✔ **Computer records:** Most pharmacies now have all their prescriptions on computers, so they can keep track of the medications your child has taken and what your child currently is on. This safety measure is designed to keep your child from receiving two different medications that may be harmful when taken together.

> ✔ **Medicine summary for the prescription:** Pharmacies now provide medicine summaries that describe what medicines are for and any possible side effects. Please read this summary carefully!

Because of computer record-keeping systems, it is better to go to the same pharmacy, so that it has a complete record of your child's medication history.

The Alternative Choice of Homeopathy

When your child gets an ear infection, a medical doctor looks at his ears and then prescribes a medicine to get rid of the infection. This doctor won't try to fix what caused the infection in the first place.

When you take your child to a homeopathic doctor, he looks at your child's body to figure out what the body is reacting to that produces the ear infection. This doctor then gives a remedy (that is not a chemical pharmaceutical but rather a natural ingredient) that helps your child's body to heal itself. Thus, no chemicals. Homeopathy attempts to stimulate the body to recover itself, much like coughing is an attempt of the body to clean the lungs.

Homeopathy . . . cures a larger percentage of cases than any method of treatment and is beyond all doubt safer and more economical and the most complete medical science. — Mahatma Gandhi

Then again, Gandhi was supposedly obsessed with his bowel movements.

How homeopathy works

A homeopathic doctor's job is to educate you to the point where he works himself out of a job. The more you know about things that make you sick, the more you can do to prevent yourself, and your children, from becoming ill.

Homeopathic doctors treat the whole person, not just the infection, by learning about you and your relationship to food, hygiene, your environment, your health education, and a host of other topics.

Once homeopathic doctors discover your background, they then prescribe a *remedy* that strengthens your body so that it can heal itself. They use natural ingredients that are free of toxins.

Homeopathic medicine has been around for 200 years. It's less expensive than going to a doctor every time that your child has a runny nose and fever. You can also keep the remedies at home and use them for prevention measures. That way, a runny nose and a fever don't turn into a bad ear infection.

General homeopathy stuff

Homeopathic medicine is not a group of whackos who sit around lighting candles, humming chants, and sticking pins into little dolls. It's an honest-to-goodness science that works. Be aware, however, that many medical doctors do not believe in homeopathy, similar to the way many M.D.'s do not believe in chiropractors. So, you may encounter some resistance with your pediatrician if you bring this topic up.

✔ I use both a pediatrician and a homeopathic doctor. I go to the pediatrician for the well-baby checkups, immunizations, and for sewing up deep cuts. We take our kids to the homeopathic doctor when they get sick.

✔ Homeopathic remedies are available in most of the national drugstore chains. It is important, however, to tell your pediatrician what medicines the homeopath is giving, if any.

✔ Homeopathic doctors also are used for behavioral problems.

Some great Web sites are dedicated to homeopathy, such as www. homeopathic.org, if you're interested in more information.

Hearing and Vision Problems

When you take your child on regular visits to the doctor, he will check hearing, vision, and the development of your child's teeth. For the hearing and vision, these simple checkups usually are enough. Schools also offer additional hearing tests when you think your child is developing a real hearing problem — other than the general ignoring you get when announcing that it's time for bed.

Taking care of your child's vision is an important part of preventive health care. Your baby's eyes are examined in the newborn nursery at the hospital, and by a doctor during the six-month and later well-baby visits. You need to make an appointment for your child to visit an ophthalmologist between the ages 3 and 4, and then every year following that.

No matter what the age of your child, make an appointment with your doctor if any of the following happens:

✔ Your child squints or rubs his eyes a lot (other than when tired).

✔ Your child's eyes move quickly either up or down or from side to side.

✔ Your child's eyes are watery, sensitive to light, or look different from the way they normally do.

✔ The pupil of the eye has white, grayish-white, or yellow-colored material in it.

  ✔ The eyes stay red for several days.

  ✔ Your child's eyelids droop, or the eyes look like they bulge.

  ✔ Pus or crust in either eye doesn't go away.

Speech and Language Milestones

Speech and language are associated with hearing. When a hearing problem exists, speech and language milestones may be delayed, and you'll need to talk to your doctor. The following is a brief outline of some general milestones:

  ✔ Newborns can follow sounds to their right or left side shortly after being born.

  ✔ Infants can imitate speech sounds by 3 to 6 months.

  ✔ Babies can make isolated sounds, usually beginning by 4 to 8 months.

  ✔ Babies can usually begin understanding single words like mommy and daddy by 6 to 10 months.

  ✔ The first word usually is usually spoken by 9 to 14 months.

  ✔ Your child should be able to say four to six words by 11 to 20 months.

  ✔ Your child should be able to tell you what he wants using single words by 16 to 20 months.

Starting a Good Dental Hygiene Program (Happy Teeth for Kids)

Your dental program for your kids starts when they are babies. Your child's first teeth start coming in between the ages of 3 months and 16 months. Because of early teeth development, their gums must be kept clean. You want them to have strong, healthy teeth so they can bite really hard when you foolishly stick your finger in their mouths to see how many new teeth they have.

A diet full of fruits and vegetables, dairy products, lean meats (like fish and chicken), and starches (like bread and potatoes) helps your children grow these really nice sharp teeth. Foods that are high in calcium are good. Potato chips, fruit rolls, and ice cream don't exactly fall in these food groups.

In addition to a good diet, your children need their teeth cleaned daily, fluoride treatments (which they may get in their water), and regular visits to their dentist to make sure everything is going okay.

Watch for signs of baby-bottle tooth decay. This early tooth decay is caused by too many sweet drinks and babies going to bed with a bottle.

Keeping baby's teeth in good shape

Do you want to save some money? Start your children on a good dental program while they are young, and you'll save a ton of money in dental costs when they get older. Trust me, a visit to the dentist can be quite costly.

✔ **Your children's teeth need to be cleaned daily.**

Once-a-day teeth cleanings are good, but twice a day is preferred. Clean a baby's gums with a wet washcloth. Use a baby washcloth and not one of your extra fluffy, extra absorbent cotton cloths. Otherwise, you'll end up gagging your kids and making them hate what you're doing even more than they're going to hate it anyway.

✔ **Flossing is important and should be done as soon as your children's teeth start touching (back molars usually are first).**

You'll have to floss your children's teeth for them until they're about 7 or 8 years old. Once they start doing it themselves, be sure to supervise their flossing.

✔ **Give your kids, including your baby, water to drink.**

Drinking water is a great way to clean out their mouths. Babies will make an awful face when you first give them water, but they'll learn to like it.

✔ **As soon as your children develop teeth, use children's toothbrushes and gently brush their teeth.**

Be careful not to brush too hard around their gum area. Brushing too hard can push their gums back too far and damage their teeth.

✔ **When brushing your children's teeth, use just a tiny amount of toothpaste and only when they can spit it out (age 3 years).**

If normal toothpaste is too strong for them and burns their mouths, you can pick from a variety of children's toothpastes, or you can go to a health food store and buy toothpaste that is milder and doesn't contain artificial sweeteners. Make sure the toothpaste is ADA (American Dental Association) approved.

✔ **You'll need to brush your children's teeth until they are 7 or 8 years old.**

Most kids have a hard time learning the up and down brushing motion that adults normally use to clean the tops of their teeth near the gums. You may want to help them out only one or two days a week by the time they reach 5 or 6, but always inspect their teeth after brushing and send them back for a second try when you see food stuck up around their gums.

> ✔ Don't forget to brush the tongue (gag, gag, gag) and the roof of the mouth.

Your kids should brush their teeth for at least two to three minutes (and so should you!). Two minutes is an eternity for kids, so use an egg timer or play a song that's about two minutes long.

Fluoride is important for strong teeth that resist decay. If fluoride is not added to the local water supply, the America Academy of Pediatrics and the America Dental Association recommend a fluoride supplement for children who are between the ages of 6 months to 16 years of age. This treatment can come in a daily fluoride vitamin that is available through a prescription from your dentist or through a dental program at school (sometimes called the Swish Program) or even a daily use of fluoride toothpaste.

When to go to the dentist

You can try to take your child to the dentist as early as 3 years old. Some children may be happy to sit in the dentist's chair and gladly open their mouths while some stranger with gloves on sticks his hands in their mouths. Some kids may not be able to handle this experience until much later. When you have a concern about your children's teeth, don't wait. If your children start to develop brown spots or places where it looks like teeth are beginning to rot, if their gums are swollen or they bleed during brushing, or if their gums or teeth hurt, make an appointment right away.

Developing a relationship with a dentist and getting your children on regular every-six-months checkup schedules are important steps to take. Be warned, if you make an appointment for your children, the dentist eventually will lure you in, too. Here are some pointers to finding a dentist:

> ✔ A small number of dentists specialize as pediatric dentists, concentrating on child development as well as in psychological and behavior management techniques.
>
> ✔ Shop around for dentists the same way you would for a doctor.
>
> ✔ You want to visit your dentist as soon as possible to determine whether your children are getting enough fluoride. Some places (like where I live) don't have fluoride in the water, so you'll have to give fluoride supplements.

Sealants

Sealants have saved my children from cavities! I know this may sound like a commercial, but I recommend that you ask your dentist about sealants, if he doesn't automatically offer this treatment.

Sealants usually are applied to the back teeth helping to protect those hard to reach teeth that are usually the first to develop cavities. A sealant is a plastic material that is applied to the teeth and hardens, protecting against plaque and other harmful substances. Sealants need to be applied to the first and second *permanent molars* and appropriate premolars as soon as possible after they erupt, which is usually after 6 years of age.

What's a dentist, and does it hurt?

You need to develop the same kind of open, trusting relationship with your dentist that you have with your pediatrician. Your children need to know that a dentist is someone who makes sure their teeth are healthy, strong, and growing well. Some do's and don'ts about visiting the dentist include:

✔ **Do allow your children to go back to the dental chair by themselves.**

This is one more step in their independence, and they're more likely to do better without you hanging around. Besides, dental exam rooms don't have that much space, and you truly aren't needed. However, if this is a first visit for a young child, the dentist may allow you to go back until your child feels comfortable with the situation.

✔ **Do always thank the dentist after the appointment is finished.**

✔ **Do check out books on going to the dentist.**

Find one that has pictures of things your children may see in the dentist's office.

✔ **Don't use going to the dentist as a type of threat.**

✔ **Don't talk about any possible pain or anything hurting.**

It may not have even occurred to your children that there could be any pain. Leave the subject alone.

The Berenstain Bears Visit the Dentist by Stan and Jan Berenstain (Random House) shows pictures of dental equipment that your child will see while at the dentist's office. Read it a few times before the first appointment so your child feels prepared.

Handling dental emergencies

Bumping their mouths is a common childhood incident that can cause children to injure their teeth. They may even crack, chip, or even completely knocked out one or more of their teeth. If your child's tooth is knocked out, place it in a glass of milk and take the child and the tooth to a dentist or an emergency room as soon as possible. Saving and reattaching permanent teeth is possible, if quick actions are taken.

Chapter 20

Making Life Safer

You've no doubt worked hard making your home warm and comfortable — and, of course, tastefully decorated. You'd think Martha Stewart herself decorated your house with all its beautiful little knickknacks and little baskets of potpourri strategically placed among things made of old jelly jars (and who'd guess those Christmas snowmen once were lint balls?). Be it ever so humble . . .

Okay, so your house may be in the Show of Homes, but how safe is it for your kids? You may have the coolest car in the neighborhood with flames painted on the side and big fuzzy dice hanging from the rearview mirror, but is it equipped for a safe ride for your children? And are you prepared to take your kids on an outing and make the event as safe as possible? This chapter covers procedures for making your home and your immediate environment safe. Safety is a vital thing, especially when you have wee ones wandering about.

Knowing Your Children

You can consider some facts as *givens* for all children. Babies will put anything in their mouths, regardless of whether it's a piece of dirt, a screw, a penny, or even dry paint chips. They do this as a way of exploring because their fingers aren't yet agile. Taste and size aren't important. When you have stairs, they'll want to crawl either up or down them. When you have cabinets, they'll want to open them and take whatever is in them out. Kids apparently consider this kind of fun right up there with the way adults think of taking a cruise or winning money.

Not all kids like to do the same things. Some kids are climbers, and some aren't. Some kids like to pick at things (like wallpaper), and other kids let small things like that go unnoticed.

The *better* you know *your* kids, the easier it is to foresee any potential problems and do something about them before something bad happens. If your child is a climber, for example, make sure all the chairs to tables are pushed in, stairs have gates on them, and drawers always are shut (they can be used as stairs). And don't leave furniture near open windows. If your child likes the dog and follows her everywhere, watch out for pet doors, which can just as easily be renamed *kiddy doors*.

Do your older children leave doors open for your younger ones to pass through? Do they leave their LEGO sets or their action figures with the 1,000 tiny parts out so that your baby can start eating the pieces like they're appetizers? Make sure your older children are well versed on house rules to keep the little ones safe.

Safety Procedures (The Do's and Don'ts)

Don't ever underestimate what your kids can do. They'll crawl, walk, reach, snatch, grab, jump, and run sooner than you expect. And they aren't even nice enough to forewarn you of their newfound talents. All of a sudden, out of nowhere, they'll stand up tall, reach over the coffee table, and spill your hot cup of tea — before you even know it.

Erring on the side of being extra safe, take it for granted on the day you bring your little ones home that they have amazing talents and can do everything anyone else can do. They're just waiting for the right moment to spring those abilities on you.

Looking at each room from a child's point of view is best thing to do. Go ahead and sit on the floor to see what a child sees. Try to be as critical of the room as you possibly can. Is there anything that can hurt a child, or anything that she can get into or put into her mouth that she shouldn't?

When something happens to your children, you're not going to have the time to open a book and start reading about stopping a lip from bleeding or treating a burn. Learn basic first aid now. Then you'll be prepared for the worst — whenever it happens.

General household safety

Look at your house in a general sort of way. Overall, how well-equipped is your house for safety? Look at the following list to see how well your house rates. If you don't have any of the stuff listed, get out that checkbook and go shopping!

- **Smoke detectors**

  Make it a practice to test your smoke detector batteries once a month. Do it at the same time you pay your rent or mortgage — some time that you'll remember. Change the batteries periodically to keep them fresh.

- **Fire extinguishers**

  Different types of fire extinguishers are available. The ones with dials on them are obvious to check: When the gauge is in the red, toss the thing. You can check the ones with pokey buttons on top (you guessed it) by pushing the button down. If it pops back up, the thing is still good. They typically last a long time.

  The fire department can also check your fire extinguishers. Your insurance company can put you in touch with an agency that recharges older-style extinguishers. Most home models are not of the rechargeable type.

- **Escape ladders**

  Great kid-friendly escape ladders are available that easily drop from a window.

- **Carbon-monoxide detectors**

  These are especially needed in the mechanical room or wherever the furnace is located. Unlike smoke, carbon monoxide is colorless and odorless, so you can't detect it unless you have a special carbon-monoxide detector.

Get fire safety information from your local fire department. They provide information on family fire drills, which you should plan and practice, how to protect your home from fire hazards, and what to do in case of a fire.

The bedroom (It's more than a sleeping place, it's an adventure)

Start with your baby's bedroom. This room can be scary when you think about it. Bedtime is the only time your child is going to be alone. You want to be almost microscopic when looking at this room. Remember, tiny fingers can peel, dig, and pry more than you may think. Start with your crib. It should be from a known manufacturer, such as Simmons, Child Craft, or Furil Baby.

- **Don't let babies sleep with plastic covers on their mattresses.**

  Unlike the tags on pillows that say, *"Do Not Remove,"* you're supposed to remove the plastic from the mattresses.

✔ **Babies should never sleep on adult waterbeds (which can cause hypothermia), cushions, beanbag chairs, adult comforters, or pillows.**

These surfaces are too soft for babies who are too young to move themselves around. Babies can easily smother.

✔ **Never, under any circumstances, walk away from or turn your back on a baby who is on the changing table.**

Even when a changing table is equipped with a safety strap, a baby can roll over and fall off — a baby as young as 4 weeks old can do this!

✔ **Don't use homemade cribs or antiques.**

They aren't tested for safety. If the bars on cribs are too far apart (more than 2 inches), your baby's head can get caught between them, and she can strangle trying to get free.

✔ **Keep bedding simple.**

A sheet, blanket, and bumper pads are enough. Newborns can't move around, and they can either become overheated — which is thought to be associated with the cause of SIDS (Sudden Infants Death Syndrome) — or they can suffocate.

✔ **Don't use pillows.**

Babies don't need pillows, and again, using one may cause them to suffocate.

✔ **Get rid of bumper pads when your children are old enough to pull up.**

A baby can stand on the pads and get more leverage when trying to jump out of the crib. And like any good POW, it's a baby's job to attempt escape.

✔ **Remove any toys strung across the crib when your children are old enough to pull up.**

If a child gets ahold of that kind of crib toy, the risk of strangulation increases.

✔ **Don't put cribs or toddler beds near blinds, drapes, or wall hangings with cords that hang down.**

Cords can become wrapped around your child's neck. Watch out for wallpaper or borders. Little fingers like to pick at these tempting papers so that they can rip them off the wall with much more ease than it took to put them there. The danger comes when a baby decides to eat the wallpaper.

✔ **Put plastic covers on all the electrical outlets, and plastic boxes over cords that are already plugged in.**

You can find these covers and boxes at any store that carries baby stuff, like Target, Kmart, Sears, or Wal-Mart.

✔ **Make sure that the toys in the room are appropriate for the age of your children.**

Young babies shouldn't have toys or games that have small pieces. They wouldn't play with them, anyway. They'd just eat the parts. You should also be wary of ribbons on dolls or stuffed animals. They can be pulled off, popped into the mouth, swallowed, and choked on.

✔ **Wash and dry all toys regularly.**

Toys collect dirt and dust, not to mention baby drool, dried snot, slimy cracker juice, and they eventually end up in your child's mouth.

✔ **Don't put toy chests or children's furniture near windows.**

If your windows are fairly low, your child can crawl up on the furniture and even fall out the window.

✔ **Use toy chests made of light material, like plastic, with a lid that either comes off or hinges and stays up.**

Babies get hurt by trying to get toys out of a toy chest and then having the lid fall on their heads.

✔ **Make sure purses and fanny packs are out of reach.**

Purses and fanny packs usually contain small coins, medications, or other small objects that you don't want your children playing with.

Children's accessories (junk for the little ones)

Like you, your kids will have their own stash of personal belongings. Things that they need to keep them happy. Your job is to continually inspect this *stuff* and make sure that none of it begins to break, crack, tear — or do anything that can potentially hurt your child. You need to:

✔ **Check toys for missing parts.**

When plastic toys break, they leave sharp edges that can cause scrapes and cuts. Throw those toys away.

✔ **Check pacifiers to see whether the plastic nipple is still in good shape.**

If the nipple becomes too old, it cracks and breaks. Throw old pacifiers away.

✔ **Wash pacifiers often.**

Wash them just like you would a bottle and nipples, to get rid of germs and dirt that collect.

✔ **Never tie a pacifier around your child's neck, and never place a rubber band around their heads to keep it in their mouths.**

Don't use these pacifier tethers when they're sleeping.

✔ **Remove crib mobiles when your children are old enough to pull up on hands and knees.**

Your baby will try to reach for the mobile and, if successful, can pull it down and shove everything possible into her mouth. The mobile's cords can also wrap around a child's neck.

✔ **Don't put your children to bed with toys in the crib.**

A baby can roll over onto one and get hurt.

✔ **Don't use a baby carrier or a baby swing as a car seat or as a seat when riding bicycles.**

Cars and bicycles have special seats for you to use.

✔ **Follow all manufacturers' directions for assembly when using a baby swing.**

Use the belts and straps when a child is in the swing. Never let older or heavier children play in the swing. Not only can they break it, but they can also fall from the swing and hurt themselves.

✔ **Don't put highchairs too close to walls, counters, or tables.**

Children will use their feet to push against these things to knock over their chairs. Likewise, don't put them too close to hanging objects that they can pull on, and never let them stand up in their chairs.

✔ **Use your strollers with all the safety equipment they come with.**

Always use the seat belts in strollers, and lock the wheels when you're not pushing the stroller. This precaution prevents the stroller from rolling away.

✔ **Watch out for little fingers when setting up the stroller or folding it.**

Fingers can be pinched!

✔ **Don't hang heavy bags, purses, or diaper bags from the handle of the stroller.**

The weight of these bags can pull the stroller over.

✔ **Don't use a baby walker.**

In 1993, 25,000 children between the ages of 5 and 15 months were treated in hospital emergency rooms because of walkers. Most of the injuries were caused by children falling down stairs in these walkers. A good alternative to the baby walker is the "Exersaucer." The name alone gives you a good indication of what this gadget is all about.

Living/family room

Because these are rooms where you and your family spend most of your time, you need to take extra precautions to make them safe.

✔ **Put plastic covers on all the electrical outlets, and plastic boxes over the cords that already are plugged in.**

These covers make it impossible to plug or unplug cords.

✔ **Put gates on all the stairs going up or down.**

You don't want to find out that your baby has learned to crawl up the stairs by seeing him teetering on the top step.

✔ **Take portable gates to place in the doorways of staircases when you're traveling to someone's home.**

Remember to ask permission before you start setting up your gates.

✔ **Put breakable items either away for a while or in higher, less accessible places.**

At least until your child is old enough to learn what's okay to touch and what's *not* okay.

✔ **Don't leave babies and young toddlers unattended on furniture.**

The moment you do, they'll fall off. It doesn't matter how many pillows or blankets you place around them, the day will come when they figure out how to get over those obstacles. You'll find out their new trick when you hear a thud — and a scream — and you find them on the floor.

✔ **Scrape, sand, and repaint all old paint areas.**

Old paint may contain lead, which is poisonous. It's pretty much a given that once children are tall enough to reach a window, they'll suck or chew on windowsills. Remember to do all this work without your children in the same room. This is toxic stuff, and your kids shouldn't be around it. In fact, to be really safe, you should wear a mask yourself.

✔ **Have furnaces, fireplaces, and gas barbecue grills checked for carbon monoxide leaks.**

Carbon monoxide is a poisonous gas that you can't see or smell, but it not only can make you very ill, it also can kill you if you breathe it for too long. Likewise, don't use charcoal grills indoors (it's the gas thing again), and get rid of the charcoal. You don't want your kids playing with that stuff.

✔ **Clean air filters from heaters and air conditioners once a month.**

This practice keeps your air cleaner and reduces the amount of germs flying around.

✔ **Don't keep your car running in the garage.**

Not only will your car spew out carbon monoxide, which can make you sick (and even kill you!) when you're in the garage with the car, but those fumes also will seep into your home if your garage is attached to the house.

✔ **Keep the cords to blinds or draperies tied up, out of the reach of children.**

If these cords are looped at the bottom, cut the loop, and tie the ends around the tops of the blinds, so your kids can't reach them.

The kitchen

You'll be trying to cook dinner, and there your kids are, perched on your toes begging to be picked up or wanting something to eat. Kitchens, however, are one of the most dangerous places for your kids to hang out.

The kitchen is full of wonder with lots of shiny toys, like butcher knives, neat knobs that turn machines on, and — if you're a wild cook — lots of goodies to nibble on from the floor. Protect your children from this Fun House.

✔ **Put locks on all your cabinets.**

You don't want your kids juggling your china, sucking on a knife, or gargling with Liquid Plumber.

✔ **Use the back burners when cooking on the stove.**

Little fingers can reach up and grab hot pans and pull them down.

✔ **Turn the handles on your cookware inward.**

You don't want little hands reaching up and grabbing a hot pan. It's sad how often this happens.

✔ **Keep drawers locked.**

Eating utensils, knives, and even the stuff in the "junk drawer" can all be dangerous to kids.

✔ **Keep the small kids out of your way when cooking.**

If they're too small to help prepare dinner, put them in a highchair or at a table to color or play with a toy. If they're big enough to help, put them to work. Beginning chores for your youngsters are setting the table, filling water glasses, and putting condiments on the table.

✔ **Lock up or throw away plastic bags.**

That includes shopping bags, garbage bags, plastic wrap, plastic sandwich bags, plastic dry cleaning bags, or plastic film of any kind (such as the kind used to wrap toys).

- **Keep alcoholic beverages away from children.**

  Their little systems can't handle alcohol, and they can get alcohol poisoning.

- **Keep chairs away from counters.**

  You don't want to find out that your little one can climb by finding him sitting on top of the counter.

- **Keep important phone numbers on a list, displayed right next to the phone.**

  These numbers should include the Poison Control Center's number (look in your phone book for your region's number), fire, police, 911 if it's in your area, and a couple of neighbors' phone numbers that you can call for help.

- **Keep *Syrup of Ipecac* in your medicine cabinet.**

  But don't use Syrup of Ipecac unless you're instructed to do so by a physician or someone at the Poison Control Center. Syrup of Ipecac is used to induce vomiting, which is what you want your children to do if they take something poisonous. It's the quickest way to get whatever they took out of their system. But remember to use this stuff *only if* you are instructed to do so by your physician or the Poison Control Center. *Never* use this stuff on your own.

The bathroom (otherwise known as the potty room)

The bathroom is another room that kids should not use as a playroom. It takes only 1 inch of water for someone to drown, and your toilet has more than one inch of water in it. When your kids are old enough to pull themselves up, they'll go over to the toilet and reach in to play with the pretty water. A baby who is old enough to reach into the toilet is old enough to fall in and drown. Some other bathroom safety tips include:

- **Keeping bathrooms blocked off with gates or installing safety locks high enough so that your children can't reach them.**
- **Keeping lids to toilets closed.**
- **Keeping shower doors closed.**
- **Never leaving water standing in sinks, bathtubs, or buckets used for cleaning.**

  Little people are attracted to standing water. It's an open invitation to them to come and play with it.

✔ **Keeping cleaners, perfumes, deodorants, and any other *foofoo* stuff locked up and out of baby's reach.**

Your kids will start imitating your morning hygiene ritual, if they see you doing it, and will want to play with all the stuff that you play with.

✔ **Always keeping medicines in the medicine cabinet and away from children.**

Most adult medicines can kill a child.

✔ **Using child-resistant packaging for anything and everything that you use.**

✔ **Keeping small appliances like blow-dryers, curling irons, electric razors, and irons unplugged and put away.**

Putting Your Child in Danger

Accidents are one of the biggest reasons why kids get hurt. Some of the falling down and bumps and bruises can't be helped. But kids also choke, get burned, and are cut for unnecessary reasons (as if there were good reasons to get choked, burned, and cut). You can take measures to prevent some of these accidents. The checkbox list in Appendix A can serve as your to-do list.

Burning

Fire, hot objects, scalding liquids, and children do not mix. You want to do everything that you can to avoid having to treat your child for burned fingers or worse. Cautionary measures are called for, so it's essential that you:

✔ **Put your coffee cup toward the middle of tables and counters.**

Just when kids get old enough to reach over the edge of coffee tables or counters, they grab for that steaming-hot cup of coffee or tea. And don't use tablecloths or doilies that can be pulled so that the coffee comes tumbling down.

✔ **Don't hold your children when you're holding a cup of hot liquid.**

As sure as you do, your child will stick her hand in it. Please don't assume children know better, because they don't.

✔ **Use your back burners to cook whenever possible.**

You may also want to buy a stove guard that doesn't let little fingers touch hot pans and guards that go over the burner knobs, so that toddlers can't turn stoves on.

✔ **Turn pot handles toward the rear of the stove.**

Even the professional chefs do that.

- ✔ **Keep kids away from floor furnaces or area heaters.**
- ✔ **Hide your disposable lighters, or don't use them.**

    Many fires start when children play with disposable lighters.

- ✔ **Don't let your children use the microwave oven.**

    They get burned by hot food or steam that comes from bags of popcorn or dishes that have lids or plastic on them.

- ✔ **Never hold your children while you're cooking.**

    Grease can pop up on children, or they can reach down and grab something cooking before you can stop them.

Keep an *Aloe vera* plant at home to relieve pain from minor burns. Cut a small piece off the plant, peel back the top layer, and squeeze or rub the gooey middle onto the burn.

Choking

Kids put the darnedest things in their mouths. They can find the tiniest microscopic item just so they can gag and choke and scare the bejesus out of you. Choking typically occurs in children because of how small their windpipes are. If your child is choking but still is able to talk or cough, then she probably can handle the stuck item on her own. If she is unable to cough, talk or if she turns blue, then she isn't getting any air to her lungs, and you need to help her right away. Call 911 immediately for help. In older children, you can perform the Heimlich maneuver, but this cannot be done to babies under 1 year of age. Attend a CPR class so that you can find out how to handle choking children of all ages.

Kids choke the most on the following items.

- ✔ Grapes
- ✔ Hard candies
- ✔ Deflated or burst balloon pieces
- ✔ Coins
- ✔ Raw vegetables cut in circles
- ✔ Buttons
- ✔ Nuts
- ✔ Popcorn
- ✔ Pins
- ✔ Small toys and toy parts
- ✔ Hot dogs cut in circles
- ✔ Plastic bags

You can also do your part by making sure you that provide a calm, relaxed environment for your kids so they don't feel rushed to eat. Rushing causes eating problems later in life, but it can also contribute to the choking problem.

Playing

Playing should mean fun, good times, yippee, let your hair down, be wild and free, go for it, let it all hang out. For adults, maybe. For kids, playing can be just as dangerous as walking a tightrope. If they aren't careful, playing can be very dangerous.

Kids' play needs to be restricted to children's games and activities and steered away from adult activities. That is why you don't see a 9-year-old playing craps in Vegas.

Don't put your kids in potentially dangerous places or areas, thinking that you'll keep a close eye on them. Kids can squirm around and move quicker than you can react. That is why places like the top of the Empire State Building sport signs that say not to set kids on the wall. Kids can slip through your fingers before you even know it. Some other don'ts about playing are:

- ✔ **Don't let your kids ride on the lawn mower with you.**
- ✔ **Don't let your kids ride in the back of pickup trucks.**
- ✔ **Don't leave your kids on the edge of a swimming pool, thinking that they'll sit there quietly.**
- ✔ **Don't let your kids ride on four-wheelers, motorcycles, personal watercraft, or other recreational equipment when they are younger than the recommended age limit.**

Get real. How often do kids sit quietly anywhere unless, of course, they're doing something they shouldn't? Too many accidents are caused by parents doing things, like sharing the riding lawn mower with a child, not knowing how dangerous it is.

Homemade toys that are fun for kids to play with are cardboard boxes and Tupperware with wooden spoons to bang on. Unsafe toys are anything with plastic bags or cellophane wrappers. Children can easily choke on plastic and cellophane. Kids also like to put bags on their heads as pretend hats. Plastic bags over the head cause suffocation.

Go to the Web site www.uni.edu/playground. This is the National Program for Playground Safety Web site. This group rates your playground for safety.

Tugging toddlers through tantrums and tenderness

Toddlers are the hardest to hold, especially when they don't want to be held. They squirm. They push against your chest to be let down. They arch their backs obviously not caring whether they can fall on their noggins (*noggin:* very technical term for head). When toddlers want down, nothing will stop them.

If holding resistant toddlers seems like a chore, try picking up a toddler who doesn't want to be picked up: She throws herself on the ground as if, for some reason, being that extra foot away from Mom and Dad makes it impossible to reach her. Toddlers also raise their arms up and drop to the ground. This technique is taught in self-defense courses for escaping from an assailant. I have no idea how kids know this stuff. They must sneak off at night and watch Bruce Lee movies.

Even though toddlers often like to behave like rag dolls, you still must resist dragging them by their arms. This action can dislocate their delicate shoulders and elbows.

Avoid roughhousing with toddlers, because that type of activity can lead to accidents. Typical rough play includes tossing children in the air or hanging them upside down by their ankles. Even the famous "airplane" game can be dangerous. Not only are you stressing their shoulder and hip joints, but you also can fall and end up hurting yourself while sending a kid into a suborbital flight pattern that may anger the FAA.

Personal habits

If you're taking the time and putting forth the effort to make your home safe, you also need to look at any personal habits that may be harmful to your child.

 Even if you go out and buy every safety gadget available, put locks on everything, put gates on all stairs, and clothe your children in rubber suits, they'll still get hurt. Nothing you can buy does as much good as parents who are attentive to their children.

Smoking

No matter how much you try to justify your habit of smoking, it's still a bad habit that not only will eventually kill you, but while you're busy making yourself sick, you'll also be making your children sick.

Second-hand smoke is bad for your children, and has been linked to premature babies, low-birth-weight babies, SIDS (Sudden Infant Death Syndrome), learning disabilities, an increased risk of asthma, pneumonia, and other medical problems. Even when you try to rationalize your smoking by saying that you only smoke outside, you nevertheless must realize that your children aren't stupid. They'll eventually realize what you're doing. Remember Chapter 1 and the section on setting good examples? Smoking anywhere, inside or outside the house, sets a bad example no matter how you look at it.

Research also has found that pregnant people who are around smoke also are exposing their unborn babies to that same smoke.

Drinking

Just two things. Don't get drunk around your children, and don't leave alcohol lying around so that your kids can get into it. Drinking around your children teaches them that you think drinking is acceptable. If you must drink, do so responsibly.

Guns

If you're going to have guns around the house, then take your kids to a gun safety course and remind your kids that *it is always loaded.* All guns are loaded. Period. Rather than keeping your kids ignorant of guns, show them that a gun is a loud and dangerous thing. Warn your kids that when they see a gun, they are not to touch it, and they should go get an adult immediately.

Virtually every city has gun-training courses for children, which I highly recommend. Kids who are familiar with guns and who have taken gun safety courses don't get into accidents . . . unlike kids who are unfamiliar with guns and haven't been taught the proper respect.

A study once was conducted on two groups of kids; one group had gun safety training, and the other did not. Both groups were placed into a room with an unloaded handgun. The kids who had the training saw the gun, but ignored it. The kids who didn't have the training picked up the gun and pointed it at each other. Education is the best avenue toward gun safety.

Drugs

What can I say? Don't use illegal drugs — ever. Even if you use drugs privately, where your children won't see you using them, drugs still slow your mind and reaction time, which are two things that you need to have when you're a parent. If you use drugs in front of your children, you're teaching them that it's okay — and then you've gone and ruined *their* lives as well.

Making Kids Waterproof

Water is such a scary thing when children are around it. Keep these safety tips in mind:

 ✔ **Always supervise your children when they're around water of any type.**

   That means water that is in a bucket, a child's pool, or even big water puddles from rain.

 ✔ **Use swimming-pool safety.**

   Your pool should have a four-sided, 5-foot fence around it with a self-closing, self-latching gate.

✔ **Wait until your children are at least 3 years old before starting them in a swimming program.**

The American Academy of Pediatrics advises against infant swimming programs. They claim that babies can get parasitic infections from swimming pools. Babies can also swallow too much water, which leads to water intoxication. The AAP also believes that parents develop a false sense of security, thinking that their infants can swim.

✔ **Check to make sure your old spa, hot tub, or whirlpool is equipped with new, safer drain covers that the U.S. Consumer Product Safety Commission helped develop.**

Hair entanglement and body part entrapment have been known to cause drowning deaths in the older models of spas, hot tubs, and whirlpools. Have yours checked for safety.

The saddest thing to hear is a parent who has lost a child to drowning say, "I was only gone for just a minute."

Traveling: Car-Seat Safety

Everyone who rides in your car should wear a seat belt. If you're in a car accident and only your kids are in seat belts, you can just as easily hurt them by flying around the car when you're not buckled in.

Several types of car seats are available: those that face forward, those that face backward, infant car seats, and toddler car seats.

✔ **Always, always, always use a car seat when traveling.**

Even if you're only going a short distance, take the time to put your kids in car seats. Besides, it's the law!

✔ **Use only the type of car seat that is age- and weight-appropriate for your children.**

Don't stick your 6-month-old into a toddler seat. It won't provide enough support.

✔ **Fasten the car seat down with the seat belt.**

When your child is in her seat but it isn't fastened down, she instantly becomes a large projectile: Something that can easily fly around the car and either go out a window or smack you in the back of your head.

✔ **Always use the car seat's safety belt.**

Car seats are not meant to be glorified booster chairs. If you don't use the safety belt to hold down your child, the seat is useless.

✔ **Read the directions on the car seat and FOLLOW THEM!**

If you have a rear-facing car seat, face the car seat only to the rear. Never face it forward. Manufacturers make these clarifications for a reason.

✔ **Don't put car seats in a front seat equipped with an air bag.**

Either have the air bag disabled or put your child in the back seat. The force of an expanding air bag is too strong for a car seat.

✔ **Children weighing less than 20 pounds should always face toward the rear of the vehicle.**

Up until children reach 20 pounds, they don't have enough head control to face toward the front. Their heads will bobble around like rag dolls.

The safest place for your baby is in the middle of the back seat. In a car seat, of course.

Your child *must* be in a car seat — it's the law. If your kids are riding in the car without car seats, you are breaking the law.

You also want to remember to keep your car and trunk locked at all times. You don't want a child playing inside of a car, especially in the summer. The temperature inside of a car parked in the sun can reach 130 degrees F. If a child becomes trapped in those conditions, she can suffer dehydration, burns, and die. Never leave your child in a car alone, and show your kids how to unlock a locked car from the inside.

You know those straps you see on shopping carts that are intended to keep kids in the shopping cart seat? Yeah, use them! Between 1985 to 1996, an annual average of 12,800 children ages 5 and younger were treated in emergency rooms because they had fallen from a shopping cart, according to the U.S. Consumer Product Safety Commission.

Air bag safety

A baby or small child riding in the front seat can be seriously injured or even killed by an inflating passenger-seat air bag. An air bag is not a soft pillow. The force of this bag often injures adults who sit too close to it. If you have a rear-facing child seat, never use it in the front seat of a vehicle equipped with an air bag. Use rear-facing car seats in the back seat! In almost every case in which a child was killed by an air bag, the baby was riding in a rear-facing safety seat being used in the front passenger seat. The back of the safety seat was so close to the dashboard that the air bag broke the back of the safety seat when it deployed. The back of the seat then struck the child in the head, causing a fatal brain injury. These child safety seats were not designed to protect against the impact of an air bag.

Chapter 21

Finding Good Child Care

● ●

In This Chapter

▶ Considering your choices

▶ Taking a look around — up-close and personal

▶ Using a referral service

▶ Programming the first day for minimum stress

● ●

*F*inding someone to care for your child when you can't is a difficult topic to write about. No one is a better caregiver for your children than you are, even though day-care facilities will try to convince you that what they do is healthy and good for your child. Yeah, right. But reality hits home real quick. At times you'll need someone to watch over your children.

Picking a child-care provider is scary, plain and simple. Giving your child to someone and hoping that provider will love and care for your child the way you do is difficult. This chapter is meant to help you make good decisions about who will watch your child.

Looking at Your Options

You must promise yourself something: You'll be optimistic about finding someone to take care of your children. Many wonderful people and schools have great programs where your children can play, have fun, and become little geniuses. Recent studies have shown that if your child is in a *good* day care, he will thrive and continue to develop appropriately. Because undesirable and rat-infested schools do exist, your job is avoiding such places and finding what you *really* need and want. Your first decision concerns what kind of care is best for you and for your particular situation.

Whatever you choose as a means of child care, always consider the location. As is true with real estate, everything is *Location! Location! Location!* You want something that is close to home, and, preferably, close to work, or at lease close to whoever will be picking up your child. You don't want to spend a good chunk of your mornings and afternoons driving to and from the child-care center. And, you want to be close in case your child gets sick or has an accident.

Trust your gut! Even though the person or center you choose for your child care may have all the qualifications, if you don't *feel* right about this person or place, keep on looking. You must feel good about the person and place where you're going to leave your child.

The ever-popular day-care center

Your first option for child care is a day-care center. These centers are easy to find, they're staffed with teachers, and your child's day usually is organized with arts, crafts, and music. Look for a day care that actually tries to teach the basics like the alphabet, counting, and printing.

The good news

You can find centers where teachers have teaching credits or credentials and the environment is bright and clean. Your child will have other kids to play with and a nice area to play in. Furthermore, these centers are required to have licenses and are reviewed by the licensing agencies to make sure they're following day-care standards.

Don't even look at any place that isn't licensed. Get nosy, poke around, and ask many questions. If you find a place that doesn't have a license, turn around and run: Places that have no license are not held accountable by anyone to operate safe and sanitary centers.

The bad news

The bad part about day-care centers is that parents who feel too obligated to work to think sensibly (and thus keep their sick children home) often send their sick children to school. Yes, that means if you put your children in a day care, they will get sick, harboring the latest strain of flu from their playmates.

You also may have problems finding a day-care center that accepts children who haven't yet been potty trained. Or the center may just charge you an extra fee to change diapers.

A third concern with day-care centers is that your children may not get much individualized attention, especially when classes are at full capacity. What is full capacity? It depends on the ages of the children and the square footage available at the center. Call your local Child Welfare Department to find out what your local requirements are.

To prevent illnesses and germs from spreading from your children to you, give your children a bath as soon as you pick them up from day care. This strategy helps prevent the spread of germs.

Watch to see whether day-care workers wash their hands — which they should do every time that they change a diaper, wipe a nose, or help someone on the potty. Toys should be washed daily, and the staff should be wearing plastic gloves when diapering little bottoms or handling food — which hopefully isn't happening at the same time.

Your friendly corporate day-care center

Corporate day-care centers, supported by individual companies, are becoming more popular. If a day-care center is the route you're going to take, check to see whether your company has one available. These centers are in the same location as the company, so your child simply goes to work with you every day.

Company-sponsored day care is a great idea. Your child can go to work with you, you can visit your little one during the day and even have lunch together, and you're close enough to breast-feed your baby (if the center accepts babies).

Private Sitters (not some Army guy)

The old-fashioned baby sitter is still alive. Maybe you remember getting hired by the neighbors for 25 cents an hour to watch their kids. Those types of baby sitters are still available, but it'll cost you more than 25 cents an hour.

Two options are available for private sitters:

- At their home
- At your home

Generally, you have to be careful with private sitters. Most aren't governed by any regulations unless they have more than a certain number of kids they're watching, and that number varies from state to state. No certification means they don't have to comply with any cleanliness, health, or safety standards. Remember that most of the questions at the end of this chapter should also apply to private sitters, so be sure to ask before you hire anyone.

Sitting on your children at their home

Keep your eyes open when interviewing a private sitter. Go to the prospective sitter's house to see whether it's clean and tidy. Are there safety locks on cabinets and on electrical plugs? Is there a place for kids to play? In addition to the questions at the end of this chapter, you need to ask about the number of kids the private sitter takes care of at one time. Does the sitter ever leave the house with the kids? Does the sitter entertain much company during the day? Is the sitter certified in CPR and first aid? You may also be concerned if the private sitter doesn't plan and schedule activities for the day. You don't want your little one getting bored.

Private home sitters usually are less expensive than day-care centers or having a sitter come to your home. They typically have a small group of children, so your child gets more attention than at day care, and if your child is ill, you usually still can use the sitter (although some sitters won't allow sick children). Some home sitters will allow your schedule to be a little more flexible, as opposed to day cares, which require you to pick up your child at a certain time or else pay a humongous fine.

The bad news is that private home sitters may not have a backup person for when they become sick. They also may not be required to be licensed (again, this varies from state to state), so there's no way to monitor their work. You also have to be careful that your private home sitter doesn't decide to take every December off to take hula lessons in Hawaii. Having a sitter gone for an entire month can really leave you in the lurch.

You want someone whose main concern is taking care of your child. Finding a sitter who offers arts and crafts and games similar to those used at day-care centers would be nice, because you don't want someone who looks at child care as going about the day as usual only with someone's kid hanging around.

Baby-sitting is one step better than parenthood; you get paid for it, and you can quit when you want. — My sister, Debra Coppernoll

Sitting on your children in your own home

When you have a private sitter who comes to your home, you can determine what you want your children to do all day. If you want them involved in art projects or park outings, you're the one who makes the decisions.

You also don't have to worry about other children making your child sick, or you having to stay home from work with a sick child. If you're really lucky, your sitter may also do some housework.

The only problem with private sitters is that they're hard to find, they tend to be expensive, and you need a backup person for when they get sick. You also aren't able see how a sitter does during the day, because no one is around except the sitter and your kids. Similarly, a sitter isn't required to be licensed; and you also must keep in mind that this person coming into your home every day will be alone with your children. Finding someone you already know and trust would be nice. If that isn't the case, then you must remember to thoroughly check references, and if the sitters are willing, have them finger-printed by your local law enforcement agency.

Preparing your sitter for your children

When you begin using a private sitter, you want this sitter to be as well informed about your children's schedules, their likes, and their dislikes as possible. Before your sitter starts, have that person come over and spend time going over the following:

- ✔ The eating and nap schedules.
- ✔ Favorite toys and any nicknames that your child may use (example: your child may call her favorite doll "Bud").
- ✔ Food favorites or allergies. Start out with a list for the sitter.
- ✔ Fears your children may have (like the vacuum, thunderstorms, *Teletubbies*, and so on).
- ✔ Calming tactics for when your child is upset.
- ✔ A list of phone numbers for emergencies.
- ✔ A release form (see Figure 21-1) in case of an accident.

Figure 21-1:
A release form you can make at home, simple and to the point.

RELEASE FORM

_____ has my permission to authorize
Fill in the complete name of your sitter

medical treatment to my child(ren) _____ in case
List the names of your child(ren)

of a medical emergency.

Signed,

_____
Sign your complete name

Communication between you and your child-care provider is important. The same way you want to be told about school events, your child-care provider needs to know about what's going on in your home. For example, if your child was up all night and unable to sleep, your child-care provider needs to know. That way he or she can adjust for your child's moods or tiredness during the day.

The joy of night-out sitters

Your concern for daytime sitters should also carry through for nighttime sitters (for those special dates between you and your loved one, who hopefully is your husband or wife). These sitters should also know CPR and first aid.

If this is the first time a sitter is watching your child, have that person come over at least an hour early. If the sitter is able to spend time with you before you leave, your kid adjusts to having a new person around. Take time going over the following with the sitter:

- The evening schedule
- The bedtime
- Household rules (like no jumping on the bed or eating in the living room)
- A list of emergency phone numbers and the phone number where you're going to be for the evening
- Any allergies your children have
- A list of *Do's* and *Don'ts* (For example, *do* keep the doors locked, *don't* stay on the telephone all night.)

Take any sitters on a tour of the house, so they know their way around. Clue them in on any quirks your house has, such as a door that automatically locks or what switches will blow the fuse box. Leaving a flashlight on the kitchen counter isn't a bad idea. If the electricity goes out, you don't want your sitter and your children sitting in the dark screaming. Are you worried yet?

Write out your children's evening schedule for your sitter and make it as detailed as possible. Include favorite foods, what snacks are allowed, what your children like to wear to bed, whether your children prefer certain blankets, and whether they like to sleep with certain stuffed animals. Don't hide any information. When your child still is wetting the bed, for example, let the sitter know the evening routine and what to do if that happens.

Having a sitter can be more fun when you let your kids do extraspecial things only when you're going out for the evening. Let them build a fort made out of chairs, blankets, and pillows, eat popcorn, and watch a favorite movie. They may even start looking forward to your evenings out.

Co-op programs

A co-op program is organized by a group of mothers who all share baby-sitting time. If you have a full-time, 9-to-5 job, this program won't work. But, if you work part time, or don't work outside your home, a co-op program is a great way to get a baby sitter for lunch dates or just time away to do shopping. Payment is made in kind. In other words, you baby-sit for other members of your group when they need a sitter. Hours are logged so that one parent isn't doing all the sitting and another is doing all the shopping. It works out so that everyone gets equal time.

When you first meet with your co-op group, go over all the rules, especially situations regarding sick children.

After-school programs

Many day-care centers, private sitters, and even some public schools offer after-school programs. These programs are for school-age children who need some place to go after school until their parents can pick them up.

You need to ask the same questions about after-school programs that you do when your children need an all-day caregiver. In addition to these questions, you need to find out the following:

- ✔ Is the afternoon organized?
- ✔ Is time scheduled for kids to do their homework?
- ✔ Do kids get an afternoon snack or are they expected to bring their own?
- ✔ What arrangements are in place for transporting children from their school to the after-school program (when it's at a different location)?
- ✔ How are kids released to their parents?

Hunting for Good Child Care

You must be aggressive when hunting for child care. Don't be shy or timid; don't hesitate to ask questions and poke your nose around where it probably doesn't belong. Be bold and brave. You're making an important decision and you have every right to act like an overprotective parent — maybe even on the paranoid side.

Keep your eyes open

The two main things you need to look for when you tour a child-care facility with the intention of placing a child are the physical environment and the nature of the child-adult interaction.

The physical environment

The room where your child will spend most of his time should be clean and safe but not necessarily too neat and tidy. After all, it is a room filled with kids. Look at the toys and equipment (such as tables and chairs). Are they appropriate to your child's age? And are they in good condition? Does the artwork on the walls look like the teacher did it with some help from the kids, or is it the product of a child who was allowed to be creative on his own?

Try looking at this room from your child's point of view. Are the toys, pictures, and working material at your child's level? Now look at the room with safety in mind. Are the room dividers (if there are any) low enough so that a teacher can see what's going on in all areas? You may find that new buildings are designed with many windows, low walls, and open spaces; some may even have video monitors to protect children from abuse.

The child-adult interaction

Next, you need to look at what's *happening* in the room. Do the children seem happy, healthy, and involved in activities? Remember, this is a room full of kids. Sooner or later an argument or accident is likely to occur. That's to be expected. You need to watch to see how the caregiver handles the situation. Ideally, the caregiver will stay calm and step in to help the kids solve their own problem.

It is hoped that you'll find a staff that looks happy and enjoys their work with the kids. You don't want to see caregivers who look like they're on the verge of a nervous breakdown, or someone who doesn't seem in control of his or her class. You also want a teacher who practices good communication skills.

Don't be shy — ask many questions

Arm yourself beforehand with questions. Write them down and document the answers. When you've researched all the places and people who are possible candidates, sit down and go over the answers. With a written record, you won't have to try to remember which person said what and who promised this or that.

Questions to ask are . . .

✔ **May I have some names and phone numbers of parents whose children currently attend this center (or of parents whose children you've cared for in the past)?**

Ask for a list of parents you can call as referrals. If you can't get this list because some people may not want their phone numbers given out to strangers, stop other parents and ask them how they like the facility or the teachers. The best time to do this is during afternoon pickup time when parents are a tad less hurried.

✔ **Do you allow visitation during the day?**

Avoid places that are hesitant for parents to pay surprise visits or that don't allow visitation during the day. Stopping in, inspecting their work, and seeing your child are your rights, if that's what you want. After all, it is *your* child.

✔ **What kind of snack or lunch program do you offer?**

Avoid places that serve only sugary or nonnutritious foods.

✔ **May I see the play areas?**

Play areas should be well-lighted and well-supervised. The area underneath slides, jungle gyms and other climbing structures should be covered with cushion-type materials like bark chips, sand, or rubber. This covering minimizes injuries if your child were to fall. Outside areas should have a fence so that little ones can't walk off — and big mean bad boogey men can't walk in and snatch someone.

✔ **What is the procedure for releasing the children at the end of the day?**

You want a system with a sign-in/sign-out ritual. No place should be so relaxed that anyone is able to walk in and take a child without someone seeing what's happening. Having a place with a prerelease form attached to your child's application describing to whom your child may be released would be nice. That way you can restrict it to grandma, an aunt, a neighbor, and so on.

✔ **What are the rules regarding sick children?**

You want to hear something about the school or caregiver separating a sick child from the other kids when they realize that someone has come down with an illness. The caregiver should also have a policy on sending home a sick child whose temperature reaches a certain point. That may be anywhere from 99 to 101 degrees F.

✔ **Do you give out medications? What is your policy?**

Schools and private caregivers, like most places, are afraid of legal problems, so many facilities won't give out medications. Others will with written release forms and well-written directions. You can count on your child getting sick and needing to take medication, so these answers should mean a great deal to you. When the facility or caregiver won't give out medications, ask yourself whether you work close enough so that you can leave work to give your child his medicine during the day?

✔ **What will you do if my child is injured?**

Injuries can mean anything from a bump on the head to a broken arm. Most places handle minor injuries because kids have many of them, especially when they're playing with other kids. If it's important for you to know about every bump and bruise, you may want to include in your child's file the stipulation that you're to be called *anytime* your child gets hurt.

✔ **When your caregiver calls only for an emergency, what constitutes an emergency?**

Is anything that involves blood or are only accidents that involve broken bones considered an emergency? For your own comfort, you need to know how the center defines an emergency situation.

✔ **What are your fees?**

Be prepared for heart failure here. Child care, in general, is expensive. And, the younger your child, the higher the cost. The reason for the higher fees is that more staff is needed to care for younger children, because their teacher-to-child ratio must be lower than with older children. Ask whether the fees include any meals or snacks and whether additional fees are charged for diapering and other such services.

✔ **Do you have a late pickup charge?**

Most day-care chains charge late pickup fees that can be anything from a flat fee to as much as $1.00 for every minute that you're late. These people want to go home when it's time, and these charges are in place so that parents won't get the idea that being 10 to 15 minutes late every day is acceptable.

✔ **What is your teacher-to-child ratio?**

You're basically asking how many kids each teacher is responsible for handling. Every state has different requirements. You can call your local Health and Welfare Department or Child Welfare Department to find out what your state and city requirements are. You need to know this number, because when the state says that a child-care facility can't have more than ten 2-year-olds to one teacher, you don't want your 2-year-old with a teacher who has twenty to look after. These laws also apply to registered private sitters.

✔ **What are your teacher qualifications?**

You want a child-care facility that requires its teachers to have credits in child-care or child-development classes. These classes include CPR, first aid, and child development. Private sitters should also be certified in CPR and first aid.

✔ **What is the turnover rate of your teachers?**

Finding a center that has a low turnover rate of teachers is good for your child: You don't want your child involved in a situation where he never is able to develop a relationship with a teacher because the teachers are always leaving. A high turnover rate also reveals a problem at centers that can't seem to keep teachers employed.

✔ **Do you do background checks on your employees?**

It is unfortunate that you have to ask this, but you don't want a convicted child molester caring for your children.

✔ **How do you discipline children?**

If the response is "We beat first, ask questions later," you may want to look elsewhere. Knowing how your caregiver handles discipline problems is important — if only so that you can use the same language and discipline style at home. Day cares usually are pretty good about discipline. They rarely fall into the bad habit of saying, "I'm going to give you until the count of three before I act like I may start to do something." They give one warning, and then they act.

On the other hand, you don't want to keep your child at a facility that doesn't discipline at all. You'll have plenty of work on your hands when your child is with someone during the day who lets him get away with anything he sees fit to do.

Conversely, you also want to find out how teachers reward good behavior. They may give out stickers or candy; or, the teachers may simply allow special privileges. This reward system may be important to you, particularly if your child happens to be diabetic and can't have candy, or if you hate stickers because your younger child always finds them and eats them.

✔ **What kind of communication will I have with my child's caregiver?**

You should receive some type of information about what your child is doing during the day and any behavioral problems that occur. Daily or weekly newsletters are good.

✔ **How well does my child have to be potty trained?**

This question is for the facility or private sitter that only takes potty-trained children. Your child may have accidents up until the age of 4 or 5. You need to know whether the facility will handle accidents and how well caregivers will clean him up afterward. You don't want to bring your child home and find pants full of poop. You also don't want your child with someone who believes in the old school of thought that a child should be potty trained by 1 year of age and shames your child every time he has an accident.

✔ **What kind of payment schedule do you have? Do you allow time off for vacations?**

Many facilities make you pay whether you're there or not. They use the payment as a means of holding a spot for your child. Others allow you time off during the year for vacation. Each facility handles this situation differently, but you need to know whether you're going to have to pay for day-care time even when you're not going to be there.

✔ **What is your daily curriculum for the children?**

You want to know whether the school has the day scheduled with organized activities or whether it's a free-for-all during the day. Your child doesn't necessarily need to be put in a preschool environment and forced to learn the *ABC*s at 6 months old. In fact, forced learning in itself can be detrimental to young children. But children need organization during their days. Take time to discuss the center's educational goals and philosophies with the teachers and the director. You want someone whose goals are the same as yours.

✔ **Do you have a naptime during the day? What is your policy on children who no longer take naps?**

Your child may not be a napper, but the facility you choose may require all children to at least lie down to rest. You want to find out so that when your child comes home complaining about having to lie down, you can talk about just *resting*. You can explain that the day care has naptimes so the other kids can rest. When your child doesn't even like to lie down, you need to talk to the center about a separate activity for your child.

✔ **Can I see your last licensing report?**

This document gives you an idea of how well the center measures up to state requirements. You can also call the licensing agency and ask whether a particular center has been cited for any violations.

✔ **Do you have NAEYC accreditation?**

NAEYC stands for National Association for the Education of Young Children, a private association whose accreditation goes beyond the state level. Its inspectors look at a variety of criteria ranging from child-teacher ratios to developmentally appropriate teaching practices and multicultural curriculum. Basically, when a facility has this accreditation, it's looking mighty good.

You can also go to the NAEYC Web site to find a center close to you that is accredited. Type in the name of your city, state, and zip code, and then click the *Find Programs* button. The centers in your area are listed. The Web site is `www.naeyc.org/accreditation/center_search.asp`.

Using a Child-Care Referral Service

Whenever you can't seem to find a private sitter who is close to you, call your local Health and Welfare Department for the number of your area child-care referral service.

This service provides names and phone numbers of sitters who have been accepted into the department's program as certified sitters. Candidates must complete an application showing current certification for CPR and first aid to qualify to be a sitter for the Health and Welfare Department, and they must list their procedures of discipline, food for snacks and lunches, daily schedules, and activities.

This service can recommend people close to either your work or your home but can't guarantee the type of care that your child will receive. So, this is when you would want to do your research by talking to other parents, viewing for yourself what the home or facility looks like, and making a few surprise visits to see what happens during the day.

A great Web site called Child Care Aware is located at www.childcareaware. org. It can help you find child care in your area. This Web page belongs to an organization called Local Child Care Resource and Referral (CCR&R). Its purpose is to help parents by giving them referrals to local child-care providers, information on state licensing requirements, and other information that help them find the best child-care provider in their area. You can also call 800-424-2246.

Starting Your New Child Care

You never know how your child is going to act on the first day of day care. Your child may see all those toys and other kids his age and forget you ever existed. Or, what is more likely to happen is that your little one will want to go exploring — but with you close by.

If this is the first time you're leaving your child with a sitter or at a day care, gradually make the transition. You don't ever want to just go in, drop your child off, and then leave. That would be hard not only for your child, but also for the people who are responsible for taking care of your child — and, ultimately, for you.

Try this process of easing into a new day-care situation:

- ✔ **Day 1:** Go with your child for the morning and have lunch with him. That gives you both an opportunity to find out how lunch is handled. After lunch, you both can go home for the day.

- ✔ **Day 2:** Go with your child for a few hours. Sit back, watch, and encourage him to go and play without you. Having you there within eyesight makes your child more comfortable with the whole situation. After a couple of hours, leave for a while. Come back and get your child later. Make sure that you let your child know that you're leaving and that you'll be back soon. Never sneak out. That's mean and can turn into trust issues later on with your child.

- ✔ **Day 3:** Go with your child for a few hours, kiss him good-bye, let him know you'll be back later, and then leave. Come back at the end of the day.

- ✔ **Day 4:** Go with your child for a few minutes. Make sure he is settled in and then kiss him good-bye; let him know that you'll be back later for him, and leave.

The idea is that you want to gradually make your exit. Dropping your child off to a new place without him warming up to the idea is harder on him (and perhaps you, too) than weaning yourselves from each other.

You don't have to follow this schedule exactly. You can make up your own schedule of how you gradually wean yourself from your child.

Give your child a few pictures of your family to take to the facility. Being able to look at these throughout the day can be comforting for your child.

Here are a few other guidelines to make leaving your child at a sitter or day care a little easier on you both. Use the checkbox list in Appendix C to be sure you're following these guidelines.

- ✔ **Don't rush in the mornings.**

  Kids hate to be rushed and don't handle it well at all. Give yourself plenty of time to get ready at home — even if it means getting your child up a few minutes early so that he can lollygag around. And spend a few minutes getting your child settled in at the day care. Never rush in, drop your child off, and rush out.

- ✔ **Spend some time together in the morning.**

  Take breakfast with you to your child's room at his day care and share it together. Allowing an additional 15 to 20 minutes is sufficient.

- ✔ **Never sneak out while your child is doing something else.**

  Tell your child when you're leaving and that you'll be back at 5:00 p.m. (or whenever). You'll turn any kid into a clingy child who's afraid to let you out of his sight if you're always disappearing.

✔ **Make your good-byes quick and to the point.**

Some children never seem to get over the separation, no matter how much time you devote to making them feel comfortable. When you decide to leave, kiss your child good-bye and *leave*. Don't hang around and go into long explanations as to why you must leave — just leave. You can't reason with a mad or upset child, so simply go. Rarely does any child cry all day; they usually get over it pretty quickly. Once you finally leave, your day-care worker or sitter can help your child become involved with something else that takes his mind off your departure.

✔ **Don't scold a child who cries because you're leaving.**

Being upset is a natural response when a parent is leaving. Asking your child not to be sad and to instantly stop crying is unrealistic. Just let him know that you love him, you're sorry that he's upset, and you'll be back, and then leave.

✔ **Don't be too hard on yourself.**

Children aren't the only ones who shed tears on the first day of a new child-care situation. Parents shed a few themselves. Try holding back these tears until you can hide in the safety of your car. Your child doesn't need to get the impression that the place where he is staying is a bad or sad place.

✔ **Don't be upset if your child isn't as *tidy* as when you left.**

Go ahead and be upset if you pick up your child and there's snot smeared all over that once clean face. In fact, you should talk to the director or teacher about something like that. However, if your child's clothes are on backwards, he may have been practicing his independent self-help skills. If your child has red paint in his hair, clay in his pockets, and Play-Doh under his fingernails, chances are good your little one had a great day.

Read the book *The Berenstain Bears and The Sitter* by Stan and Jan Berenstain (Random House) to your kids. It's a great book to get them accustomed to the idea of a sitter.

Tossing the Coin for Sick Kids

When your child is sick, someone is going to have to stay home. If one parent is a stay-at-home parent, then a problem doesn't exist; however, if both parents work, something must be done. Relieve the stress of trying to answer the question, "Who's going to stay home today?" by talking and working out a backup child-care plan in advance. You parents need to talk to each other about work schedules, time-off options, or other family member options. Play fair here. It doesn't always have to be Mom that stays home. You need to work out an equitable plan that you're both happy with.

Part V

Developing a
Good Person

The 5th Wave   By Rich Tennant

"SCREAMING OR NON-SCREAMING?"

In this part . . .

Raising your child to be a well-balanced, confident, responsible, and independent person is what the chapters in this part are all about. These chapters contain guidelines, suggestions, and tips that can be used every day in helping your child develop into a person who you'd be proud to know; someone who is confident, respects others, communicates well, has good habits, and has a nice set of moral values. This stuff is as important, I think, as the rest of the book. However, the subject matter in these chapters directly relates to the guidance and development of the kind of good person that others want to be around.

Chapter 22

Raising Your Child (12 to 24 Months)

- -

- -

*1*n the movie *Raising Arizona,* Holly Hunter tells Nicholas Cage, "If you love me, you'll get me a child." And so he does. Of course, he has to steal one for her, but that's beside the point. Once they have their beautiful little boy, they sit him down and look at each other. Holly Hunter breaks out in tears and says, "I love him so much." After that point, they're a little unsure about what to do with this child they both love so much.

That's the dilemma this chapter addresses. Here are more guidelines and some general things to practice once you have that child you're destined to love "so much!"

Treating Your Child Like a Person

Don't misinterpret this section's title, "Treating Your Child Like a Person," to mean "Treating Your Child Like an Adult." Those are two altogether different things. The difference between them is that adults make lifelong decisions . . . not necessarily good decisions, but they make them. Your kids may not be able to decide what to wear to the park. They do, however, deserve the respect that all people deserve.

Treating your child like a person means treating your child with respect. Don't take advantage of children or embarrass them because they can't fight back. You wouldn't even think of it, right?

Consider this scenario: A man and woman are going to the grocery store. The man tells the woman he has to go to the bathroom. She says, "Okay," and he goes. No big deal.

Now change the players: A mother and her son are going to the store, and the son says he has to go to the bathroom. The mother grabs the boy by the arm and jerks him, while at the same time saying, "I told you to go to the bathroom before we left. Can't you hold it?" The boy, with tears in his eyes, says, "No, Mom. I really have to go." So the mother yanks her son to the bathroom, all the while saying, "I can't believe you do this to me."

Ever see that happen? I witnessed this scenario just the other day, and it's embarrassing and humiliating for the child. Can you imagine this woman saying to her husband, "Dave, I told you to go to the bathroom before we left. Are you *sure* you have to go? Can't you *hold it* until we get home?"

Most parents don't realize it when they're humiliating their kids. It just happens because parents either lose patience or just don't think about what they're doing or saying. It's easier to overlook children's feelings when they aren't capable of saying, "Hey, knock it off, you're embarrassing me!"

Taking the time to understand and care for another person is a true sign of love. — Wise Old Lady

Another embarrassment and potentially humiliating situation for children is making them perform their little "tricks" or talents when they don't want to. When you make your children perform before others, like playing the piano, when they don't want to, you risk ruining their enjoyment of that talent. Their talent may be a personal thing that they enjoy doing privately but not for an audience.

If you *are* able to get your kids to perform their tricks, understand the difference between laughing *at* them and laughing *with* them. No one likes to be laughed at.

Talking to Them and about Them with Respect

Children are the most amazing things you ever create. They're like precious stones that must be treated with care and shown with great pride. Even when your 3-year-old dumps juice all over the floor, remember that she's special. She dumped that juice with such pride and precision that even a diamond cutter would be envious. How else could someone dump juice and not only get it on the floor but *also* in your purse, in the drawer, and on the chair across the room? You need not go into an explanation to your friends about how clumsy your son or daughter is. Your child is being a child, and there is no explanation necessary for that.

Too many parents are comfortable bad-mouthing their children. You're supposed to be your children's greatest supporter, their cheering squad. That can't be done when you're always pointing out their shortcomings. After all, they've managed to keep their mouths shut about how you can't pull out of the driveway without knocking over the garbage cans.

Your children are bright. They catch on to more than you realize. Imagine how crushed you'd be if you heard your best friend talking about your big butt, your inability to drink without spilling it on your shirt, or your body making mysterious noises in public.

Your children share the same feelings that you do about being embarrassed. They like to know that when you talk about them, you bring up the good things they do and not the bad. This practice may sound like bragging on your children. So what, if it is? You have something to be proud of, and it's okay to tell other people that you think your children are *terrific.*

Children are likely to live up to what you believe in them. — Lady Bird Johnson

Using Positive Communications (Or What Most of Us Call Happy Talk)

The best way to tell your kids that you think they're special is to treat them special. Do this by the way you talk to them. Don't talk down to them in a superior way, don't be condescending, don't use foul language, and don't yell.

Your communication style needs to be positive, upbeat, and cheerful. Sort of like Mr. Rogers. Mr. Rogers is cool. He never says anything bad about anyone, he always says nice things about the people he meets, and he looks at life in a positive manner. He doesn't even yell at his train friend when he's late. Mr. Rogers uses *positive communication.*

Your kids will use your style of talking. If you speak in negative tones, calling everything *stupid* or *dumb*, so will your children. If you think positively, you'll use positive words, and your kids will do the same.

Read more about communication skills in Chapter 23.

Good and positive communication skills also require good listening skills. Mirror back what your child says and then ask for more information. Having someone ask you to talk is a positive experience, and your children benefit greatly when they grow up with positive communication experiences.

Children have never been very good at listening to their elders, but they have never failed to imitate them. — James Baldwin

Interacting with Your Children

As is true of your communication, interacting with your children needs to be fun and positive.

Recognize the difference between being in the same room with your kids and interacting with them. The difference is when you interact with your children, you become a part of their lives, and you participate in their conversations and their playing. Too many families think that if they all sit in front of the television together, they're doing the *family togetherness thing*. That way doesn't work. You can't be interacting with each other when you're sitting in front of the TV, mesmerized by the latest basketball-shoe commercial.

Your goal as a family must be to schedule your life so that you have as much time as possible to interact with your children. That means making choices. You can either work late every night, or you can choose to go home and spend time with your family. You can opt to have everyone grab snacks all evening, or you can all work together to make dinner, sit down, and eat together, and then all clean up together. You can decide to watch TV after dinner, or you can do something that everyone in the family can have fun doing together, like playing a game. Leave your activities open to things that encourage communication between you and your family.

Don't fall into the dreaded pit of thinking that your job is more important than spending time with your family. If you were to ask your kids what they'd like most — money, or to spend more time with you — *time* would be the answer.

As your kids grow older and start having outside interests like sports or clubs, you may actually have to schedule a *Family Night*. This night should be a time when everyone commits to staying home and spending the evening together. Make it a rule that no friends are allowed over, no telephone calls, no working late, and no plopping in front of the TV all night.

Letting your kids choose what nights to have the TV on and what nights to have "No TV Night" will help eliminate TV wars. — Denise DeLozier

Television robs you of time with your family

The most interaction you can get from spending all your time in front of the TV is when you ask each other who has the bag of chips. Because it's unrealistic to ask people to go without their television (because, after all, it is a form of entertainment), *limit the amount of TV that you watch.* Keep to shows that you and your kids are able to discuss afterward, and watch it only for special occasions. Plan your TV watching. Never fall under the lure of let's-see-what's-on-next or watch TV while you're waiting for your show to come on.

Is TV evil? Studies on declining values and the disintegrating family have drawn this conclusion or that. Recent statistics indicate that the average child spends almost an entire day per week in front of the TV. Yet everything ties into the introduction of TV into American life. TV probably isn't evil; however, it can rob you of valuable time that you can otherwise spend with your family. Don't let it do that to you. Control your TV and your TV viewing habits. Remember, the thing has an OFF button.

Giving Kids Time

Your kids don't know, and won't know for several thousand years, what the concept of time is. In kindergarten, they begin learning what yesterday, today, and tomorrow mean, but that knowledge really won't *mean* much. And certainly the phrase, "You have 15 *minutes* to brush your teeth and get in bed," means zilch. You may as well say, "You have 15 *minogranits* to brush your teeth and get in bed."

If you want to minimize your stress levels, allow your kids plenty of time to prepare for things. Buckets of time. Oodles of time. If they have one hour to get dressed, make their bed, and brush their teeth, you'd think that was enough. Generally it is. But, you never know when they must engage in battle with ten invisible Putties, duel with the Joker, or re-dress all their Barbie dolls.

To keep your sanity, practice these steps:

- Give your kids only a few chores at a time rather than a long list of things to do. You may have to give only one chore if you're dealing with a 2- or 3-year-old.

- When you give your kids a chore, tell them how much time they have to finish it. Be realistic: Give them a little extra time. Don't assume that if it takes you five minutes to sweep the porch, it'll take them five minutes. Because kids are oblivious to what ten minutes means, for example, show them a clock and let them know what the clock will look like when their job is to be done. I do this every morning when my kids are getting ready for school. I show them the clock so they know what 8:20 looks like, which is when they have to brush their teeth, and what 8:40 looks like, which is when we're walking out the door.

✔ Check on your kids periodically to make sure nothing is getting in the way of their finishing a chore. You know, land mines, three-eyed monsters, the Princess of the Galaxy, and so on.

✔ Give them a countdown every 10 to 15 minutes. This intervention helps explain to them the concept of time, so they're not surprised when you walk in and say, "Time's up."

✔ When they've finished their chores, have them come back and give them something else to do. This doesn't leave room for the whining "But I forgot!" line that kids dish out so easily and that probably is the truth.

Sharing with Your Mate

Unless things have changed radically since this book went to press, the women are the ones who get pregnant, who go through labor and delivery, and who breast-feed. That's the way it happened at our house. If it happened differently at your house, we'd be interested in hearing about it. But just because Mom seems to have so much to do at the beginning, parenting isn't always left up to her. Both parents need to be involved in *The Parenting Game.*

Both parents need to know how to change diapers (yes, even the explosive, stinky ones), clean up puke stains, discipline, put the kids to bed, and do all the other joys and chores of parenting. Not only will you miss out on a lot of fun and quality time with your kids if you don't help with the kiddy chores, but you're really going to irritate your mate when you don't help and end up making him or her do all the work.

Putting Moral Fiber into Your Day

I've got to warn you, I'm going to talk about religion here. The purpose isn't to shove any specific type of religion down your throat, because really, so many cool ones are out there. The only point of this section is to bring this issue to the table and have you consider it as a part of raising your children. Much like the fact that you have to consider how to handle other topics your child will raise — things like sex, divorce, death, and eating cookies for breakfast — it's just a fact of life.

When do you tell your children they should be kind to everyone? I hope it's before they've punched the neighbor kid in the stomach. How do you relay the message that they need to honor and respect their mother and father? Your actions should be teaching them these things, but is that always enough? Sometimes bringing an outside source in is more effective when teaching things as important as moral issues. These lessons are best taught by bringing a spiritual aspect into your child's life.

Children who go to Sunday school are seldom found in court. — Reverend John Coppernoll

At home, you should be teaching lessons about honesty, making good decisions, being kind to others. When you go to your church or place of worship, these lessons also are taught, but rather in the form of, "This is the problem that Peter had and this is how he handled it." This example is helpful to your children, because they not only learn that their problems are real (and that other people have them), but it also gives them a path to follow when these problems occur again.

Religion, regardless of what religion you're talking about, shouldn't be scary or unapproachable for children. In fact, children are the people who usually have the greatest faith and openness about religion. They're also the ones who aren't afraid to bring up religious topics for you to answer.

The best way to teach kindness, love, and honesty is to be that way yourself. (Oh yes, it's the set-a-good-example theme again.) Teach your children the importance of being fair and honest. Tell them that it's always best to do the right thing. Cheating is bad; telling the truth gets rewards and makes other people trust you.

If there is anything we wish to change in the child, we should first examine it and see whether it's not something that could better be changed in ourselves. — Carl Jung

Somewhat good reasons to go to church

If you or your kids need some good reasons to go to church, other than the moral lessons and guidance for life, then here are some. Personally, I think the moral lessons are pretty good reasons, but you may need a little more coaxing.

✔ You get to wear nice clothes.

✔ It keeps your kids occupied for a while.

✔ You get to go into a large room and sing off-key with other people who are also singing off-key.

✔ It sets up the day to go out for lunch (no cooking).

✔ Free coffee (and even donuts at the nicer places).

✔ God likes it — what more can we say?

Going to your local house of worship is another way that you, as a family, can spend time together. You'll learn that sometimes things taught by Mom and Dad aren't taken to heart as much as when someone else teaches them. As a parent, we need all the reinforcement we can get to teach children right from wrong. It's great to be able to ask your child, "Now Jordan, do you think Jesus stuck his tongue out at his mother?"

Many children have invisible friends that they make up so that they can have someone to talk and play with. Having someone like God as an invisible friend couldn't be a better choice. He's tons better than a Pokemon.

Religion is a foundation. It's there for your children to build their lives upon. This foundation can always be there no matter what kind of problems your children encounter as they grow up. Don't underestimate the power of being able to answer the question, "Where do babies come from?" with, "From God."

Your children are going to rely on everything you do and say to make them the kind of people they grow up to be — not to put any pressure on you or anything.

Chapter 23

Communicating with Your Child

• •

In This Chapter

▶ Talking effectively

▶ Explaining to your children what you expect of them

▶ Teaching good communication

▶ Answering questions

▶ Communicating with stickers and notes

• •

Good communication skills are the foundation for building a great relationship with your kids. However, so many different elements get thrown in the way that listening and communicating aren't always easy or effective.

This chapter covers things that you can do to improve communication with your kids. It doesn't necessarily mean they'll mind you or agree with what you're saying, which is okay, but at least they'll hear what you're saying. This chapter also tells you how to avoid problems caused by a lack of communication — in addition to providing some ideas about how to teach your kids to be good communicators.

Talking and Being Heard (It Isn't Always the Same)

Mother: "I've informed you a googolplex times to abstain from vexing your sibling."

Child: "Huh, Mom?"

When you talk to your kids, you must keep a few things in mind.

If you have something to say, and you want to be heard, do the following:

- ✔ **Get down to your children's level.**
- ✔ **Use simple words.**
- ✔ **Get to the point.**
- ✔ **Don't yell.**

Getting down to your children's level

When you really want your kids to hear you as you talk, physically get down to their level. If you can't squat, pick them up and put them on your lap. Look them right in the eyes, speak calmly and slowly, and say what you have to say. Don't be vague or babble and don't try to impress your children with your fabulous expanded vocabulary.

Encourage your children to look *you* in the eye. Kids can be standing right in front of you and have a bobbly head like those dogs that sit in the rear window of old-lady cars. *Bobble, bobble, bobble.* They're not paying attention.

You certainly don't need to get down to your children's level to say, "Good morning," or "Are you hungry?" Save this kind of action for *serious* conversations such as, "Now, Simon, what did you do with Mommy's keys?" or, "Do you understand why you got into trouble for hitting your brother over the head with the bat?" But don't forget that the most important part of communicating is being a good listener. Communication can't work both ways when you're doing all the talking and none of the listening.

God gave us two ears and one mouth so that we can listen twice as much as we talk. — Old proverb by someone important

Using simple words

As adults, parents sometimes are brave enough to say, "What *exactly* does that mean?" They do this hoping they don't sound too much like a dork. Kids, on the other hand, will smile at you, and nod, or better yet, stare at you with blank looks on their faces.

Talk to your kids by using words that they understand. Getting your point across is easier when your kids know what you're talking about. If you don't think they understand, ask them to explain what you've just said. That is a great test to see how well you're getting your message across.

Real-life examples you need not read

Here are some real-life comparisons of interpretations from your mouth to your child's ears.

What you say: "Jordan, you need to be responsible and put your dirty clothes in the clothes hamper every night."

What he hears: "Jordan, you need to be rahpitty-blah and put your dirty clothes in the clothes hamper every night."

What you say: "Jeremiah, don't piddle. You're supposed to clean your room."

What he hears: "Jeremiah, don't pid hole. You're supposed to clean your room."

What you say: "Don't be sarcastic to your sister."

What he hears: "Don't be sark a stick to your sister."

Always ask children whether they understand. If they seem unsure or hesitate, then ask them to explain it back to you. That's really the only way you'll ever discover whether you're getting your point across. Of course, you may have a child who doesn't hesitate to ask you what certain words mean. Then there's no question as to what is understood.

When you don't talk to your kids using words that they understand, you may as well be speaking Swahili. That's why you hear many successful parents talking in short, blunt sentences, using simple commands. Although they sometimes sound like they're talking to a pet: "Sit. Stay. No, no, no! Stop, stop, stop! Good boy."

At some point you'll have to expand your vocabulary; you won't always have to talk on a preschool level. When you begin introducing new words to your children, take the time to ask whether they understand what you've just said. Many times, they'll smile meekly and say, "Yes," insincerely. Just ask them to explain what you said. If they're missing your meaning, explain it to them in another way or define the word that's throwing them off.

Getting to the point

Pretend that you're being timed on a conversation egg timer. If you don't say what you need to say within a short period of time, you've lost the attention of most children. On the other hand, when you're too brief, they'll ask for more information, if they need it.

Your kids understand you a lot better when you're specific and when you get right to the point, so:

- ✔ **Don't ramble on and on.**
- ✔ **Don't go into long explanations.**
- ✔ **Say exactly what you mean.**

Children don't have to listen to you. They can choose not to listen the same way that you choose not to listen to certain people. You can't force, bribe, beg, or plead enough to get them to listen. They don't care. Even if you're in the middle of a sentence, they'll walk away when they get bored or are just tired of listening. Good communication between you and your children is the foundation for a long, happy, and growing relationship. If your children aren't listening to you, you've lost that foundation to build upon.

Don't yell

Yelling is the worst way to communicate. Let me say that louder in case you didn't get it:

YELLING IS THE WORST WAY TO COMMUNICATE.

Here's a guarantee: When you yell at your kids, they're not listening to a thing that you're saying. All they're doing is sitting there teary-eyed and upset because you're yelling or they're getting angry themselves. Your point is lost, they're upset, and you're upset. *Nothing* has been accomplished.

When you yell, your message won't get across. So whenever you reach the point where you're about to yell at someone, stop and leave the room. Just for a second, mind you. Take a few deep breaths, get your composure back, and approach the situation again.

You're trying to be a role model and teacher. Yelling isn't a trait that you want to pass on to your kids. In fact, it comes back to haunt you as your kids grow older and their hormones get all stirred up. After all, when you yell, you're only teaching them to yell.

If you have to yell at your kids, you're not close enough to them. — My dad, Virgil Hardin

Explaining What Is to Be Expected (Or, How to Avoid Those Ugly Grocery-Store Incidents)

Outbursts in grocery stores and other temper tantrums can be reduced by a simple method of communication: Explain to your kids what you expect of them. Tell them how they are to behave.

Kids like to know what's going on just as much as you do; they like being prepared and informed. Set the ground rules before you go anywhere or do anything. Use this strategy when you can, and you'll see things go smoother with your kids. For example:

> "Jonah, we're going into the toy store to buy Simon a birthday present. We're not buying you a present. You can look around. You can tell me what you like. But we're not buying you anything today. Today is for Simon. Do you understand?"

Don't be surprised when your child protests, whines, or still comes up to you with a toy, explaining that he's always wanted this special LEGO Millennium Falcon, and if you get it for him today, he never will ask for anything again.

Your response needs to direct your child back to the original conversation about Simon's birthday and explain that you both had an agreement. You'll be in trouble whenever you give in to the whining and the major fits. Your kids won't believe you the next time, if you tell them they can't buy anything and then give in and get them that one little toy. Buckling under the pressure only leads you to more tantrums because, obviously, the tantrums work. Here are some pointers for avoiding tantrums:

- ✔ Before whisking your children out of the house, give them time to prepare whatever things they need. That's important. Their preparation may mean only tucking Barbie in her Malibu Barbie house before she leaves. It may mean searching for ten minutes for a toy to bring along. Whatever it is, give your children time to do their thing before you leave, and that way they won't feel rushed. Giving your kids a countdown helps. Tell them you're leaving in 30 minutes. Then tell them you're leaving in 15 minutes. Then give them a five-minute warning. Walking out the door is a breeze when your children are prepared.

- ✔ Look your children in the eyes when you get to where you're going, making sure that you have their attention, and then tell them what your expectations of them are and why you expect this behavior. Be precise and clear about what you mean. You don't need to go into long explanations unless they ask for more information. But don't expect miracles. Children are children, and they'll behave as such. They squirm and wiggle and make noise and voice their opinions.

- ✔ Never assume your kids know what you want. When you stop talking and start assuming, you get into trouble. For example, suppose that you're going to your cousin's wedding. Tell your kids what a wedding is, and what it's going to be like. Then tell them their job is to sit quietly and watch. No talking or getting up is allowed. Tell them that they need to get a drink and go to the bathroom *before* the wedding starts, so they won't have to do those things during the ceremony. Be a smart parent and bring a pen and pad of paper so your child can at least draw during the wedding. And, again, understand that kids are kids. Weddings and other formal events aren't exactly fun for them.

Plan wisely before putting your kids in an environment that's going to be difficult for them. Don't expect a 2-year-old to sit quietly in a theatre, at a wedding, or in an upscale restaurant. And, remember that it's unfair of you to scold a child for being a child when he's in an environment that he shouldn't be in to begin with.

If you have to put your child in a situation that isn't appropriate for his age, then giving him instructions beforehand is much easier than trying to set the rules while you're already involved in that activity. You end up saying, "Shhh-you-need-to-be-quiet," or, "No you can't have anything," way too much. Instead, you'll be giving a few reminders of the rules you've already gone over.

Explaining things to children in advance works really well, too, especially when you're in a hurry: "We're going to the store for just a few minutes. Don't ask for anything." It may take awhile for them to believe that you really mean what you said, so they may go ahead and ask for something. But, don't give in, and eventually they'll get the idea.

Advanced planning works only when you don't give in to whining and change your mind about the rules. If you set rules but don't stick by them, you're in serious trouble. Your kids will always push you, whine, and throw fits whenever you go back on your word. This is a parental behavior that also is known as not being consistent.

Teaching Basic Communication Skills

Everyone loves a good communicator. Someone who's charismatic is without a doubt an excellent communicator. Look at top executives, and you'll find enthusiastic communicators. These are the kind of people you admire, and the kind you want your children to grow up to be like.

The problem is that communication skills must be taught. Doing so is part of your job as a parent. And communication, like everything else, has rules. The rules are simple, and if you currently aren't using these rules, now is the time to learn them:

- **Use correct English.**
- **Look children in the eyes.**
- **Speak slowly and clearly.**
- **Let children express themselves.**
- **Set an example.**
- **Allow disagreements.**
- **Listen and hear.**

English as it is speaked

"Him was des da cutiest iddyy bitty precious lovey lamb. An him is jus da sweetes iddy bitty singie, yes him am. Wis his cunnin ittle toot-sies. An him sayin goo goo goo. Him iz muzzies ittle lambie boysie. Oochie chochie coo."

To this the baby listens by the hour and day and week. And yet his mother wonders why he never learns to speak.

As told to me by Grandma Marcia Gookin. Author: Unknown

Kids who have good communications skills do better in school. They make friends easier. And they grow up to be more confident people.

Using correct English (don't use baby talk!)

Baby gibberish and baby talk are two different things. Baby gibberish, the "goo-goo, gah-gah" thing we all want to do to babies actually is good for babies. New research has shown that these high-pitched exaggerated sounds that adults use with babies can actually boost their learning potential. So go ahead and "goo-goo, gah-gah" until you can't take it any more.

Baby talk, however, is different. Toddlers use baby talk. It sounds real cute to everyone else. But if you ever expect your children to speak properly, you must speak well. When you speak babyish, your kids assume that's the way adults talk, too.

Baby talk is basically using incorrect English. It's saying things like, "Does baby want his blankey?" instead of "blanket." When you call a blanket a blankey, your children call a blanket a blankey. That's neat for awhile. But when you see a 5-year-old walking around calling a blanket a blankey, it isn't cute anymore.

Teaching your kids to talk one way only to change it later on isn't fair. It's just as easy for you to say, "bottle," as it is to say, "baba." Your children will say, "baba," when they first talk. You need to follow that up by saying, "Yes, bottle." Say "bottle" a few times slowly. They'll eventually catch on. English is hard enough. Don't make it any harder than it already is.

Looking children in the eyes

Looking people in the eyes establishes a sense of confidence and trust. Moms and dads look at babies in the eyes all the time. I don't know anyone who avoids looking a baby in the eyes. It just can't be done.

Start looking your kids in the eyes when you talk to them, and do that from the moment your baby is born. As they get older and more mobile, getting them to look you in the eyes is harder, because they're too busy watching the cat spit up hairballs.

Younger children automatically look at you when they start trying to communicate. Look back at them. But as your kids grow older, eye contact is lost. You eventually must ask them to look at you when you're communicating. When there's eye-to-eye contact, everyone is paying attention.

When your kids start talking to you and telling you stories about things that happen to them, take the time to stop what you're doing and listen. Pay attention! This is the best way to teach eye contact, and it shows your children that you're interested and that you think what they're saying is important.

Speaking slowly and clearly

Your kids will talk much like you do. If that's a disturbing thought, now is the time for you to make some changes. Do you speak too fast, ramble on and on, or sound like you have mush in your mouth? Then don't be surprised when your kids do, too.

The only two ways to teach kids to speak well are:

- ✔ Speaking slowly and clearly yourself. Your children will pick it up and eventually do the same.
- ✔ Telling kids to slow down when they're overexcited and start talking too fast.

Don't make it sound like you're scolding them. On the contrary, just tell them that you can understand them better when they slow down a little. Once they've slowed down, they'll naturally begin speaking more clearly. For example, you might say, "I'm sorry, Sarah, but I can't understand you when you talk so fast. Please slow down."

Letting children express themselves

"There are some days that all I want is for my kids to be quiet, and now you're telling me to encourage them to express themselves? You've got to be kidding!" I don't know how many times I've heard this, but it seems to be the common response from many parents I speak with about their children and freedom of speech.

It's true. Having your kids express themselves is a wonderful way to teach them to communicate. When you express happiness, anger, disappointment, confusion, or whatever, you must formulate your thoughts and then try to say what you feel. It isn't easy to do. Many adults haven't been able to master this feat. When you encourage your kids to communicate, they grow up not only being better communicators, but they also discover how to express their feelings.

When you think that you've done something to make your children mad — like not giving them a second bowl of ice cream — ask them whether they're mad. As they're sitting there pouting, they may say, "No." Tell them that it's okay to tell you whether they're mad and that you won't be angry. Encourage them to tell you how they feel.

When you start training your youngsters how to open up to you, communicating their fears and frustrations will be easier for them by the time they have to go to school. That is the moment when many of their feelings will pop up and need to be discussed.

Another way of encouraging your kids to communicate is by using the words, "Tell me more about that." Your child stomps in the house and yells, "I'm mad!" Sit down and say, "Really, you're mad? Tell me more about that." Your child builds a neat spaceship and shows you the place where the pilot sits. Say, "Tell me more about that." This method is a simple but powerful tool to gather information and encourage your child to talk.

Setting an example

The best way to teach anyone is by example, which means that you must follow the same rules you that you set for your kids. You must remember to be a good listener, don't interrupt, don't finish his sentences for him, and ask for more information to encourage conversation. Resist the urge to hurry him up when he's telling a story, because it may seem to take forever.

Setting a good example may mean making changes in the way you communicate. Read the following and see how many of these apply to you.

(As you read the items in the following list, think of better ways for your children to express themselves. Give them words that may be better suited for them to use. They may be using words or phrases that they've picked up from friends or the evil television and may not be aware that what they're saying is inappropriate for their age or the situation.)

✔ **No cursing, damn it!**

Don't use any words that you wouldn't want your kids to share at school. Whenever you do, they're sure to take that word to school and share it with all their friends.

If you hear your children saying something that you think is inappropriate, even when it's something like, "Shut up!" tell them that they can use better words; tell them to say, "Be quiet," instead. Don't ignore children when they use bad language. They may interpret your silence as you not caring. And don't overreact by yelling or getting mad. Doing so may be the reaction they were hoping for.

✔ **No sarcasm.**

Sarcasm is contagious and can be extremely hurtful to others.

If your children are too young to understand sarcasm, you won't make any sense when you use it. If they do understand sarcasm, they may be hurt by it. Sarcasm is an unnecessary form of communication.

✔ **No yelling.**

Talking louder doesn't make things more understandable or clearer. If you don't understand, I'LL TALK LOUDER, OKAY?

Your job is communicating your ideas to your children in a calm manner. Yelling lets them know that you've lost control of yourself. And, believe it or not, they're not listening. They're just watching your face turn red and get all distorted.

✔ **No arguing.**

Disagreement is great. Arguing or fighting over the disagreement is not good. When you and your kids have a disagreement, let both sides of the disagreement be heard and work calmly to resolve the disagreement. Understand that you both think you're right, and sometimes disagreements remain unresolved. Thinking that every conversation is going to have a "winner" is unrealistic. You both may have to agree that you both disagree. That's okay.

Whenever you find that your conversation is on the brink of an argument, calm yourself down and remind your kids that they also need to calm down.

✔ **Don't lie.**

It's possible that you may be asked a question for which you don't have the answer. Admitting that you don't know something is okay. Never lie to your children or make up an answer to a question when you don't know. Simply tell your children that you don't know and that maybe you can find out the answer together. Then follow up by finding out the answer. Your kids won't think less of you because you were able to admit that you didn't know something.

The *smartest* people in the world are able to say that they don't know something. The *dumbest* people in the world are the ones who think they know everything.

✓ **Mirror the speaker and ask for more information.**

Mirroring keeps you involved in the conversation and lets the speaker know that you're paying attention. It's also a process of making sure that what you heard is what the speaker meant to say. So, when a child comes home and says, "I hate my school. I don't have any friends, and everyone is mean!" your mirroring response would be, "So you hate school." You'd then follow that up with, "Tell me more about that." Now be quiet and let your child talk. You don't ever want to invalidate your child's feelings by saying, "Oh Jonah, you don't hate school, you're just tired tonight." No, no, no. Bad parent. You're job isn't trying to make things better by talking your child into a good mood. Your job is to listen to your child, make sure you understand what he's saying, and then ask for more information.

The mirroring and asking for more information technique is good to use with anyone. This is an excellent communication skill that is highly underused. Practice these two things and watch the communication grow!

Allowing disagreements

The first response that you may have is: "Kids naturally want to disagree, because they're kids. That's what they do." This may be true for many or even most kids, but your role as a parent is *not* to discourage disagreements. If your children disagree with you, it doesn't have to mean they're arguing, which is how many parents interpret disagreements. It just means they have a different opinion, which is good.

When you encourage your kids to express their differing points of view by saying, "Tell me more about what you think," you're doing the following:

✓ **Helping your children to explain their feelings**

As I mentioned in the previous "Setting an example" section, verbalizing your feelings is a great practice for perfecting communication skills.

✓ **Encouraging discussions**

Believe it or not — and please accept this in the best way possible — you're not always going to be right. Sometimes your kids can bring up a point of view that you may not have thought about. It happens, so be prepared.

✔ **Allowing your children to be heard**

Being able to express yourself is such a great feeling. Your children also will appreciate being able to express their feelings and knowing that their opinions have been heard.

✔ **Teaching fairness**

Allowing people to voice their opinions is only fair. With this approach, however, your children also learn that just because they can voice their side of the story or their opinion, that doesn't mean they'll always get what they want. And sometimes they may even have a good argument for why they need to spend the night with Aunt Debra.

Thank your children for participating in the discussion. Tell them that you've heard their point of view by saying, "I hear that you're angry at me for not letting you spend the night with Aunt Debra," and point out that you appreciate their input. Nevertheless, don't be afraid to veto their request. Parents have the final decision. But you need to explain your decision. "It seems to me that you've really thought out why you should be able to spend the night with Aunt Debra, and I appreciate your input. However, Aunt Debra is having guests, so she's not going to be able to have you come over tonight. How about if we arrange it for another time?"

Listening and hearing

Listening and hearing are not one in the same. Both are extremely important and yet overlooked at the same time. Being a good listener means not interrupting your children and not finishing their sentences for them. It also means practicing mirroring skills as mentioned earlier in this chapter.

Hearing is different than listening. You can be hearing what your children are saying, but you may not be listening. Hearing means that the noise is hitting your eardrum. Listening means that you understand what they're saying, or even what they're not saying but are really meaning.

Do You Have a Question?

Your goal as a good parent is to be someone who communicates well and someone your children can approach. You want your children to be comfortable enough to ask you complicated or awkward questions.

"What are you going to do?" — Dr. Tim

Try this the next time your daughter or son comes to you with a problem: Listen carefully without interrupting, then pause for a second before asking with all seriousness, "What are you going to do?" If you're like most parents, limiting yourself to this one simple question can be a challenge. Why is that? And why is this question so different from what we usually say to children? In my experience, this rarely asked question is one of the more useful "lines" a parent can learn.

Packed within it are powerful, complex messages. Most of these messages are for children: "I'm aware that you have a problem and I'm curious about how you're going to solve it. I'm not giving advice or fixing the problem because I truly believe you can solve it on your own. I also know that you're upset. That's certainly understandable. But strong feelings don't entitle you to act badly or to fall apart. Even when you *feel* upset, you can still *act* in a way that is right, more times than not. I will be here to support you, but I'm going to wait and see what you do before I offer to help."

This question also contains messages for parents: "My child is upset and confused. It worries me to see him struggle, but my own distress is no reason to take on his problems. I'll fight the urge to fix his problem so I can give him an even greater gift. It is the gift of his parent witnessing his persistence and celebrating his success when he overcomes the problem in his own. It may seem like I'm not helping, but the truth is I'm helping in a different way, a better way."

Listed below are some other, useful lines. See if you can uncover the messages contained in these lines.

"This has been a rough day for you."

"I know that you're mad, but that doesn't give you the right to hurt other people."

"Is there something you would like me to do?"

"We probably won't agree on this, but here's how I see it."

"I didn't know that about you."

"You really don't like my rule."

"I've been thinking about what you said the other day . . ."

You can answer awkward questions effectively by following four rules:

✔ **Rephrase the question — also known as mirroring.**

Make sure that you understand exactly what they're asking. The more you understand about what they're asking, the easier it is for you to answer.

- "Why does Uncle Richard like to wear Aunt Robin's dresses?"
- "You want to know *why* Uncle Richard likes to wear Aunt Robin's dresses?"

✔ **Keep your responses simple.**

Your children don't always want a textbook answer.

- "Where do babies come from?"

- "From mommies."

When you answer their questions and they skip off happily, you answered as much as they needed to know at that time. If they continue asking for more information, you may have to go into more detail and drag out the visual aids.

✔ **Try responding as quickly as possible.**

If you're unable to answer at the time your children ask a question, follow up later. You don't want your children to feel that you're unwilling to answer their questions.

- "What is sex?"

- "Well dear, *sex* is an interesting topic. How about we sit down after dinner and talk about it?"

Then remember to sit down with your children later.

✔ **Be observant.**

If your children seem bothered by something or if they ask only vague questions (but never want to go into detail), sit down and talk. Maybe something is bothering them that they're having problems talking about — or perhaps they're confused about something and don't quite know what to ask.

- "Daddy, do you *love* me?"

- "Yes, I love you. Why do you ask?"

An unusual child is one who asks his parents questions they can answer.
— E. C. McKenzie

Alternative Forms of Communication

Tired of telling your kids *every* morning to make their beds and brush their teeth? As a parent, you hope that they'd finally understand that they have to do this every morning regardless of whether you've told them to do it or not. How is it possible for kids to remember that three days ago you promised to buy them Fruity Pebbles cereal, yet they can't remember to brush their teeth? Maybe it's time to change the way you're telling them.

A few of the traditional answers to commonly asked (yet unanswerable) questions

Q: Why is the sky blue?

A: It has something to do with chromatic filtering.

Q: What's chromatic filtering?

A: It's the stuff that makes the sky blue.

Q: Why can't I stick my elbow in my ear?

A: Because it would get stuck.

Q: Where do babies come from?

A: Mommies.

Q: Where do the mommies get them?

A: Daddy helps Mommy make the baby in her tummy.

Q: How?

A: Want some candy?

Q: Where does the sun go at night?

A: Well, the earth revolves, but the sun stays where it is . . . isn't the sun pretty?

And if all else fails, you can always satisfy them with:

A: Because *God* made it that way.

However, and in all seriousness, please don't be ashamed to say, "I don't know," to your children. It's much better to say, "I don't know," than it is to always sound like a punch line.

A good way to get kids to do things that they don't like to do is making those tasks as fun as possible. Tell your kids what you want them to do with notes, charts, and pictures (See Table 23-1 and Figure 23-1).

When you can't get your kids to remember to make their beds every morning, make a chart that lists their daily chores. After they've done their chores, let them put a sticker beside each chore that they've finished. Give them an award for the completed chart. If the chart is completed by a certain time (one that you set), tell them that they can do something special, like watch a favorite video, or you can promise to play a game with them. If they don't complete their chart, don't let them do whatever you've set as their special reward. Be consistent. Don't give in to whining or big Bambi-eyes filled with tears. This strategy works only when your kids know that you're serious.

Make time to talk

You're busy and so are your kids. But during all the hustle and bustle of your lives, you need to *make* time to sit down with and talk to your kids. It isn't always possible to *squeeze* in this extremely important time. But when you don't make this time, you may find that you and your kids are using the moments right before bedtime to try to cram in an entire day's events. You need something better.

Table 23-1	Good Morning!						
CHORES	*Mon.*	*Tues.*	*Wed.*	*Thurs.*	*Fri.*	*Sat.*	*Sun.*
Make your bed	☺						
Put pajamas away	☺						
Brush your teeth	☺						
Get school work done							
Feed dog/cat	☺						
Kiss parents good-bye							

Writing notes to your kids (like Figure 23-1) is a great way to praise them for a job well done or simply to show them that you love them.

Figure 23-1:
Notes are an easy way to praise your kids — and say "We love you."

> You did a great job
> making your bed
> this morning!
> Thank you so much.
> We love you,
> Mom & Dad

Chapter 24

Your New Big Job: Teacher

Congratulations! You're getting a teaching position without going to the college and taking the state-board tests, and you don't even have to move to the cramped on-campus dormitories. The only small drawback to your new job: You have to work seven days a week without any vacations, sick days, or weekly paychecks. You got this job the day you became a parent. Your students are your children. Your job description includes — but is not limited to — teaching English, math, science, social behavior, communication skills, gym, health, and hygiene. And the list goes on.

You're evaluated every day. Look at your kids. How do they behave? What kind of people are they turning out to be? Do they seem well-balanced, or are they habits that you wouldn't be happy to live with?

Good or bad, you can look to yourself as part of the reason why they are the way they are.

You're Teaching All the Time

Your kids constantly are learning. You begin teaching them to recognize your voice even before they are born. The day they're born they start learning by listening to you talk and sing and interact with them. They watch your smile, your actions, and the way you talk and walk. Their personalities, the issues they carry throughout the rest of their lives, some of their habits, and essentially who your kids are develops within the first seven years of their lives. Some of this development is directly related to you. Their goal is to do what you do. It's like a lifetime game of *follow the leader* — and you're the leader. That is the nurture theory. Part of who they become is also the nature theory, meaning that they are born to be who they are.

Knowing that you play a big part in your child's development, embrace the fact that you'll be teaching your kids every day of their lives. Heck, I'm $*#& years old, and I still go to my mom for advice, and I imagine I'll still go to her when I'm old and gray. Well, I'll never be gray thanks to Lady Clairol.

Thinking about your kids trying the things that you've done is scary. So, you need to take a close look at your lifestyle. If your 3-year-old spills her crayon box, puts her hands on her hips, and yells, "Damn it!" think before you get mad. Where do you think she learned that? She had to get it from someone. Maybe you'll find the culprit in your mirror.

Setting a Good Example

The easiest and most effective way to teach is by example. Even adults learn better by seeing other people do whatever it is that they want to learn to do. Can you imagine learning how to paint pictures without first watching someone else paint?

You are the bows from which your children are as living arrows sent forth.
— Kahlil Gibran

Once your kids see you do something, they practice what they've learned. They see you walk, and then slowly they start trying to walk. They hear you talk, and then they start babbling. They see you smoke, and then they head for the Bic lighter.

When your kids first learn to speak, they're imitating the words you say. Even when they say, "Dada," it's their attempt at trying to say, "Daddy." I hope that when they say, "Baba," it isn't short for *Bud Light*.

Don't compare

Don't be tempted to teach your children by comparing their behavior to that of their siblings or to that of yourself. You need to keep this warning in mind when you set expectations for your children. Address each child separately and accept them for who they are. It really doesn't matter that one child takes longer to walk, or talk, or ride a bike. Each child has a personal timetable.

A friend relayed a story about when she was driving on the highway one day with her daughter when another driver, a man, quickly cut them off and drove away. The daughter, seeing that her mother was mad, said, "Mom, why don't you just flip him off like you always do?" Oops.

Avoiding making a spoiled brat

Parents do not maliciously do things to harm their children, at least they're not supposed to. So be aware of the things listed below so that you don't turn your precious darling into a spoiled brat.

- **Don't buy love.**

  Do you give your children everything they ask for? Some parents try to compensate for the fact that they aren't with their kids as much as they'd like to be, so they give their kids everything they want. A better way of making up the fact that you aren't able to spend as much time with your kids as you'd like is to take a day off or come home early and play games. Your child receives more enjoyment from an afternoon of sitting on the floor playing games and eating popcorn than from any toy that you could ever give her.

- **Reward work.**

  Your kids can earn the extra stuff that they want by doing extra chores for you. They'll appreciate their possessions more when they've had to work for them.

- **Watch yourself.**

  How do you act? Is your behavior less than perfect? Criticizing others, acting hard to please when someone wants to do something for you, frequently returning or exchanging gifts, placing too much importance on the monetary value of something are actions that set poor and bad examples for your child.

Read the book *The Berenstain Bears Get The Gimmies,* written by Stan and Jan Berenstain (Random House), to your children. It offers a good lesson on kids (or bears) who ask for something every time they go to the store.

Good habits

You've put it off long enough. Now is the time to start developing *good* habits and getting rid of bad habits. Don't even think about saying that you don't have any bad habits. Everyone has bad habits. Some, admittedly, are worse than others.

You can't have the attitude: "I'm going to pick my nose if I want. I'll teach my kids not to do it. They'll know better." Alas, it doesn't work that way. You are your kids' heroes. You are their role models. Whatever you do, your kids will want to do it, too. Whenever you think that your bad habits aren't going to affect your kids, your reality is distorted.

How sharper than a serpent's tooth it is to have a thankless child!
— Shakespeare

Please and thank you (alias: manners)

Don't underestimate the importance of good manners. Do you remember that woman who flipped you off on the highway this morning? She didn't have good manners. You don't want your kids to grow up to be one of those finger-flipping, road-hogging, inconsiderate drivers who are plaguing the highways and byways of our lives.

Your children will grow up to be kinder and more considerate of others if you teach them how to be that way when they're young. Again, you can do that by setting a good example. You must always say "please" and "thank you" to your kids. Even when you are saying, "Please get your bicycle off my foot," or "Thank you for the dead slug."

And don't forget good table manners. Everyone tends to be a little too relaxed at the dinner table when it comes to proper behavior. Maybe you think it's funny when Daddy balances a spoon on the end of his nose or one of the kids makes a hat out of his napkin and wears it on his head all during dinner. If you don't mind this kind of monkeying around, even when you're dining out, ignore this advice. But, if you're like me, and you don't think it's appropriate to do this kind of stuff in public, then teach your kids what you think is acceptable and what isn't acceptable, and then make sure that you're consistent about the rules.

Kids have a hard enough time remembering household rules. They have an even harder time remembering rules for *dinner at home* and rules for *dinner out,* when those sets of rules aren't the same. Some general table manners include no gross jokes, no throwing food, no leaning back while sitting in the chairs, no talking with food in your mouth (including no "see food" jokes) — and definitely no loud farting or belching.

Yes, in some cultures belching after a meal is acceptable and even encouraged. However, don't let someone's excuse about practicing multiculturalism sway you. If belching isn't allowed in your culture, don't allow it at the table. And if you do happen to burp (and who doesn't?), say, "Excuse me." If you laugh about burping, you've created a family precedent, and your kids will belch and laugh about it the first time they have dinner at a friend's house.

Only worth reading if you want a lesson on bad habits

Bad habits include smoking, getting drunk, taking drugs, yelling to get your point across, drinking out of the milk carton, cursing, lying, cheating, littering, crossing the road on a red light, farting in public, picking your nose, belching out loud, talking with food in your mouth, interrupting, ignoring, forgetting your mother on Mother's Day. Just to name a *few*.

Good manners that you can teach your children include not interrupting people while they talk and not shoving your way in front of others to always be first, two things that kids are *infamous* for doing. Teach your children how to write thank-you notes, make get-well cards for sick relatives, say *please* and *thank you,* acknowledge when someone is talking, say *good-bye* to someone who is leaving, share cookies with a friend, and always give their parents the green M&Ms.

Teachers in the local school system tell me that a growing problem in schools these days is that children lack good manners. Children don't treat teachers, staff, or classmates with respect. So schools now are teaching good manners and respect in addition to conflict management. And yet, good manners still begin at home and should be taught by parents. Here are some guidelines that you can use at home:

✔ **Be kind to others.**

Telling kids, "Do unto others as you would have them do unto you," doesn't really mean anything to them. Instead, stress the importance of treating others the same way they'd like to be treated, especially when you see them doing something that you know they themselves don't like. My son Jonah hates to be interrupted, and yet he interrupts people. I remind him, "Jonah, you really don't like it when people interrupt you, so please don't do that to Jeremiah."

✔ **Understand their actions.**

Help your children understand the harm they can cause by doing or saying thoughtless and unkind things. Ask them, "How would you feel if someone pointed at you, and started to laugh?" In the beginning, you may simply be doing damage control, but eventually you'll be helping them to avoid harmful words or actions.

✔ **Show them the way.**

Children do whatever they have to do to express themselves. Sometimes that comes off looking and sounding pretty bad. Playing a role reversal game with your child can help show them how to handle situations. Let them ask the question or behave a certain way, and you respond by showing them how their behavior should appear.

✔ **Be a good role model.**

"Do as I say, but not as I do" is a joke. Your kids probably want to respond with, "Yeah, like you'd catch *me* playing bridge with a bunch of 50-year-old women!" When you want your child to show good manners and respect, you must also practice good manners and respect. Say please and thank you, admit your mistakes, apologize, and treat people, in general, with kindness and respect. That is a great lesson that I learned from my father, and I'm working to pass it on to my kids. The reward of this behavior is that, like my father, your children will grow up having many friends and a family that loves being around him.

✔ **Share.**

Share with your children so they understand the importance of sharing with others. Compliment them when you see them sharing with others.

✔ **Keep kids healthy.**

Children tend to behave badly when they're tired or hungry. Kids need sleep and nutritious foods to survive. It's that simple.

✔ **Practice family politeness.**

Everyone in the family must practice "please" and "thank-you" policy in which, for example, no request is considered unless the person asking says "please." When one of your children forgets, just give him or her a look that says, "I'm waiting." They soon catch on. Use the same approach for saying "thank you."

✔ **Thank-you notes.**

My friend was pleasantly surprised to receive a thank-you note from one of my kids. Teach your children the importance of thanking people for gifts. Show them how to write notes and make sure that they are sent promptly after receiving gifts.

✔ **Praise good behavior.**

Praise is a wonderful teacher. Tell your children how proud you are when you notice them being polite and following the "please" and "thank-you" guidelines that you've set.

Many children's books are designed to teach children about manners. I strongly recommend that you take the time to read these stories to your children. Examples of books on manners are *Manners* by Aliki (Scholastic Inc.), *Perfect Pigs* by Marc Brown and Stephen Krensky (The Trumpet Club), Richard Scarry's *Please & Thank-You Book* (Random House), and *The Berenstain Bears Forget Their Manners* by Stan and Jan Berenstain (Random House).

Boring safety and emergency information (but read it anyway)

Remember the movie *Kindergarten Cop?* Arnold Schwartzenegger asks how many kids were born in Astoria. Everyone in the class raises their hands. And then he asks how many kids were born outside of Astoria. Again, everyone raises their hands. What's the lesson here? As a parent, teaching your kids some basic information is your job. That includes having them:

- Memorize their complete name and phone number. If they can remember their address, teach them that, too.

- Memorize the complete names of their parents or guardians.

- Memorize the phone number of a neighbor or family member in case of an emergency when you can't be reached.

- Know what 911 is, what it means (and the phone number for 911 is nine-one-one), and what constitutes a 911 emergency. Also tell them that the police will come out and visit with them whenever they play with 911. We had that little visit ourselves!

- Know who a stranger is and what to do when strangers try to get them to get into their cars.

- Know who to go to in case they get lost in public places like shopping malls, fairs or carnivals, movie theaters, or parks.

It's an unfortunate fact of life, but there are people out there who steal children. Investing in a home fingerprinting kit can help protect your children from this awful situation. It contains forms for information about your children and the supplies you'll need to do your own fingerprinting.

You and your children also need to have a private password that only you and your family know. When someone tries to pick up your children, tell them to ask for the password. When anyone tries to pick them up and doesn't know the password, make sure that your children know they are not to go with that person. If you don't know how your children need to respond to strangers or getting lost in public places, go to your local police station and ask for public safety information.

Read *Never Talk To Strangers* by Irma Joyce to your kids. It's a fun book about who is a stranger.

To help keep your kids safe in cyberspace, take a look at www.safekids.com. There are some great things on this Web page that all deal with the safety of your children. *Guidelines for Parents* and *Family Contract for Online Safety* are great resources. Some downloadable items such as the *Kids' Pledge* and the *Parents' Pledge* would be good to sign and post at the family computer.

Teaching Honesty and Responsibility

Your new teaching job keeps getting harder and harder. Teaching honesty and responsibility takes a considerable amount of time and patience, and it isn't anything like teaching your kids how to tie their shoes, where they understand the basic concept after a few lessons. You'll have to keep hammering away at these lessons for a long time.

Can we be honest?

You teach honesty by encouraging your kids to tell the truth and to let you know what's on their minds. Having your children tell you what's on their minds shouldn't be a frightening thought.

When you've taken a toy away from your child because she was throwing it, you know she's going to be mad. Ask her how she feels. Tell her that it's okay to tell you whether she's mad, and let her know that you won't be angry. Then ask her why she's mad. This strategy teaches your kids that they can talk to you honestly without you getting upset or yelling. Your part in this business is that you must be prepared for this kind of input from your children.

A second way of encouraging honesty is avoiding confrontations in which telling a lie is made easy for your child. Instead of saying, "Simon, did you color on the wall?" say "Simon, you know you're not suppose to color on the wall." Avoid direct confrontation when you already know the answer. Asking him if he colored on the walls, when you saw him do it, sets your child up to tell a lie. Don't put your kids in situations where fibbing is easier than telling the truth. Even as an adult, when someone asks whether you ate the last chocolate chip cookie, you get a little nervous — like maybe you did something wrong. Learn, however, to stick out your chest and proudly announce, "Yes! I ate the last cookie, and I must be honest, it was the best cookie out of the whole package."

Now, if Simon really didn't color on the wall, he can easily say, "But Mom, I didn't color on the wall, it was Dad!" Figures.

Pretty much all the honest truth telling there is in the world today is done by children. — Oliver Wendell Holmes

The third and most important way of teaching honesty is being honest yourself. Don't ever lie to your children. You're setting an example. When you lie to your children, they'll think that it's okay to lie. But, on the other hand, when your children lie to you, you get mad. You can't have double standards.

Thinking that you'd never lie to your children is easy. However, you must be careful about unintentional lies (see Table 24-1): "I'll be back in just a few minutes" — and you're gone for several hours. These kinds of *white lies* can teach your kids not to trust you.

Table 24-1	Traditional White Lies
White lie	*Truth*
"It's just medicine. It tastes good!"	It tastes like lighter fluid.
"This won't hurt."	Gestapo-approved torture tactic.
"I just have to grab one thing from the store."	Two hours later, you own the store.
"We're going to Aunt Mildred's. We won't stay long."	Any time at Aunt Mildred's is a long time.

The correct ways to make the intended statements represented by the white lies in Table 24-1 are:

1. "The medicine helps to make you feel better."

2. Not saying anything about pain is best. When you can't get away with that strategy, say, "This may not feel so good."

3. Either grab your one thing and leave or say, "I have some shopping to do. I don't know how long it's going to take."

4. "We're going to Aunt Mildred's. We'll leave by 11:30." Show your children on the clock what 11:30 looks like when they don't know.

Kidding and teasing can be fun. Everyone does it and thinks that it's a hoot. But be careful not to overdo the kidding with your kids. They don't have the knowledge and experience to determine what's a joke and what isn't, so they take everything you say to heart. When your kids get to the point where they follow everything that you say by asking, "Really?" then perhaps you ought to hold off on some of the joking until they start believing what you say without questioning it.

Being responsible boys and girls

Teaching your children responsibility starts out with small tasks and chores. When your children are old enough to understand simple commands, start giving them a job or two. I don't mean sending your 2-year-old out for a paper route but rather simple tasks. Ask them to give the book to Grandma, take the paper to the trash, and put the spoon in the drawer. After they've completed the jobs, let them know what a terrific job they did. Give them lots of praise — and, of course, hugs and kisses. Your children will beam when they realize that they've completed a task that made you happy.

As your kids grow older, you can start adding to their responsibilities. Teach them how to make their beds and put their dirty clothes in the hamper. You're not only developing their sense of responsibility, but you're also starting good habits and teaching them valuable lessons about how important it is for everyone to help clean up around the house.

An important part of teaching chores to your children is to *do* the chores with them until they understand how you want the chores done. After they've learned how to do their chores, follow up by making sure that they don't start slacking off. They'll need your constant supervision for a long time — even though they may think they don't need it.

Avoid giving money for housework. Paying your child to make their bed leads down a path you don't want to go. Your kids need to know that all family members must work together as a family; therefore, everyone is expected to help with chores. When you want to pay your children for work, give them extra work like raking the yard or painting the doghouse or additional household chores that are not a part of their usual chore list, like washing windows.

Steps to follow when teaching chores

People are not born knowing how to make the bed or wash the dishes. There's a definite right and wrong way to do these things, and you must teach it to your children.

1. Do the chore with your children. Explain each step and why it's necessary.

2. Go through the chores with your children, but only observe. Have your children do all the work by themselves. If they need your help, that's a sign they aren't ready to do the chores by themselves.

3. When your children can do the chores by themselves without your help, leave them alone and let them do their chores. After they're done, have them show you what they've done. This practice not only gives you a chance to observe their work, making sure that they did it right, it also gives you the chance to praise their work.

4. Reduce the amount of time you have to observe their work. They'll slowly become more independent and responsible, and you'll be comforted in knowing that they can consistently and correctly do their chores.

5. Make sure you use a chore chart so that your children can keep track of their chores on their own and so that you won't be put into the position of nagging.

Make tasks and responsibilities fun. Your kids will enjoy doing them more when you turn setting the table into a game, or picking up clothes into a race. When giving your children responsibilities, avoid the let-me-help-you-with-that syndrome. Your children need find out how to handle small tasks and may not want you to help.

Sometimes your younger kids may be too preoccupied with something to want to stop and help you. That's okay. You can't force a 2-year-old to do something if she doesn't want to (short of picking her up and physically moving her). And you really *don't* want to use force. Having responsibilities should be fun. As your kids get older, you can start using gentle persuasion when they decide they can't break away from Superman Saving the World.

Be aware that your kids may go through a stage when they don't want to handle their responsibilities. Don't let them whine their way out of their jobs. And don't let them put their jobs off until later. This behavior starts them down that road to procrastination.

Building Independence, Self-Confidence, and Self-Esteem

Some adults attend expensive seminars and faraway camps to help them *find themselves*. They want to build their self-confidence and self-esteem. They dance around fires beating tambourines and eating bean sprouts. Then they feel *empowered* (or something) — until they get the bill.

Building this kind of character into your children needs to be done before they have to go away to a camp. It's a long process of giving your children little responsibilities every day. Add on to their responsibilities and praise them when they succeed in doing them. When they say that they *can't*, let them know they *can* do anything — if they just try. It doesn't have to be done perfectly.

Independence and self-confidence begin when you let your children do things for themselves that you'd normally do for them. Allowing them to order their own food at a restaurant or tell the doctor how they feel are good ways of building their confidence. They can also start getting their own bowls of cereal, calling friends to confirm birthday parties, picking out their own clothes for the day, and making decisions about what movie the family should go out and see together, or where they should eat for dinner. Giving your children options to choose from is a better way to start these decision-making steps. For example, tell your children about the two movies you'd like to see and then let them choose the one that you'll see. Your children also must learn that making these decisions is a special event and that making *all* the family decisions is not up to them.

All the efforts that your children put forth need to be rewarded. They need help so they can succeed. Unrewarded effort can wear down self-confidence and often results in low self-esteem. Here are some tools and strategies for helping your child to succeed:

- ✔ **Help your children set realistic goals.**

  Discuss your child's goals and then leave opportunities for each of you to review and change the goals as needed.

- ✔ **Give your children positive feedback.**

- ✔ **Show your appreciation.**

  Tell your children how much you appreciate them for helping you.

- ✔ **Use constructive criticism.**

  Giving feedback is important. Acknowledge their good effort and then talk about the areas that you suggest they can improve upon.

- ✔ **Encourage your child to be independent.**

  This one is tough for many parents. Kids need to learn how to be independent. They must learn how to help themselves, start and clean up their own activities, and how to take responsibility for their own actions. Encouraging your child to plan her own activities and take risks every now and then is best.

All the *positive* things you do and say for your kids are the best ways to develop their confidence and self-esteem. If you believe in their abilities, and you let them know that you believe in them, they'll believe, too.

All of this *praise* stuff may sound ridiculous to you, but that's because, as adults, we aren't always told how special we are and that we're doing a good job at something. We're basically confident (except for that small group of people off at camp dancing around fires and eating sprouts). Your kids aren't adults. Be careful not to tear down your children's self-confidence by always pointing out weaknesses rather than focusing on strengths:

> *Michelangelo, what a nice painting you did on the Sistine Chapel. But you know, you really didn't clean your brushes out very well. I think they're ruined now!*

They need to know that what they're doing is wonderful, and that you think they're special:

> *Goodness Virgil, look at that fence you built. That is a terrific fence. You should be so proud of yourself. Hey Shirley, come over here and look at this great fence.*

Whenever your children use the word *can't*, tell them there is no such word. *Try* or *do*, there is no *can't*.

Last but Not Least: Respecting Others

I can't say this enough: Kids learn by example. When you don't show your kids how to act respectfully toward those around them, they won't learn themselves. They won't understand that it's rude to interrupt people or to ignore someone who is talking. They need to learn to be good listeners, to be polite and kind to people, and to be helpful at all times. Okay, this sounds like the Boy Scout creed, but it's true.

The biggest brats around are those kids who don't do any of the things just mentioned. They talk back to their parents or to any adult, for that matter. They aren't loving to their siblings, and they don't play fair with their friends.

Kids learn respect not only by watching you and how you interact with others but also by receiving gentle reminders. You have to teach them how to behave. If they start interrupting you, ask them to wait until you're finished speaking. When someone else is talking, and your child is obviously not paying attention, put your child on your lap and tell her that she needs to listen to the person who's talking.

A moment of self-reflection: Could this be you?

If you're someone who doesn't let others finish their thoughts before you jump into the conversation, stop it! Your friends have neglected to tell you how annoying it is. Not only is it annoying, but it's rude — and you don't want your kids to do the same thing.

Ways of teaching respect

Set a good example yourself. Have your children do volunteer work. Encourage the relationship between your children and their grandparents. Go to your local house of worship. Develop a good relationship between you and your children. Enroll your children in a sport or club. Buy children's books that emphasize respecting others.

Chapter 25

Social Skills That Make You Proud

In This Chapter

- ▶ Dining with baby (and toddler and child)
- ▶ Preparing for the dining experience
- ▶ Traveling with your kids
- ▶ Knowing what to pack
- ▶ Spending your family vacation time wisely
- ▶ Eating on the road
- ▶ Enjoying a film with family in tow

Someone well versed in social skills knows that you don't pick your nose in front of others. Another way of putting it is having the knowledge that you don't comb your hair at the dinner table, belch out loud, or scratch yourself in front of guests. This stuff should (I hope) be pretty obvious. Moreover you must deal with the more subtle social skills, such as starting with the fork on the outside and working your way in when you find more than one fork on the table, sending a thank-you note to someone who gives you a gift, and never telling your Aunt Debra that her hair looks orange after she's colored it.

Social skills aren't easy to learn, but they're a necessary part of life that we need to teach our children. The hardest part of it all is that you must take your kids out in public to practice.

Great Social-Skill Expectations

Dining out, going to parties, traveling, or even playing with others are learned social skills, behaviors that take a lot of practice and, in some cases, advance planning. You need to keep certain things in mind while you train your children to be proper little ladies and gentlemen.

It's insane to expect too much from your little ones. They're just learning and, quite honestly, this is hard stuff to learn. Many adults haven't learned any social skills — like your Grandma Shirley who puts her false teeth on the table after dinner. Some things just shouldn't be done.

Many social activities require long periods of sitting, which can be boring to children. As adults, parents usually amuse themselves when they're bored; however, when children are confronted by boring social activities, amusing them is the parents' job. If parents don't amuse them, children find their own amusements like kicking the backs of the pews in church, throwing spitballs at waitresses, screaming just because it sounds cool, making fart sounds with their armpits during your best friend's wedding, and more.

Any type of social activity turns out better when you remember to make sure that you go to them when your child isn't tired, sick, or hungry. In addition, tell your child what is to be expected of him at the event and what is to be expected from his behavior.

Children prefer playing with other well-behaved and well-mannered children. You'd be doing your children an injustice by not taking the time to teach them the proper way to act and play.

Dining Out with Children (Other Than Fast-Food Restaurants)

Yes, it's possible to eat out at other than fast-food restaurants. Your children don't have to be going through puberty before they realize that not all restaurants have Golden Arches out front and that some places actually put your food on real plates.

Eating with the little ones

Eating out with infants is a breeze. They're *easy*. They're happy to sit quietly, be cute, and look around. Occasionally they'll spit up just to impress those dining around them. Just follow these guidelines:

✔ **Try arranging your restaurant meal during your child's naptime.**

Ideally, if you can feed your baby when you first get to the restaurant, the little one can sleep while you and your dinner date enjoy your food.

✔ **Ask to be put in a booth.**

Booths are usually wide enough to place a baby seat so that your child can nap next to you. In addition, booths are a little more secluded, darker, and better for napping kids. When you're breast-feeding, a booth gives you a little more privacy so your baby can nurse. The perfect booths are in corners.

✔ **When you can't arrange the outing around naptime, bring plenty of supplies for keeping your baby happy.**

Nothing is more annoying for you and those dining around you than to have dinner with a screaming baby. Your supplies should include plenty of diapers and diaper wipes (otherwise known as butt wipes); milk, juice, and water bottles; a spit-up towel (or two); a blanket (because restaurants can be drafty); and clean soft and cushy toys that are good for biting.

✔ **Avoid giving your child hard toys, like the hard plastic rattles, to your infant.**

Babies don't yet have enough arm control, so they eventually hit themselves on the head. This act may be funny in a Three Stooges movie, but it isn't so funny when your baby does it.

Dining with older babies, toddlers, and up

Dining out with the toddler age group takes more planning and imagination than what you need to summon up with infants. Older babies, toddlers, and your older children aren't as happy just being cute; instead, they want to be entertained. They want to get up, cruise around the restaurant, and check to see what others are eating (maybe even taking a bite or two). Follow these guidelines when dining out with older babies, toddlers and such:

✔ **Have enough supplies with you.**

These supplies include your own bib (the restaurants may supply them, but they are typically flimsy and don't work well), diapers, diaper wipes, milk, juice, water, food (if your child is not going to eat off the menu or from your plate), a blanket, and toys. Again, don't bring hard toys: Hard plastic toys are great for banging on the highchair or table. And that's a no-no. Good toys to bring are soft picture books, crayons, and a coloring book. Many restaurants already supply some of these things. Give your child toys and finger food only when needed, and, even then, only one at a time. In other words, don't dump the whole bag of goodies on the table or the highchair.

✔ **Go out to eat when it's time for your children's meal — not when that time has past.**

The best way to keep children or anyone else quiet is having them eat (nice to know for when your in-laws come to visit). Chances are good that whenever you go out to eat, your children aren't hungry, and they'll quickly become antsy. Nothing is more boring than sitting around waiting for someone else to eat.

✔ **Ask the server to bring your children's food as soon as possible.**

But do this only when your children are acting cranky because they're really hungry. Otherwise, just have them wait for their food like everyone else.

✔ **Don't permit your children to fill up on premeal stuff (like crackers, juice, or milk).**

Keep children happy by quietly playing games with them. That's why you need to have a book or crayons with you. For little ones, spoons or napkins can be a source of great amusement.

If your children seem to be getting cranky and the food hasn't yet arrived, you and your dinner date may want to take turns taking them for walks. Go visit the enticing restaurant lobby but avoid meandering around other eating guests. And never let your children walk around by themselves unless it's in the lobby — away from the other guests.

Restaurant rules and regulations

The sooner you and your children learn the basic lessons about going out to eat at a restaurant, the easier eating out will be for you both.

No loud screaming or talking

Remove screaming children from the restaurant until they've calmed down. Most people can tolerate a whimper or crying because you're not getting food to your kids fast enough. But you need to handle the *getting-mad* type of crying elsewhere.

Obviously you can't teach a baby not to cry, but you can try finding out why a baby's crying. Go through your list of reasons why babies cry (see Chapter 7). Is your baby hungry or thirsty? Does your baby need a pacifier? Does your baby have a wet or dirty diaper, need a change of positions, or is he simply tired? Of course you'll encounter the "I'm-mad-because-I-can't-play-in-your-mashed-potatoes" cries and the "I hit-my-head-with-this-stupid-rattle-you-gave-me . . . and-it-h-h-hurts!" wails. You can handle these types of crying with hugs or by leaving the restaurant for a moment. A change of environment sometimes makes kids forget why they're crying.

When you practice these guidelines, your children will grow up understanding what's acceptable and what isn't while they're eating out. As your children grow older, you still may have to offer the occasional reminder for them to hold their voices down while they talk. Kids' voices tend to get louder the more excited they get.

No wandering

When your children are at the age when they can walk, that's what they're going to want to do. Don't let them. They must learn that walking around a restaurant and picking food off other people's plates is unacceptable behavior.

No unnecessary lingering

When you eat out with your youngsters, realize that long, casual dinners are a thing of the past. When you want to linger over dessert while sipping coffee and talking about the pros and cons of national healthcare, get a babysitter and leave the kids at home. When you want a good meal with the kids, go someplace where children are welcome and the restaurant is equipped for them. Such restaurants have a children's menu, maybe some crayons, highchairs, and booster seats. Order your food, eat, and then leave. This strategy doesn't mean that eating out can't be fun. It just means that it may need to be quicker than when you were alone. If you keep your outings short and sweet, your children will be less likely to lose their patience with the situation. As they get older, you can try expanding the time. Just be sensitive to how they're acting. If your kids seem happy sitting there and playing with the napkins, sit back and enjoy. If they're getting antsy and beginning to squirm, take their hint and leave.

Having a long, relaxing dinner with 5-year-olds and older children is possible. All that you need is a pen and pad of paper for them to draw on. That usually keeps them happy while you complain about your job, neighbors, the government, and so on.

Practice politeness

You're in a public place. Practice your good manners while you're out. No food throwing — by anyone. That includes you, too, parents. Don't leave a huge mess for your server to clean up. Be respectful of the fact that tidiness is greatly appreciated. Say "please" and "thank you" to your server. The server's job is not exactly easy.

Children on the Go

Traveling with your children can be fun. No, really. Say this out loud:

Traveling with my kids can be fun.

All you have to do is prepare for the trip. This advice applies regardless of whether you're traveling by car or by plane. Remember, much of traveling with your kids is your attitude. You're taking your kids with you, so you must act as a *family*. Gone are the days when you took off for Europe with a duffel bag and your dad's credit card. Things are different now.

Hither and thither with the kids (general travel information)

Traveling with your kids can be fun, provided that you keep a few basics in mind. Make sure that you tell your kids what's going on and give them an idea of your schedule. Traveling often involves a great deal of waiting, so let them know that, too. Like everything else, when you inform your kids what's to be expected of them, they'll be better able to comply.

If you have a young one, try leaving before naptime. Everyone is much happier when your baby or toddler is able to sleep through most of the trip.

Finally, take plenty of snacks, drinks, and entertainment. Sometimes the entertainment may mean you, so be prepared to sit with your child and play some games (only if someone else is driving). If that doesn't appeal to you, all sorts of travel toys are available for keeping your little one happy.

Here are a few tips that can help make traveling with your kids less like an episode of *The Simpsons:*

- **Allow yourself plenty of time to get to wherever you're going.**

  Remember that you'll have to stop for potty breaks, rest stops, and stretching your legs.

- **Ask your travel agent about vacation sites that are equipped for children.**

  A travel agent should be able to give you a list of hotels that accommodate children, along with resorts that have special children's packages. For example, the Hyatt Regency in Scottsdale, Arizona, has a water playground and a special all-day camp designed for kids.

- **Have snacks and toys close at hand.**

  You don't want to be contorting all over the place, or digging in the bottom of bags trying to reach the things you need.

- **Take your doctor's phone number with you.**

  Kids get sick, even when traveling. Don't forget your insurance card, too. You never know when you'll have to pick up medicine on the road.

Some children don't sleep well in unfamiliar places, so take along a favorite blanket or stuffed animal to make them feel more comfortable. You may also find that you'll have to stay with them until they fall asleep.

See the USA in your SUV (automobile travel)

No one enjoys trying to do marathon trips where you drive and drive and don't stop until you've driven to your destination. Keep these things in mind when traveling by car:

> ✔ **Make regular stops.**
>
> Even when no one needs to pee. Stop for stretching and letting off energy. Your kids will get tired of sitting and want to stop on occasion.
>
> ✔ **Clean up.**
>
> Stopping at a roadside park not only means playing tag and going on short walks, but it also is a good time to change diapers, wash hands and faces that may have gotten sticky, and clean out your car. Your trip is much more enjoyable when everyone feels clean and isn't having to fight trash that's piled up on the floor.
>
> ✔ **Exercise caution.**
>
> Play tag or chase only when you're in an area that is away from cars. Don't play in driveways or parking lots, and never let your kids play unsupervised.

No matter what else happens, don't let your young ones out of their car seats while you're driving. It takes only a second to have a car wreck and have your little ones thrown from the car. When your kids get tired of sitting, pull the car over to a McDonald's and let them play on the McPlayground, on the McSlide, and in the McBall cage.

Up, up, and away (airplane travel)

Basically the same rules for car travel apply to airplane travel. The only difference is you can't pull the plane over to a roadside park and let the kids run around. The same routine of x-ray machines, searching backpacks, and even random body searches also apply to children. It's been reported that children as young as 4 years old have been pulled out of the line to be searched. I hope this changes soon but just in case it doesn't, have a conversation with your children about the x-ray machine and the people who may go through their backpacks or any carry-ons they have. Of course, airport security procedures do make you think carefully about what to carry aboard a plane.

Here is a list of things you want to make sure you do have with you, though. Let them search all they want — you still need to make an airplane trip successful and comfortable for your children.

✔ **Pack extra diapers and clothing.**

You never know when you're going to encounter extended layovers on connecting flights. Don't forget to pack plastic bags for dirty diapers and dirty clothes. You'll also want to pack an extra set of clothes in case diapers spill over or the eating process doesn't go so well.

✔ **Be prepared for ear unplugging.**

Bring something to suck on, such as a bottle, pacifier, sucker, or piece of candy (hard candy and gum work well for older children who know how to suck on a piece of hard candy without choking on it). Breast-feeding also works. The hardest parts of flying with a child are the takeoffs and landings. Changing air pressure hurts those delicate little ears, and they'll not hesitate to let you know.

✔ **Take a car seat whenever you travel with your toddler.**

Yes, you'll have to pay for the seat your kid occupies, but flight-safety experts will tell you that a child is better off in that seat than in your lap. Besides, your toddler will be used to the seat. And because he knows that when he's in the seat he isn't allowed to get up and stroll around, and he'll therefore be less likely to want to get up and walk around the plane.

✔ **Take snacks and beverages with you.**

Your kids may not be happy with the airline-provided snack of stale peanuts and a thimble of soda. So bringing along snacks and beverages that your kids enjoy is better.

✔ **Limit your carry-ons.**

Airplanes have a limited amount of space, and just because you have children doesn't mean that you're allowed more than your two carry-ons. A purse, a diaper bag, an overnight case (leave the metal fingernail file at home or it will be confiscated), and a stroller are *more than* two carry-on pieces. The less you have to carry with you, the better off you'll be.

Combine your purse and the diaper bag, check the overnight case at the ticket agent's desk, and check the stroller at the boarding gate. If you let the ticket agent know that you want to check the stroller, the agent will ticket the stroller. That way you can drop it off at the gate as you're about to board the plane. Airport personnel will have it ready for you as you leave the plane (just let them know that you'll need it to get off the plane).

Give your child a carry-on bag, such as his own backpack, for personal items. Things like toys (but no guns, knives, or any toy with small removable parts), snacks, and ID card are good.

> ✔ **Don't let your kids walk the aisles.**
>
> The flight attendants have a hard enough job getting all those drinks to everyone. The last thing they need is a bunch of kids bouncing up and down the aisle while they're working.
>
> ✔ **Reserve a bulkhead seat when flying.**
>
> Bulkhead seats have extra room in front of you, which you may need while juggling kids, bags, food, and toys. You get the idea.

Kids up to 2 years old fly free, but you have to hold them in your lap (and that rule soon may change). Those older than 2 can sometimes get lower fares, but it depends on where you're flying. Whenever you travel by plane with your child, always call a travel agent and let the agent know that you'll be flying with your child. Every airline is different, and sometimes children's fares are more than the lowest excursion fares. It's too confusing. Just call 'em.

Kids can be great on a plane. The rocking and the low hum of the plane usually puts them to sleep.

Remember that your children must have their own passports when traveling to a foreign country. And call the National Center for Infectious Diseases Hotline (404-332-4559) for information about immunization requirements. You may need immunizations when traveling outside the country. You can also visit the NCID Web page at www.cdc.gov/travel.

You can make traveling a little more fun for your kids by packing them a new toy or surprise. The newness of the toy keeps them busy through most of the trip (all of the trip if you're lucky). Don't bring any toys that have too many small pieces. Otherwise, you'll be spending most of your trip trying to find all the parts.

Warnings: Please observe these flying-safety guidelines

Do not put your children through the x-ray machine.

Do not check your children as luggage.

Do not store your children in the overhead baggage area. They may shift during the flight and fall out when the door is open.

Do not use your children as flotation devices.

Do not tamper with, disable, or destroy the smoke detector in the lavatory.

In case of an emergency, the oxygen mask will fall from the overhead bin. Do not fight with your children as to who gets the oxygen mask first.

Every time you need to take a trip, go through this list checking off your supplies.

❑ Diapers

❑ Baby wipes (or hand wipes when your child is past the diaper stage — get the travel size)

❑ Spit-up towel

❑ Bottles and nipples

❑ A light blanket

❑ Eating utensils (cups, spoons, and so on)

❑ Plastic bags for dirty diapers and dirty clothes

❑ A change of clothing

❑ Beverages (juice, formula, and water)

❑ Food

❑ Entertainment for the kids (books, stuffed animals, crayons, or small portable TV with attached Nintendo)

❑ Current passport (when traveling outside the United States)

❑ Names and phone numbers of your pediatrician and medical insurance carrier

❑ Medications (Children's Tylenol — or similar acetaminophen product — diaper-rash ointment, and any other medications your children are taking)

Lovin' those family vacations

When you're traveling with your family and little kids are involved, keep these things in mind:

✔ **Don't overschedule.**

Vacations are for rest and spending time together. The goal isn't shoving everything possible into one day. You'll all get too tired and cranky when you think that you're rushing from one place to another. In fact, when we travel as a family, we schedule periods of *down time* when nothing goes on. It's better that way, and it makes things more relaxed.

✔ **Keep your kids on their schedules.**

Eating and sleeping schedules must be kept as much as possible. If your kids become overtired or too hungry, they'll become unpleasant. Very unpleasant.

✔ **Have plenty of free time for goofing off.**

Playing in the pool, going on hikes, building sand castles, or frolicking in the lake is the ultimate in fun for kids. Don't overbook your vacation so that you leave out time for relaxing, reading, and letting the kids run around and explore.

✔ **Don't eat too much junk food.**

Snack on some healthy stuff every now and then. You don't want your vacation cut short because someone is puking all the time after having ingested too much of the cotton candy/grape soda combo. Worse yet, you don't want your little ones to get stomach cramps because they haven't eaten vegetables for four days and they're now constipated.

Do I need to remind you never to allow your kids to play around water alone? And don't leave an older child in charge of younger ones when it comes to water. Older kids can become distracted and forget that they have the job of watching their younger siblings.

Food on the road

Consider this nightmare: You're driving down the road on your family vacation and you see a sign that says, "Last stop for the next 50 miles." The last thing you want is to be 20 miles past this stop and have your children announce that they're hungry. For kids, that means they're hungry NOW!

Remember these feeding tips the next time you take a trip:

✔ **Have enough supplies.**

Take a bib, baby spoon, juice cup (the kind that has a *closable* spout so juice or milk doesn't leak everywhere).

✔ **Keep enough food on hand.**

Put dry cereal in plastic bags to add milk to later. Bring small jars of baby food (although you'll have to throw away the extra when you aren't able to refrigerate the leftovers). Bring along dry finger foods like Cheerios, crackers, and chewy granola bars.

✔ **Keep plenty of liquids with you.**

For bottle-fed babies, put dry formula in bottles and add water when needed. Avoid using canned formula. You'll end up throwing away the extra formula that you aren't able to immediately use. Try to avoid having a bunch of sweet sodas as your only liquid. Water works best for quenching thirst, and it's better for you.

✔ **Keep a bottle of water from home with you.**

Water is great for a quick swig, or for adding to formula bottles. Your home water is less likely to upset your child's stomach.

✔ **Keep a supply of juice.**

You can refill your child's juice cup by keeping a large jug of juice with you, or buy the boxes of juice. Remember, buy the fruit *juice* and not the fruit *drink*. (Fruit drink has added sugar that your child doesn't need.)

✔ **Limit fresh fruit.**

Unless your trip is short and you can store the fruit in a refrigerator or a cooler, avoid taking it with you. It gets hot and mushy (with the exception of apples — but don't drop or step on them).

✔ **Yum, restaurants.**

Don't forget the joys of eating out while on vacation.

See Chapter 8, for more information about feeding babies while traveling.

Children and the Movies

Keep an open mind and realize that although you may be going to a movie, you may not be watching it. Every child is different and doesn't respond to the movies the same way. Some kids, no matter what their ages, will sit quietly and watch the movie. Some kids won't be able to sit still until they're 5 or 6 years old. (And even then, they'll have a hard time not announcing, "The dog isn't really dead!")

Now is a great time to rediscover those comfy aisle seats in the back. When you have a child who won't be quiet, take him out to the lobby until he quiets down. If he won't quiet down, leave. Don't sit in the theater with your crying or fussy child. Other people have paid to watch the movie, too. But they didn't pay to sit in a dark room listening to your little one — even if your kid is adorable.

Chapter 26

Punishment and Discipline

● ●

In This Chapter

▶ Sorting out the differences between punishment and discipline

▶ Setting the household guidelines

▶ Dealing with repeat offenders

▶ Becoming a creative disciplinarian

▶ Making decisions with your partner

● ●

*A*lthough it may be hard to fathom, at some time or another, your dear, sweet child is going to do something that makes you want to pull your hair out and scream at the top of your lungs. You don't want to do that. You also don't want your kids to be brats. So now you're faced with some strong decision-making.

This chapter covers what you can expect when disciplining your child. It also covers punishment, which is what you do when your child chooses not to follow what you've said.

The Big Difference Between Discipline and Punishment

Some parents are afraid to discipline their children. And some parents think discipline is the way parents push their will on their child, regardless of what the child wants. Both attitudes are wrong.

The whole point of discipline and punishment is *teaching* your children. It's a learning process. You can be a good parent with definite ideas about discipline and punishment without being afraid that either your children are going to hate you or that you'll mess up their lives forever.

Crime and punishment

Discipline is about setting ground rules and boundaries and making your children live by and follow those rules. Sounds easy enough. The only problem is that your kids, for their own reasons, won't always want to follow those rules and stay within those boundaries. They'll always seem to have their own agendas that may not match yours.

Although it's difficult, you must be tough and not give in to whining, crying, and big puppy-dog eyes filling with tears. When your kids cry because you don't let them jump on the couch, well, that's okay. They're crying because they're mad, not because they're physically hurt. There's a big difference. You need to know the difference between these two kinds of crying.

When your children are mad and start crying, you have these options:

✔ **Accept the crying.**

Don't get mad and spout the ever-so-popular line, "I'll give you something to cry about." Just because your children are mad doesn't mean that you have to be mad, too. One mad person is enough. It's okay that they're mad. Mad is a natural emotion, and they will feel mad from time to time. That's okay.

✔ **Try consoling your children.**

Tell your children *why* you don't want them doing something — which doesn't always work when kids are mad. If you can, simply hug, kiss, and hold them. Just because they're mad, or you haven't allowed them to do something, doesn't mean that you can't be affectionate. Sometimes crying children continue crying longer and louder when you're hugging them. So, listen closely and know when to let them go, and then tell them you love them and send them on their way.

✔ **Ignore or tune out the crying.**

Some kids scream louder and longer when they know that you're listening or that their crying bothers you. In that case, you can give your children the option of going to their rooms and coming back to you when they've gotten control of themselves or you can leave. Tell your children you'll be back after you think they've had enough time to be able to calm down.

✔ **Take their minds off it.**

This strategy works great for babies and toddlers who are easily distracted. When your children are mad, take them outside for a walk or hand them a toy. Sometimes this distraction works like shutting off the water valve. Instant happiness.

Please, oh please, don't say this . . .

You've just scolded your kids for jumping on the couch. They're upset, maybe mad, and crying. Please don't say, "You stop that crying, or I'll give you something you can really cry about." Don't you get it? They already have something to cry about. They're mad. For kids, that's as good a reason to cry as anything. Beating them for crying is really not going to stop the crying. Never has, never will. Allow them to cry. It's okay.

Kids will test your rules. Some kids will test your mettle after only a few times of saying, "No, don't sit on the cat." Some kids think it's just too much fun to resist and keep sitting on the cat, so you'll have to be just as stubborn as your children and keep pulling them off of the cat, telling them again and again, "No, don't sit on the cat."

Discipline and torture techniques

As you go about disciplining your children, you may start sounding kind of naggy. No one likes to listen to someone who's nagging. As a defense to this annoyance, your children may start tuning you out. You know, it's sort of like your husband who tunes you out when you start talking about him throwing his dirty clothes *next* to the clothes hamper instead of *in* it or like your wife when you describe the big fish that got away.

Humor (the Ha, Ha, Ha's of life)

Anything approached with humor goes over better than it does when you don't use humor. When you discipline your children, it usually isn't going to be a life-or-death situation, and a little humor may get your point across better. It's easier to remember a funny situation than a direct Marine drill-sergeant type of command:

What you want to say:

"Put your shoes where they belong."

The alternate way:

"Your shoes snuck out of your closet. Can you please help them find their way home?"

What you want to say:

"Eat with your mouth closed."

The alternate way:

"Does your mouth know how to chew and stay closed at the same time? I'd really like to see that happen."

What you want to say:

"Who left the milk out?"

The alternate way:

"Why don't you be the milk police? Your job is to make sure everyone follows the milk rules. Arrest whoever breaks this law!"

What you want to say:

"Stop hitting your sister."

The alternate way:

"I know your sister does things that make you want to clobber her, but in this family, we don't hurt each other. Instead, use your words to let her know that you're angry. Say, 'I'm really mad at you right now.'"

What you want to say:

"Did you break the knob on the TV?"

The alternate way:

"Oh, oh. The knob on the TV is broken. Did the TV blow the knob off, or did you have something to do with this?"

Put it in writing

The goal of discipline is educating your kids about knowing right from wrong and teaching them about the rules of proper behavior. But when they're tuning you out because you're beginning to sound like a broken record, your entire goal of trying to teach them something goes up in smoke. See Chapter 23 for more about alternative forms of communication for getting your point across. Writing notes and letters is one example.

If you're tired of telling your children every day to shut the lid to the toilet, simply put a sign on the wall behind the toilet (like Figure 26-1). This gentle reminder keeps you from sounding like you're nagging, and your kids will get the message.

Please, close me when you're done with your duty!

Thank You,
Mr. Toilet

Figure 26-1: A gentle reminder.

The Ordeal of Punishment

After you've established your rules and boundaries, but your children make the decision not to follow them, then it's time for punishment. This situation is different from your 10-month-old leaving toys scattered all around. A child that young hasn't learned to pick up toys yet. (For some kids, that day may never come.)

Punishment is the penalty for breaking rules that you've set up for your children. It's an *educational tool* used to show your children about why these rules are in place. Punishment comes into the picture when your 8-year-old decides to throw rocks at cars, for example, even though the kid already understands that doing so is wrong.

You can't punish your child, however, when she doesn't know or understand the rules.

Making the punishment fit the crime

So Sally just broke your car window with a rock. Actually, it was one of several rocks. Now what do you do? View punishment as a great learning device. The point here is not to physically beat your child every time she looks the wrong way, but rather it's to teach her to make good choices. When she doesn't make the proper choices, there are consequences. Keep these things in mind when setting punishments:

> ✔ **Be realistic.**
>
> Don't *ground* someone for a year when you know that you'll never be able to keep the punishment going that long.
>
> ✔ **Don't be too lenient.**
>
> If a punishment has no effect on your children other than merely taking away some time, you're being too lenient. Punishment must mean something to children for it to be a lasting and learning experience.
>
> ✔ **Consider your punishment carefully.**
>
> Sometimes just hearing a parent become upset and then being scolded by the parent is enough to crush any child. You must know your child well when you're considering punishment.

When applying punishment to the car-window-breaking incident, you'll have to assume a couple of things. First, consider whether your child is old enough to be outside throwing rocks — say, 6 years old. And second, consider whether your child understands and has been told not to throw rocks around the cars. If you child isn't old enough and doesn't understand the consequences of her actions, you have to question the punishment.

If a 2-year-old threw the rock and broke the window with a lucky shot, you can't do much, other than scold, because a 2-year-old won't understand that what she did was wrong and probably has never been told not to throw rocks around cars.

If, on the other hand, your 6-year-old threw the rock, has already been warned about throwing rocks, and has been told she will be punished if she throws rocks, you have several options:

Punishment: Timeout

Result: The only thing a 6-year-old learns from a timeout for breaking a window is that she got off really easy. This kid wouldn't learn a thing.

Punishment: Spanking

Result: Spankings don't last that long and aren't good for teaching. Again, your child probably looks at this as getting off pretty easy.

The reconnect — Dr. Tim

It helps to have a standard "script" for those times when you must switch into the role of disciplinarian. A good disciplinary script enables you to stand firm without losing control in the heat of the moment. Here's a four-step approach to discipline that you can use when custom-building your own disciplinary script. The first three steps will be familiar, but the last step may not be.

Instruct: An effective disciplinary script begins with a simple command or instruction. The goal here is to avoid any confusion about what you expect and to let your child know that you mean business. Many "problem" children who disobey their parents look rather normal when their parents begin to use simple, clearly stated commands.

Warn: Warnings are a way to remind children about a previously given instruction and to put them on notice about what will happen if the instruction is not heeded ("If you don't finish your homework, there will be no TV later"). Warnings are useful because they often allow parents to stand firm without having to impose a sanction. Warnings can also be used to remind children about a standing rule ("No toys in the kitchen"). Warnings are especially handy for children who are very impulsive or cognitively immature and need a lot of reminders. Warnings are not appropriate when children are being aggressive. Instead of learning that aggression is wrong and prohibited, they may learn that aggression is okay, but you can use it only once before you have to stop.

Sanction: I could have used the word "punishment" here, but I prefer "sanction" because some parents get locked into thinking that they have to be mean in order to be firm. It also fits better with recent studies that tell us children misbehave because it usually works better than good behavior to achieve their goals. Not that children conduct cost-benefit analyses, but their behavior does tend to match what they can get away with ("Why should I do chores if whining can get me out of them?"). So whether you use time-out, spanking, grounding, or extra chores, an effective sanction should make it more "costly" for a child to use misbehavior than good behavior.

Reconnect: This last step is designed to repair any damage to the parent-child relationship that may have resulted from the disciplinary conflict. Think of it as bringing children back into the fold. Reconnecting is also an opportunity for parents to make sure that children have not misinterpreted the disciplinary message (for example, "I'm not supposed to hit my brother when mom is cooking"; "My parents don't care how I feel"). The process of reconnecting has to wait until the child is emotionally ready to hear you. For some children, this could take quite a while (a day or two). What should parents say when reconnecting? I recommend three main points:

> "I love and cherish you, even when I have to discipline you."

> "Know that each and every time you do _____, I will discipline you."

> "In this family, we don't do _____."

If your child lets you, combine these messages with an affectionate hug or a touch of the hand.

Punishment: Working to pay for the window

Result: Doing extra chores to pay for the broken window has considerable learning potential. To really drive the point home, make a chart with a list of chores, the price paid for each chore, and the total price for fixing the broken window. This chart, along with the chores, is a good reminder to a child who made a wrong decision.

Punishment: Loss of a privilege

Result: This punishment is good when used in combination with the punishment of working to pay off the window. Instead of getting to go roller-skating, the child spends that time doing the extra chores.

Combining different punishments to drive home your point is the idea here. But apply a punishment only when your children are going to *learn* something from it. When that works, your children will think twice about breaking the rules in the future.

Making punishment a learning exercise

Discipline and punishment should be a time of learning. When your children break a rule and you think punishment is deserved, make sure they fully understand *why* they're being punished.

For example, when you see your daughter doing something horrid, don't grab her by the arm and shuttle her off to her room. If you do that, you've passed up an important disciplinary step. You forgot to let her know why she's being punished. Say, "Because you did *whatever*, I'm giving you a 10-minute timeout. Please go sit in the timeout chair, and we'll talk about this again in 10 minutes."

At some point, be sure to remind her of why she's being punished. Go visit her after the *prison* time, and explain your thinking. "You had to sit in timeout while all your friends played outside, because you called Marilyn a bad name. Do you understand?"

When the punishment has a long duration, ask your child from time to time why she's being punished. "Do you remember why you can't swim in the pool this week?" She should be able to tell you exactly why. If she says, "I forgot," remind her. Keep to these simple guidelines:

- ✔ Make the punishment memorable.
- ✔ Make the punishment appropriate to the crime.
- ✔ Make sure your child learns from the punishment.

Have you ever spoken with children whose parents spank them all the time? When you ask why they got spanked the last time, they usually reply, "I dunno." This response drives home how ineffective spanking is; if the child being punished can't remember the crime, what good is the punishment?

Whether you're trying to teach your children what the household rules are, or punishing them for breaking those rules, always stop and let them know why something is not allowed. Telling them is more meaningful, so they're more likely to remember. When your children understand that jumping on the couch can break the springs and then they won't be able to sit on the couch again, they're less likely to jump on it again in the future. If you can, stop and show them the springs in the couch so they can see what you're talking about.

Guidelines for Discipline and Punishment

Don't take lightly the idea of disciplining or punishing your children. Being on your toes and making sure that your kids are following the rules of the house isn't always easy. Deciding how you're going to punish your errant children isn't easy, either. That never is a pleasant task.

Your decisions about punishment are made easier when you make crystal clear to your children what's allowed and what isn't allowed in the house. You can't have double standards, such as letting one child get away with something while punishing another child who does the same thing. And, you must follow through with your kids.

How to be lovingly unbending (the art of consistency)

Once you establish your household rules and guidelines, you can't be inconsistent about these decisions. You also can't punish children for something one time and then act like it isn't a big deal the next. This inconsistency can cause you more trouble than it's worth.

Be tough. Be strong. When your children cry because you haven't allowed something, that's okay. They're crying because they didn't get their way, but that isn't a sign that they're going to hate you or that you did anything wrong. It means that your children are mad. They'll get over it.

For more about "Being a Consistent Parent," see Chapter 3.

Don't forget your follow-through

Follow-through must be a consequence of your children having broken a rule on purpose. When they break a rule, consider it a test that they're giving you to see whether you're really going to do something. This isn't a test you can afford to fail.

When you establish a rule that your kids can't throw balls in the house, and they do it, your follow-through is the punishment that you set forth. If you make a rule and you don't follow through with a punishment whenever the rule is broken, your kids won't think anything about breaking other rules. They'll consider your rules *bogus*.

Follow-through also means that when you've established a punishment where your children have to do something, such as write a report or clean something, you must make sure that it's done. If you fail to follow up with the punishment, you're setting a bad example for your kids. You're letting them know that even though you say that something will be done, they don't need to take it too seriously, because chances are you won't check to make sure that they actually did it.

See Chapter 4 for a more detailed discussion of follow-through.

Anger is to be specially avoided in inflicting punishment. — Cicero

Reforming the Repeat Offender

Discipline is simple. It's making your kids learn and follow rules so they can grow up to be nice people. Punishment is a little more difficult. When a child continuously repeats the same *crime*, you may want to stop and think about why this child seems so determined to do so.

Have you explained to her why she isn't supposed to do whatever it is she's doing wrong? If you have, and she seems aware that digging in your plant not only causes a mess but may also kill the plant, maybe something else is going on.

You may want to ask yourself these questions:

> ✔ **Are you giving your child enough attention?**
>
> It's always been understood that children prefer positive attention. They like playing with you and getting hugs and kisses. But if they aren't receiving that, kids will go for any kind of attention they can get. Negative attention is better than no attention at all.

✔ **Is your child bored?**

Have your child help you do the laundry or cook. Play games together. Give her projects that she can do on her own, but be sure that you check on her often and give her praise for what she's doing.

✔ **Is there a pattern to the crime?**

Does your child dig in the plant only when you're putting her little sister to bed or when you're sitting down to pay bills? If that is the case, she may be letting you know that she doesn't like you paying attention to someone or something else. In that case, tell her that as soon as you're done with what you have to do, the two of you can do something special together. Then give her something to keep her busy while you're doing your chore.

Being in Charge without Being a Tyrant

The fact that you need to discipline your children is not an open invitation to treat them with a lack of respect or decency. It also doesn't mean that you take on the role of Czar with your children as the peasant slaves.

Letting kids be kids

Kids will be kids and should be allowed to make mistakes, make messes, and get mad and upset. You can't expect miracles from people who may not be as old as your favorite suit. Kids are awkward at times, spilling and dropping stuff, knocking things over, and generally doing things that are goofy. They typically are not malicious or evil. Be careful that you neither punish typical kid behavior nor give them unrealistic expectations that they can never meet.

Don't make words less meaningful by using them again and again

Instead of always saying "No" or "Stop," offer alternatives to whatever your children are starting to do. When you see your children starting to color on the walls, say: "Don't color on the walls. Here is a piece of paper. We can color on the paper instead." If you're always yelling out "No," "Stop," "Don't," "Quit," or "Help me, my children are taking over," your words lose their effectiveness after a while.

You don't always have to win

Discipline shouldn't be a series of wins and losses in an on-going battle between you and your children. Discipline sometimes can leave room for compromise between you and your children as long as you get your point across.

It isn't important that you always win the clothing-selection war, for example. Clothing may be one of the first areas in which you find yourself coming to a mutual compromise with a child. Your goal is getting your child dressed, but your child may want to exert her independence by helping to choose the clothing. This is a situation in which you compromise by coming up with an outfit that you both can live with.

Parents tend to think that whenever they don't always get their way, they're letting their child run over them. Think about the getting-dressed scenario. Your goal is getting clothes on your child. Does it really matter whether your child wears the pink button-down oxford shirt or the Mario Brothers T-shirt just as long as your kid gets dressed? No, of course it doesn't.

It is better to bind your children to you by respect and gentleness, than by fear. — Terence

Handling situations with gentle guidance

Getting your children to do something often is just as easy as coaxing them not to do something. Likewise, being gentle about getting them to do it is just as easy as yelling and screaming at them. Don't forget that your goal in disciplining your child is to teach. Your children are more open to listening to and *hearing* you when you express what you want to say in a kind and gentle manner. Don't be surprised, however, if you can't always accomplish that. You may find yourself quickly losing your temper and yelling when you walk into a room to find mud all over your white carpet. The goal here is to at least *try*.

With soft words, one may talk a serpent out of its hole. — Iranian proverb

Using enthusiasm to guide your children

If you're trying to get your children to do something they don't necessarily want to do, approach the situation with great enthusiasm, making it sound like fun. When you make the process of getting your kids' shoes on them fun and like a game, your children will think doing it is fun, and then maybe they'll forget to scream, kick, and throw the shoes across the room.

Don't harass your children

You always need to have faith that your children are going to do what's right. You can't sit waiting, like a cat perched in front of a mouse's hole, for your children to do something wrong so that you can pounce on your prey. Neither should you fall into the trap of scolding your children before anything happens or in anticipation that something may happen. That is just nasty behavior on your part and needs to be avoided.

The Purpose of Punishment

Punishment must be viewed as a positive action. Predicting every possible scenario and then handling it in a certain way is impossible, so keep these guidelines in mind:

✔ **What will the punishment teach your children?**

When you fall into the habit of giving the same punishment for the same crime, that punishment may lose its effectiveness and its educational value. If that's the case, then change the punishment.

✔ **Your children must always know the reason for the punishment.**

If you send children off to their rooms without letting them know why, you've lost the opportunity to teach them and the punishment will mean nothing to them. Explaining punishment can be difficult to do with toddlers and preschoolers who require clearer and more specific explanations.

✔ **Don't establish punishments when you're angry.**

Decisions are never good when you make them quickly or in anger. You're also more likely to establish a punishment that is more out of retaliation than with the idea of educating your children in mind. Set the punishment after you've taken a few seconds (or as long as it takes) to cool down and think about what it is you need to do.

✔ **Give your children a chance to fix the error.**

Everyone needs a chance to correct whatever they've done wrong. Resolving the problem is your goal, not punishing whenever possible. Punishment needs to be the last straw. Lying is a good example. When you catch a child in the process of *stretching the truth*, but you can stop her before it turns into a Paul Bunyan-sized lie, you've given your child a chance to correct the error.

✔ **Forgive and forget.**

Don't hold grudges against your children. After you've had to punish them, tell them that you still love them and then forget about the crime. Bringing it up again or using it against them at a later time isn't necessary.

We can not be forgiven if we refuse to forgive. — Janette Oke

Punishment is not fun. If you enjoy punishing your children, you need some serious psychological help. The only way to avoid punishing your child is to consider it as a last possible resort. Look at the following examples of ways that you can handle problems while avoiding punishment:

- **Remove the temptation to get into things.** When you spend all your time putting your china back into the cabinets, put childproof locks on the cabinets. Make sure that the things you don't want your children getting into are out of their reach or inaccessible to them. Of course, that isn't always possible. After all, removing all the cushions from your furniture just so your toddler stops making a bed on the floor with them is a little difficult.

- **Reconsider what's important.** Did you establish a rule before really thinking it through? Like the preceding example, do you really mind when your child throws the furniture cushions on the floor to play with them? Is it so important that the cushions stay where they belong? Think long and hard before establishing a rule. In our household, furniture cushions are really tools for making forts.

- **Let your children help you solve problems.** If your daughter can't keep from throwing the skirts she doesn't want to wear on the floor rather than putting them back, ask her to come up with a solution to the problem. She may suggest changing the drawer with one that is lower so that she can reach her skirts and be better able to put them away. Or maybe it's time to go through the clothes together and get rid of the ones your child can't wear anymore.

- **Get in your children's way, so they can't get into trouble.** Physically stand in a child's way, so that she can't push the tree over in the living room. Tell her she has to leave the tree alone, and then get her interested in something else.

- **Stay calm and don't yell.** Your kids will most likely tune you out when you yell. Even when a child is yelling at you, don't fall into the trap of yelling back. Gather your patience and keep your voice calm, cool, and relaxed. This strategy not only calms your child down but also shows your child that staying calm is the better way of communicating.

- **Explain why and what you're doing.** Knowledge is powerful. If your children understand why you do something, or why something is not allowed, it makes more sense to them. Doesn't it to you? Your children may not learn at first, but don't give up hope. Eventually what you're saying will make sense, so keep explaining the *why* behind the rules.

- **Have your child start over.** When your children talk or behave rudely to you, ask them to start over. You may even have them leave the room and come back in to approach the situation again. This time, however, ask them to think about what they want to say and how they should say it.

Types of Punishment

So it's happened. You're going to have to punish a child for doing the unspeakable. The sections below give you some options for punishment. Alter your punishment so that one type doesn't become habit and lose its effectiveness. Parents must be *creative* disciplinarians.

Timeouts

Timeouts are a popular method of punishment. A timeout is where you physically remove a child from a situation and have her sit somewhere, alone, for a specific period of time. The thought here is that if your child is hitting, screaming, or just throwing a fit because she didn't get her own way, time alone will enable her to gain control of herself. And the act of taking her away from her play group can be *painful* to a young child.

Like most situations when it comes to children, you must gear the timeout to the particular child and the situation. You also must take two things into consideration:

- ✔ **The place:** Ask yourself whether your child's room is really the most effective place for timeout. Will it help make her sit and think about what she did? Isn't her room also the place where she goes to play, read, and perhaps even watch TV? If you're going to take the time to punish your child, don't send her to the place she most wants to be. It's like saying, "Okay, you've really done it this time. Boy are you in trouble. Your punishment is to take this $20 and go get ice cream."

- ✔ **The time:** Don't set a strict guideline on how long a timeout should be. If you tell your child that the designated timeout is for five minutes, but after that the crying and temper tantrum haven't subsided, the timeout obviously hasn't been long enough. Letting your out-of-control kid off the hook won't be effective, either. Nothing will have been accomplished. Five minutes, in this case, was not long enough for your child to gain control of herself.

You need to put a disclaimer at the end of your timeout rule: "You'll have timeout for five minutes. If you can control yourself by then, I'll let you out. But, if you haven't calmed down by then, you'll have five more minutes of timeout."

If the timeout is just to have her sit and contemplate what she's done, the rule usually is to make her sit in timeout the same number of minutes as her age. For example, a 4-year-old would sit in timeout for 4 minutes. A 30-year-old would sit out for 30 minutes. My mother would be sitting out for hours!

The ins and outs of "timeout" — Dr. Tim

These days, nearly all parents know something about timeout. It is widely recommended as a disciplinary technique because it is both effective and nonviolent. Having said that, I now hasten to add that many parents are disappointed and confused by the whole timeout thing.

Parents are unsure about timeout for a number of reasons. For one thing, the term can mean different things. As a disciplinary technique (which is how I am using it), timeout is shorthand for "time out from reinforcement," which means removing children from a rewarding setting and putting them in a nonrewarding setting. The idea is that children will want to behave so they can stay where there are more rewarding activities. But the term "timeout" has also been used to mean a brief intermission, especially in sports. Thus, some parents speak of their child "needing a timeout," a chance to cool down emotionally.

Parents have other, more important, concerns about timeout. For example, timeout is a technique that comes with a lot of rules, and unless you have a master's degree in education, it's hard to remember them all. But, as it turns out, many of these rules (for example, child sits in a chair, child is quiet, child stays for 1 minute for every year) are not critical to the success of timeout. There's also a sentiment among many parents that timeout doesn't work. Do you hear parents saying, "I use timeout and boy does it work"? I don't hear that. Instead, I hear parents saying, "Timeout? Yeah, right." Admittedly, timeout is not a technique that you can use with older children (past age 10). And it won't work if children are put in a room where they can watch TV and play video games. But the most common reason that timeout "didn't work" is that the child refused to stay put.

Unlike spanking and grounding, timeout requires a certain amount of cooperation on the part of the child (how cooperative does a child have to be to be spanked or grounded?). And if a child never stays in timeout, then it was never established. This is not a good thing. A child who escapes from timeout, or who stays only because the doors are locked, is not likely to benefit. The key to using timeout effectively is establishing it in the first place. It's kind of like trying to smash a cockroach: If you don't do it right the first time, it just makes a big mess.

Imagine a struggling mom and her defiant, 5-year-old son. Let's call him Teddy. Mom tells Teddy that if he bites his sister again, he'll have to go to the timeout corner. Sure enough, little sister gets bit, and Teddy is guilty as sin. Mom marches him over to the corner and says, "Teddy, you have to stay here for 5 minutes because you bit your sister." Mom turns to leave, and Teddy starts his jailbreak! What should this mom do? She can try scolding him, but that's not likely to work. He might stay if she threatens to take away some prized possession or valued privilege. But if that doesn't work, what else can she do?

Her remaining option is not a pretty one. If she wants Teddy to learn that she is serious about him staying in the corner, she will have to be more persistent than she has ever been before. She'll have to keep walking his butt back to the corner every time he escapes, or she'll have to hold him physically in the corner until he's ready to stay by himself. Either way, they won't have any fun. It won't be quick, either, if Teddy is used to having his way. In fact, I tell parents that if they're going to establish timeout, do it on a day when they have little else to do.

If it's so hard to establish timeout (in some cases), why do it? Two reasons: First, once children are convinced that parents are serious about timeout, it becomes a convenient, reusable, and highly effective disciplinary sanction. The second reason is that establishing timeout sends a powerful message to children about who is in charge. Some children are convinced that they are more powerful than their parents. But if parents persist in establishing timeout, their children will witness parents' commitment to being a person of authority.

Taking away privileges

Punishment is most effective when it serves as a learning tool that can be emphasized again and again. For example, taking away a privilege — such as no videos for a week — is something that makes an impact on your children every day of the week. Unlike spanking or timeout, which are over and done with quickly, taking something of importance away has a greater opportunity of making a lasting imprint.

I prefer taking privileges away from my kids when they've done something to deserve a punishment. I do so for a length of time that I think will make an impact. My oldest son took a hammer and dug chunks out of our deck when he was 5. Rather than spank him — because I knew he would forget why he was spanked 20 minutes later — I took away the privilege of watching *Batman* for one week. I'm sure I would have seen fewer tears had I spanked him. But for five days, every time he asked to watch *Batman*, I was able to reinforce that he'd made a poor decision (the hammer and the deck), and because of that decision, he couldn't do something that he really enjoyed. Needless to say, we've never had a hammer problem again.

Taking away privileges doesn't work on kids who are too young to remember or know that they've done something wrong.

Giving extra chores

Your children should have chores that they must do on a daily basis, such as making their beds, hanging up their clothes, taking out the trash, and so on. And your children need to know that everyone has to do chores. It's a part of life. But when a child does something that requires a punishment where chores are involved, divvy out extra chores. For example, when your children play outside all day and spread trash all over the yard, the punishment can be to clean up the yard and, while they're at it, rake up the leaves and pull weeds from the garden.

Use this kind of punishment sparingly. Your kids should have their own set of chores to do anyway, and you don't want them always thinking that they're in trouble just because they've been asked to do extra chores. But, on occasion, this type of punishment is effective.

Punishing by educating

Kids *generally* aren't evil beings sent here from another planet just to make your life miserable. Honest! So when your children do things that you consider to be wrong, like breaking household rules, keep in mind that these acts *usually* aren't done out of spite. Many times kids break rules because the outcome of breaking the rules isn't known, or they don't know the rule in the first place. Because your kids truly want to do what's right, education can be a powerful tool against repeat offenders.

For example, when a child is caught breaking a rule, such as stomping on your flower garden, try turning the punishment into an opportunity to teach your child something. Have her research and write a report about flowers, or roots. If she's too young to write, have her draw a picture of flowers and their roots. Take the time to look at flowers and other plants with your child and then talk about how roots work. Go to the library and read about roots. The more your child knows about the consequences of what she's done, the less likely she is to do it again.

This kind of punishment/lesson-learning doesn't work for children younger than 3 years old. They're too young to understand the relationship between what you're reading in a book and what they did.

Spanking yikes!

A large percentage of people still believe spanking is an acceptable form of punishment. Their reasoning: "I was spanked and I turned out okay," or "I only spank to really make my point." Personally, I don't believe that hitting someone is the best use of my time or the best educational tool. Violence toward children isn't what I consider as being kind or gentle or loving. I want to teach my kids to be tender and compassionate, and I can't do that when I'm not behaving that way.

Punishment is a learning tool. You're using it to teach your kids something. Does spanking accomplish this? No, not really. Besides, if you hit your child, what does that teach? Remember, no double standards here. Whatever you do, your children will do because they look to you for guidance.

Isn't spanking just a quick and easy way of resolving your own frustrations when you aren't able to handle a situation? After all, whacking a mouthy kid is simple. It takes much too much time to be patient and explain things, which, of course, has more positive results.

You're setting an example of how to behave with every one of your actions. If you pout when you don't get your way, your children will pout, too. If you yell when you become frustrated, your children will, too. If you hit or spank when you get mad, your children will, too. Don't rely on the old saying, "My kids know better than to hit," because your spanking teaches them something different. They can't distinguish between *hitting* and *spanking* — and the situations that make the distinctions.

Punishment needs to have an impact on your children. It must be remembered for as long as possible. When you spank your children, how long are you going to be able to remind them about why they were punished? The whole spanking process doesn't really last that long, so it's usually quickly forgotten.

A number of Internet sites are geared toward educating parents so they don't spank their children. One such site is www.neverhitachild.org.

Team Decision-making

Both parents must agree on the rules of the house and how to administer them. Mom can't believe that the kids can't jump on the couch when Dad goes in and jumps with them. Both parents must agree that the couch is for sitting on, not jumping on. Both of you must also enforce this rule whenever you see the kids breaking it. Mom can't be the one who always has to set punishments while Dad pretends that he doesn't see what's going on. See Chapter 2 for more details about co-parenting.

Behind-the-scenes decision-making

As you and your partner encounter situations that require decisions about punishment, sit down and discuss what each of you thinks are the best ways to handle these situations when they come up. Don't be surprised if your opinions differ. You are coming from different backgrounds and may have different points of views. Listen to each other, be respectful of your respective points of view, and then mutually agree to a decision on discipline and punishment.

Learning to be flexible

If you start making discipline and punishment decisions before you've had kids, in reality you may find that what you've decided doesn't work. People who don't have kids have all kinds of wonderful advice and ideas that radically change once they have kids of their own. Give yourself enough room so that you and your co-parent can regroup and think about the decisions you've made. Always discuss these changes. You don't want to upset your partner by making changes without first talking to him or her.

Chapter 27

Squelching Squabbling Siblings

*H*ey, Joey, did you see what Mom and Dad brought home? It's a really small kid. He doesn't seem to do much. Why don't you toss something into his cage and see if you can wake him up. Here, try this Tonka truck.

"Brothers and Sisters Living In Harmony" is not the title from an old *Star Trek: The Next Generation* show, but rather, it's a reality. Making it happen is your job as a parent. This chapter is dedicated to brotherly and sisterly love — and the path you must lead your kids down to get there.

> **sib•ling** \'sib-ling\ *n*. A brother or sister. The *gender neutral* for a brother or sister when you don't know which one it is.

I don't have any siblings. My parents never sibled. — Hawkeye Pierce in *M*A*S*H*

There's a New Sibling in Town

You may be at the time in your life when you expand your family. Oh happy, happy, joy, joy! But you may be wondering how your other children are going to respond to a new family member. That's a very good question, and one that deserves special attention.

The news that a new baby is going to be in the house is going to prompt many interesting questions from your children. Don't be shy about answering them. And, be sure read the "Do you have a question?" section in Chapter 23.

Here are some suggestions about how to handle the arrival of a new baby:

✔ **Don't tell your children that they're getting a new *playmate.***

Playmate may be true at some point in the future, but not for now. Don't give your kids any expectations that as soon as their little brother or sister gets home, life will become instant fun — because it won't be. Newborns don't do much to entertain, other than spitting up every now and then.

✔ **Don't forget to recognize that your children are special to you, just like the new baby will be.**

Do something special. Give them a gift "from the new baby," or make them a special T-shirt so that they know they're still special in your eyes.

✔ **Don't neglect your older children.**

Make an effort to do something with them after the baby comes. This activity is something you'll have to schedule. Having a new baby in the house can swallow up a large amount of time before you know it. Continue to share "dates" with your children.

✔ **Give them an honest idea of what life will be like when the baby comes.**

Tell them that at first the baby will demand a large amount of time and that little brother or sister will mostly just cry, eat, sleep, and not a whole lot more. Also let them know that Mommy will be tired and will have to take naps to rest.

✔ **Call your local hospital to see whether a sibling class is offered for your children to take.**

These classes go over what babies like and dislike, what it's like to change a diaper, and other basic information that your children need to know. They must learn that it isn't okay to toss a Tonka truck into the crib with baby.

✔ **See whether your local hospital has a sibling class that you can take with your children.**

These classes give you a general idea of how your children may act with a sibling around and offer some things that you can do to prevent them from being jealous.

✔ **Get your kids involved with the preparation and arrival of the new baby.**

Ask for their help. Have them draw pictures to put in the baby's room, pack the diaper bag (after you lay all the stuff out), and fetch diapers or bottles for you. Getting your kids involved with the baby helps them feel more like a part of the baby's life.

After you've done this preparation, how are your children going to act toward the new sibling? That depends on your children and their level of maturity. When you take the "new sibling" classes previously suggested, you'll find that behavior usually is sorted out by age. Normally, a 2-year-old is expected to show anger or jealousy toward a newborn while an 8-year-old may be exhilarated. But that isn't always the case. You may find that you have to keep an extra eye on your 2-year-old who wants to *help* you by carrying or picking up the baby — while your 8-year-old suddenly seems to be angry with you for no apparent reason. Whatever the ages of your children, they may experience increased bouts of crying, temper tantrums, and regressions (such as bed-wetting, acting like they can't feed themselves, wanting to be carried when they're fully capable of walking, and so on). You may find that your younger children actually try to take the baby out of your hands so they can crawl into your lap. These actions usually are signs that your children aren't being heard and need your attention.

How to Handle Siblings

When you have more than one child, you must take on some new roles. You instantly become a mediator, negotiator, referee, and judge. You find yourself walking into charged situations, and listening to both sides of the crying and sobbing to determine what happened. Most of the time you won't have a clue. Both sides will sound convincingly right. And both will think that they're right.

Here are a few general guidelines for helping you maintain your sanity while you mold your children into loving, kind siblings.

✔ **Don't compare your kids.**

It's tempting just to say, "Why don't you sit quietly like your brother?" That's the wrong thing to say. Your kids will start resenting each other when you always make them feel that one is better than the other.

✔ **Don't take sides.**

You need to be the neutral party who everyone can come to. Whenever you seem to take sides with someone rather than helping to solve the problems, your children may decide they prefer to duke it out rather than come to you.

Sometimes putting your head down and letting squabbling siblings try to work things out is better. Usually they will! Besides, you won't always be there to help them work out their differences. Of course, you need to intercede when the conversation becomes physical. Your children never should be allowed to solve their problems with knock-down-drag-out fights.

✔ **Stay calm.**

When your kids are upset and all rational thought and action seem to be gone, staying calm is your job. You need to be the one who can walk in and quietly help everyone else gain control of themselves. If you get upset, too, you won't be much good at helping solve their differences.

✔ **Keep a sense of humor.**

Laugh. And do it a lot. Sometimes laughing is the only solution to conflict. When you help your kids see the humor in situations, it defuses the problem. Besides, how can you take seriously an argument over who touched whom first?

✔ **No name-calling.**

This is a big rule at my house. Name-calling can be hurtful, and fighting is harder when you can't call someone Rhino Nose or Big Butt. Whenever someone starts calling another one names, stop the argument at once — make that a rule from the beginning. The old saying, "Sticks and stones may break my bones, but words will never hurt me," is not true. Sticks and stones do hurt, and so do words.

✔ **No hitting or pushing.**

This rule is the hard one. Wanting to lash out at someone who makes you mad is a natural instinct. I've seen kids as young as 10 months old lash out at their older siblings when they got fed up having a toy ripped from their hands. The no hitting or pushing rule is a constant lesson that isn't easily learned. You must consistently teach that hitting or pushing isn't allowed in the family. If children can't touch someone in a loving way, they shouldn't touch them at all.

✔ **Give your kids time alone.**

When your kids always seem to be attacking each other, they may simply need some time alone. If you can separate your kids and have them play in separate rooms, they won't get on each other's nerves as much and will be more tolerant with each other. It's just like cabin fever for kids: When they're around each other all the time, they sometimes need to get away and spend some time alone.

Arguments typically occur when someone doesn't feel *heard.* So the waters cannot be calmed until everyone feels heard. And telling you whether they feel they've been heard is up to the participants (adult and child). Remember that it *isn't* vital that everyone agrees, but it *is* vital that everyone be heard.

When play turns into fights

Regardless of how much you read about getting siblings to play nicely together, a time will come when little battles occur over who gets to play with what first. Your children aren't always going to have you around to break up fights and be the mediator, so you need to stay out of their way and let them work out their problems on their own.

Keep a watchful eye on the situation, because when arguments turn physical, and punching, kicking, or name-calling begins, it's your job to jump in and become a teacher again. Tell your kids that fighting and name-calling are not allowed, but also let them know that they can use words to work out their differences.

Teaching Siblings How to Play Together

The main problem with kids playing together is that, at some point in time, they all spot the same book or stuffed animal — and the fight is on. A variation on that scenario is when one child has a toy and an older brother who's decided that he wants to play with the toy.

Sharing is hard to teach. I've got to tell you, when I get a box of chocolates, I have a hard time sharing. If someone else reaches for the one and only cherry cordial, I go crazy!

What you'll want to do, but really shouldn't do, is buy duplicate toys for all your kids. If it's something like bicycles, well then, *yes,* it's more fun for kids to have their own bicycles so they can all ride together. Any toy that is more fun if everyone has one (such as Barbies) is great. But if the toy is a game, the answer is *no.*

Your kids must to learn to share. They can't go through life thinking that everything they own is theirs and only theirs. The next thing you'll end up doing is buying each child his own box of cereal because someone keeps eating all the marshmallows out of the Lucky Charms.

You can encourage sharing by showing one child how to offer a toy in exchange for a toy that another child has. Sometimes this works, sometimes it doesn't. The hard part is teaching your children that when someone doesn't want to exchange toys, they'll just have to wait until the toy has been set down. Of course, they'll watch the toy like a hawk until it's down, and then pounce on it.

Teaching Siblings How to Have a Loving, Caring Relationship

I've met enough families in my life to know that being loving and kind to your siblings hasn't been encouraged or taught in every family. You must teach kids to be loving and kind to each other. Make sure that your actions also are a part of teaching. These actions show your kids how they should behave toward each other.

✔ **Don't gang up on a child.**

Don't mistakenly join in or gang up with others against your children. You're supposed to be that child's best cheerleader and supporter, not some sporadic antagonist. Ganging up on your children is a surefire way to destroy their trust, and any chance of a future relationship with your children as an adult.

✔ **Don't tease.**

Teasing is sadistic and wrong. No one who truly loves their children teases them. Of course, teasing is an inherited trait, so if your parents teased you, chances are that you'll do it to your kids because you were programmed that way. But that doesn't make it right. Never tease. Be firm with your kids: They are not to tease others.

✔ **Don't talk bad about others in front of their siblings.**

Again, you need to be your children's best supporters, so don't talk badly about your children, but especially never do so in front of your other children. Your children need to hear that everything you say about them is positive and in a loving manner.

✔ **Don't pit your children against one another.**

Your job as a parent is not instigating fights or arguments, and then sitting back and watching the excitement begin. Some parents do this — and it's wrong. Your kids are going to have enough confrontations with each other without having you add to their fires. This type of confrontation can also result from when you compare your children with each other. Each of your children will have individual strengths and weaknesses. No one likes to hear, "Why can't you be more like your sister/brother?"

✔ **Encourage hugs and kisses between siblings.**

Young children naturally pick up on affection, especially when you're liberally passing out hugs and kisses. When you see your young ones showing affection to each other, let them know how happy you are that they're giving out hugs and kisses. Encourage them to do so often. This positive reinforcement lets them know that giving affection is a natural and good thing.

✔ **Teach children how to be gentle.**

When you see your toddler belting the baby, take the toddler's hand and gently caress the baby with it. Let your toddler know that is how to touch others. You may also have to show what gentleness is to older children who may not have been around younger children or babies.

✔ **Teach family togetherness.**

Your actions are an important way to teach this. Several chapters in this book emphasize your family doing things together. Getting everyone involved in housework, cooking, and playing together is an excellent example of how family togetherness works. This is one of the most important and valuable lessons that you can teach your children. And don't forget the power of storybooks that you can read to your children — books that emphasize family togetherness.

Don't leave siblings under the age of 4 alone together. They can easily hurt their siblings by hugging them too hard or by trying to pick them up.

Sibling Communication

Everyone is going to be a teacher to your young children, especially older siblings. Listen closely to how they communicate. If you find that an older child is losing patience and beginning to yell or be hateful to a younger child, step in and remind the older child that the best way to talk is calmly and nicely. Keep in mind that this behavior probably stems from something else. Find out why are he is losing his patience.

Your children look to you as an example. When you remain calm, don't yell, and avoid sarcasm, your kids will pick up this behavior from you. Your older children will try imitating you and your actions toward your kids. Make sure you portray a loving, kind, and gentle person.

Otherwise, your children may learn from you and their older siblings to be:

✔ Ignoring

Too many parents ignore their kids when they talk. It's a bad habit that not only frustrates children but also is a bad trait to pass on to someone. Make sure that you listen when your children are talking to you. Acknowledge what they're saying. If you hear your children playing and one child is ignoring the other, point it out.

✔ Sarcastic

Like teasing, sarcasm is sadistic. It's being dishonest at the expense of another, which betrays you on two levels to your child: First, you're lying to them, and second, you're being sadistic. If you love your children, you won't play at sarcasm with them.

✔ Bullying

Children learn to bully from their parents. It's an easy thing to pick up: "You're going to do this because I say so." In other words, I'm the master, and you're the slave, and that's all the reason I need to give for you to obey me! Kids love to play that game, too! Alas, everyone usually wants to be the master, which is the core of most arguments and fights between siblings.

The opposite of being a bully is being a friend. An older sibling is bigger and stronger, but must also be wiser and kind. Bullies don't offer any choice: "Do it my way or else!" To help teach nonbullying, friendly behavior, remember that there must be a choice: "You can be quiet now, or we will leave the restaurant now. It's your choice, but this is *not* a place for making those noises."

Teaching siblings that they don't always need to agree with each other also is important. Agreement has no intrinsic value. The value is present in disagreement, which doesn't necessarily lead to anger or frustration. Disagreement simply means both siblings are being honest about their feelings; no one is knuckling under. If Jonah doesn't want to play with Jeremiah right now, then that's valid disagreement and must be accepted. The opposite is that Jeremiah bursts into bullying behavior to get Jonah to agree with him, which is the start of a great big fight!

Part VI
The Part of Tens

The 5th Wave   By Rich Tennant

"Mr Klein, would you mind telling me the next time you plan to smash your thumb with a hammer?"

In this part . . .

The Part of Tens is composed of lists of things that can be amusing: the ten tallest mountains, the ten biggest diamonds, ten vegetables that resemble former presidents, ten people named Ned who have phlebitis, and so on. Of course, lists of ten don't always have to be corny. You can discover considerable amounts of information in these lists of tens, including the do's and don'ts of a particular issue. What you'll find in this section are some last lists of tens to help you become a better parent.

Chapter 28

Ten Things to Do Every Day

This is your friendly reminder list. If you have memorized the entire book, you don't need the list. But if you don't quite have it committed to memory, then this list is for you. Consider it a highlight of things to do every day so that your relationship with your children grows and prospers.

Give hugs and kisses

Physical contact does a great deal for humans. Throw that old myth that holding children too much spoils them out the window. That's a bunch of crap. Holding and hugging and gentle baby kisses help your children in many ways. And while you're dishing out the affection, remember your partner.

Say, "Tell me more about that"

"Tell me more about that" are the best words for helping your children express themselves more and for letting you know more about what's going on in their world. They are words that are neither condescending nor threatening. They are a simple request for more information, which opens the door for your children to open up and talk.

Tell your family members you love them

Everyone needs to feel loved. Even though you may show your love by the special things that you do for your family, hearing those ever-so-important words, "I love you," also is important.

Children need love, especially when they do not deserve it. — Harold S. Hubert

Read to your kids

Reading to your kids not only starts them down a good road toward loving books, but it also provides you with quiet time to be alone with them. Kids who are read to (and who read) are associated with higher IQs, better vocabularies, and increased language skills.

Validate your kids

Validating is immediately letting your kids know that what they've just done or how they feel makes sense. Nothing is crueler than to tell your kids that they're not feeling the way they say they're feeling. "Get up, you're not hurt!" or "Stop crying! There's nothing to be upset about!" are cruel statements that you may have heard your parents use on you. When your child falls down and cries, then validate his feeling by telling him, "Gee, that must have really hurt." Or when children tell you they're mad, then say, "It makes sense that you'd be mad because your brother won't play with you." Validating your kids is letting them know that their feelings are true and that you understand their feelings.

Feed your family nutritious food

Making sure that your kids eat the right foods is important, and so is taking care of yourself. Not only are you setting a good example by grabbing a banana for dessert, rather than that piece of fudge (ummm, fudge), you're also teaching your children about making better food decisions.

Talk to your kids

Every day you need to know what your kids are doing, where they've been, who they've been with, how they feel, and what their opinion is. Talking to your kids also starts a habit of open communication between you and your family. You all need to practice open and honest communication, which includes good listening skills.

Have a special time with each child

Spending time individually with your kids is essential when you have more than one child. You need to make each child feel special and important. By spending time alone with your kids, you help them not to feel lost in a large group; and, as a result, they feel more like a member of a family.

Provide caring behavior

Caring behavior means doing that special thing that is meaningful to the person on the receiving end of that special behavior. When your child says that he loves it when you put a surprise in his lunch box, then do that! When your partner says that he loves it when you bring him hot chocolate In the afternoons, then bring him hot chocolate. Remember, however, that caring behavior must be something that the receiving person deems as caring behavior. So ask your children (and your partner, too) what they think is a special behavior that you can do for them.

Practice patience

Practice makes perfect. Oh Lordy, _do_ practice patience! Remember to get plenty of sleep, eat right, listen carefully, find out what makes your kids do what they do, ask yourself why you're losing your patience (whenever you are), and recognize when kids merely are being kids. Don't place unrealistic expectations on your kids but pick your fights well. You're not perfect and neither are your children. Embrace that idea!

Chapter 29

Ten Things for Your Conscience to Whisper in Your Ear

• •

In This Chapter

▶ Go play

▶ Be organized

▶ Stop yelling

▶ Be consistent

▶ Speak favorably about your kids

▶ Tell the truth

▶ Do what you say you're going to do

▶ Keep a safe house

▶ Dump the bad habits

▶ Keep track of your children

• •

Relationship building is what it's all about. But that can be difficult to do when you're not equipped with the right tools. Yes, building relationships is much like building anything. You must have the right tools, the right environment, and the right attitude. So, I've decided that this list is something that your conscience needs to be responsible for. Your conscience will whisper these rules in your ear when you're tired, or stressed, or hungry, and when you forget that your job is to build a relationship with your children. Oh, I can hear your conscience talking now. . . .

Pssst! Quit working and go play with your kids!

Workaholics! Most people I know are workaholics, but no one wants to admit to it. The worst of the workaholics that I've seen are stay-at-home parents. They never seem to understand that their work can wait, probably because they're always surrounded by their work (house, kids, finances, school meetings, you name it). But don't think I'm just picking on the work-at-home parents. Volunteers can also be workaholics. They spend so much time volunteering that they're never home. Then again, those typical business-suit types also are guilty.

Listen folks, cancel that meeting. Schedule family time. Have dinner together. Go for walks. And, above all, stop making work more important than your family.

Hey, are you organized today?

Organization is key to managing a family. Schedules, lists, and chores are vital in keeping your family functional. Manage your family like a business, and things will go smoothly. Remember, I have four children, and I know what it's like when someone doesn't put his backpack on his backpack hook. We spend 10 minutes hunting down the missing backpack. That's 10 extra minutes that I didn't plan for, so we may risk being late for school. Stay organized!

Are you yelling? Knock that off!

Good communication skills are key to a good relationship. Don't fall into the frustrating trap of thinking that louder is better. It isn't. It's just louder. When you catch yourself starting to yell or scream, put on the brakes and stop! Think about what you're doing and reapproach the situation.

Wait a minute, didn't you tell them not to do that?

Parents watch their kids climb on top of the table and dance to music. Parents laugh, "*Ha, ha, ha!* Aren't they cute?" But as parents, they've made a mistake. They've allowed their children to do something that normally they wouldn't be allowed to do. Now that the children have received positive feedback for what they've done, and because of that, now they'll probably do it again. So, when they get in trouble for doing it the next time, they'll be confused. "Mom, you let me do this yesterday. What's up?"

If you don't want your children to develop habits that you eventually must stop, don't ever let them start such habits in the first place. Kids develop habits quickly, *especially* when they receive a positive response from you. Be consistent with your rules.

What did you just say?

Talking bad about anyone is a nasty, horrible habit. Speaking unfavorably about your kids is especially unforgivable and can have lasting repercussions that your kids will carry with them forever, if they ever hear you talking bad about them. Your kids always need to know that you support them and think highly of them and what they do. If you're talking negatively about them (like telling your friends about their bad habits), you're not supporting them in the best way possible. Besides, your friends couldn't really care less about your kids' habits.

Is that the truth?

At no other time in your life is anyone ever going to love and trust you more than your children. Their love and trust are unconditional. Don't lessen your children's trust in you by lying to them. Watch out for the unintentional lies, such as telling your kids that the taste of medicine is good, that shots don't hurt, that you'll be home right after work and then come home four hours late, and so on. Think about what you say before you say it. If children can't trust Mom and Dad, they won't be able to trust their friends or their future partners.

But didn't you just say. . . ?

Keeping your word is right up there with the trust issues your kids will have when you don't do what you say you're going to do. That's actually a form of lying. When you promise ice cream after dinner, then everyone gets ice cream. Period. If it's too late, then that is your fault. You didn't schedule your time well or you didn't think before you spoke. Keeping your word also means holding your ground when you say no. Giving in to a child's whining, pleading, and begging never pays. Not only does it show the child that whining means winning, but you usually end up having to pay the price one way or another.

Hey, is that safe?

Don't cut corners on safety. People in the United States are fortunate to live in a country where someone has thought of virtually every worst-case scenario in which your kids can find themselves, and those same thinkers have made a gadget for us to buy to protect our kids. Don't overlook these gadgets. They help. Invest in some cabinet locks and electrical plug guards, so that you have one less thing to worry about your kids doing. And don't overlook common sense either. Don't leave your kids alone in the bathtub (not even for a second). Don't leave cabinets open or medication within the reach of children. Be smart here.

Is that a habit you're willing to pass on?

You are who you are because of your parents and your environment. Good or bad, you've learned your habits from them. Are your habits something you want to pass on? Think about your smoking, or your drinking, or your cursing. Have these habits actually bettered your life? Even if it's the habit of blaming others for your unhappiness, take ownership in the things that you do and learn how to better yourself so that your kids can discover how to be better people too.

Where are the children?

Know your children. Know where they are, who they are, and what they are doing. Keep track of your children at all times. Even when they're visiting someone, know what they're doing. When kids start making sense and reasoning with you, parents tend to let down their guard some, which is good. Your kids need to know that you trust them, and trust is how they begin gaining the independence that they need. But don't become so relaxed that you don't know what's going on. Children are just as tempted as anyone else to try something new, maybe experiment with a blender (which is dangerous) or try the beer that Dad seems to like so much.

Chapter 30

Ten Great Resources for Parents

In This Chapter

▶ People you can count on for advice and support

▶ Organizations, publications, and Web sites for your A-List

1 need help. You need help. We all need to recognize that we don't know it all when it comes to parenting, and we need guidance and help and reassurance that we're doing this right. I just want to be a good mom, and I want to have a good relationship with my kids so that when I'm old and gray (oh wait, I'll never be gray), my kids still will want to be around me. If I screw up now, they'll stick me in a nursing home and kiss me good-bye. I don't want that, and I'm guessing that you don't want it either. So, right now, when it matters most, I want to invest in a good relationship.

The items on the list that follows are places you can go where you can find more parenting information or receive support for what you are doing. After all, sometimes I just need to hear that what my kids are going through is normal and that it isn't because I'm a horrible mother. Kids will be kids!

Your friends

My friends don't always have the best parenting skills. But what they do have is a reality check for me. I listen to the struggles and dilemmas they go through, and then I realize that everyone struggles with the same things. Parents worry about the healthy development of their kids, physically and mentally. My friends also offer creative parenting tips because they are rather brilliant. What works on their child may not work on mine, but at least I have some borrowed ideas on how to handle situations.

Parenting magazine

Out of all the parenting magazines out there, *Parenting* is my favorite. It offers good topics and good guidelines for healthy development. Every now and then, someone writes an article that I think is completely nuts, like the one by the psychologist who says she just ignores her children whenever they do something she doesn't like (bad!!), so read with care. You can find *Parenting* in any bookstore and in grocery stores that have a magazine rack. The *Parenting* Web site is `www.parenting.com/parenting/magazines/`.

School counselors

School counselors deal with kids and families all day long, and they're great resources for dealing with conflict management and learning difficulties. When your child is going through a difficulty dealing with school or peers or friends at school, make an appointment with the school counselor.

Your child's teacher

Of all the teachers my kids have gone through, there was only one that I didn't think was a good resource for anything, including being my child's teacher, so be smart about this one. Teachers are good resources when you want to know, "Is this normal for a second-grader to go through?" They see hundreds of kids of the same ages and can tell you what is typical for the age group that they deal with. Now, all kids are different, that is for sure, but milestones are reached by certain age groups. For example, first- and second-graders loose many of their teeth; kindergartners may know their name and address but can't tell you what their fathers' middle names are. Teachers can also tell you what the reality of a situation is at school. No, Rio doesn't pick on Simon all day long, when, in fact, they seem to be best of friends.

The Internet

Here's the truth about the Internet: Anyone can print anything about any subject. It doesn't make the information true or accurate, but it's there. What the Internet has done is bring people together in chat rooms so they can talk to others about their problems and concerns, and parents can offer their advice. Some advice is great; some of it is just plain silly.

I have a few parenting Web sites that I can recommend for good, accurate information:

- **Keepkidshealthy.com** is a pediatrician's guide to health and safety. Located at `www.keepkidshealthy.com/index.html`.
- **Parenthub.com's Baby and Child Safety Guide** is a compilation of information on baby product recalls and safety issues concerning your children. It is located at `www.parenthub.com/parenting/safety/baby.htm`.

✔ **Parenting.com** is like an online magazine that pulls articles from *Parenting, BabyTalk,* and *Family Life* magazines. Located at `www.parenting.com/parenting/`.

✔ **Parent News** is a parent information source page. There's a great section on homework where there is a list of sites that parents or students (and even teachers) can use for homework help. Very cool. It is located at `http://parent.net/`.

✔ **SafeKids.com** is an online service that teaches you how to keep the Internet safe for your kids. It is located at `safekids.com`.

✔ **Parentsoup** is a huge hodgepodge of information on eating, health, behavior, safety, child care, and the list goes on. Lots to read! It is located at `www.parentsoup.com`.

La Leche League

Le Leche League's mission is to "help mothers to breast-feed through mother-to-mother support, encouragement, information, and education, and to promote a better understanding of breast-feeding as an important element in the healthy development of the baby and the mother." If you have a computer, they have a nifty Web site at `www.lalecheleague.org`, or you can call them at 847-519-7730 to get information or to find their support centers.

Church

Support from your church comes in a variety of ways. The moral support helps you work to maintain a healthy family unit, but the church also offers support from child care for parents-nights-out, clothing centers for hand-me-down clothes, parenting and marriage classes, and of course Sunday school for parents and kids.

The bookstore

The bookstore is where you can find copies of *Parenting For Dummies* to give to all your friends! But I also recommend reading books on building relationships such as those by Harville Hendrix. A great title by Hendrix is *Getting the Love You Want: A Guide for Couples* and *Giving the Love That Heals: A Guide for Parents.* Don't forget places like Amazon.com (`www.amazon.com`), which is a great online bookstore.

Your parents and your partner's parents

All parents can learn from tradition and history. But how your parents raised you is instructive both on *what* to do as well as what *not* to do. If you were raised with, "Quit being so grouchy!" or "You're not hurt, get up!" and you hated those comments, then don't use them. But you also need to learn why those comments were hurtful to you so that you don't pass them on to your children. Side note: Those comments are hurtful because the "Quit being grouchy" comment is a parent trying to define who you are. The "You're not hurt" comment is erasing your feelings. If you were raised with these things, you've learned this behavior as normal. Unless you study yourself and your parents (and your partner's parents), you'll end up doing the same hurtful things to your children.

Don't overlook the valuable contribution that grandparents can offer: They make great babysitters!

Part VII
Appendixes

The 5th Wave By Rich Tennant

"I FIND IT EASIER TO SAY 'NO', IF I IMAGINE THEM SAYING, 'MOMMY, CAN I HAVE THE LATEST OVER-HYPED, OVER-PRICED, COMMERCIAL EXPLOITATION OF AN OBNOXIOUSLY ADOR-ABLE CARTOON CHARACTER.'"

In this part . . .

Here's the extra-value stuff that you love finding in books. It's the kind of information that makes you feel the way you do when you find a $10 bill wadded up inside the pocket of your old coat. You didn't know it was there, you're overjoyed that you found it, and it's definitely worth something. That's the way you'll feel after reading Appendixes A through E, which feature lists and questionnaires that you'll find useful if you bother to actually use them. Go ahead and make copies of these pages, *use* them, and share them with others. I've added cute little check boxes so you can go through each list, checking off what you've done, what you're doing, or what you've bought. An occasional fill-in-the-blank sheet also has been included as a helpful tool for you to use. So go forth and start reading, checking, watching, looking, and all that good stuff.

Appendix A

Safety

• •

*T*rying to keep the world a safe place for your children may make you feel like you're being paranoid or overprotective. So be it. It's better to feel that way than to feel sorry that you didn't spend the extra time and money to protect your children from dangers that can be found in your house or car. Use these checklists to verify that you've got everything you need or that you're doing everything necessary to promote safety.

General Fire-Safety Devices

❑ Smoke detectors

❑ Fire extinguishers

❑ Escape ladders

❑ Carbon-monoxide detectors

❑ Fire escape plan for your house that has been practiced

Bedroom Safety

❑ Don't use homemade or antique cribs.

❑ Keep bedding simple — sheet, blanket, and bumper pads.

❑ Don't use pillows (until a child is 3 years old).

❑ Get rid of bumper pads when your baby is old enough to pull up.

❑ Don't put cribs or toddler beds near blinds, drapes, or wall hangings with cords that hang down.

❑ Put plastic covers on all the electrical outlets, and plastic boxes over the cords that already are plugged in.

❑ Make sure the toys in the bedroom are appropriate for the age of your children.

❑ Wash and dry all toys on a regular basis.

❑ Don't put toy chests or children's furniture near windows.

❏ Use toy chests made of light material, like plastic, with a lid that either comes off or hinges and stays up.

❏ Make sure purses and fanny packs are out of reach of children.

❏ Take plastic covers off of mattresses.

❏ Babies should never sleep on water beds, cushions, beanbag chairs, adult comforters, or pillows.

❏ Never, under any circumstances, do you walk away from, or turn your back on, a baby who is on a changing table.

Children's Accessories Safety

❏ Check toys for missing parts.

❏ Check pacifiers to see whether the plastic nipple still is in good shape. If a pacifier is cracked, throw it away.

❏ Wash pacifiers often.

❏ Never tie a pacifier around a child's neck.

❏ Remove crib mobiles when your children are old enough to pull up on their hands and knees.

❏ Don't put your children to bed with toys in the crib.

❏ Don't use a baby carrier or a baby swing as a car seat or as a seat when riding bicycles.

❏ Follow all manufacturers' directions for assembly when using a baby swing.

❏ Don't put highchairs too close to walls, counters, or tables.

❏ Use your strollers with all the safety equipment provided.

❏ Watch out for little fingers when setting up the stroller or folding it.

❏ Don't hang heavy bags, purses, or diaper bags from the handle of the stroller.

❏ Don't use a baby walker if you're not going to put gates on your stairs.

Living/Family Room Safety

❏ Put plastic covers on all the electrical outlets, and plastic boxes over the cords that are already plugged in.

❏ Put gates on all stairs going up or down.

❏ Take portable gates to place in the doorways of staircases if you're traveling to someone else's home. (Be sure to ask for permission first.)

❏ Put breakable items either away or in higher places (until your children are old enough to learn to leave them alone).

❑ Don't leave babies and young toddlers unattended on furniture.

❑ Scrape, sand, and repaint all old paint areas.

❑ Have furnaces, fireplaces, and gas barbecue grills checked for carbon monoxide leaks.

❑ Clean air filters for heaters and air conditioners once a month.

❑ Don't keep your car running in the garage.

❑ Keep blind or drapery cords tied up, out of the reach of children.

Kitchen Safety

❑ Put locks on all your cabinets.

❑ Use the back burners when cooking on the stove.

❑ Keep handles of pots turned back into the back of stoves. Never let them point out to where you're standing, or where little hands can reach them.

❑ Keep drawers locked.

❑ Keep small children out of the way when cooking.

❑ Lock up or throw away plastic shopping bags, garbage bags, plastic wrap, plastic sandwich bags, plastic dry cleaning bags, or plastic film of any kind (like those on toy wrappings).

❑ Keep alcoholic beverages away from children.

❑ Keep chairs away from counters.

❑ Keep important phone numbers on a list, displayed next to the phone.

❑ Keep *Syrup of Ipecac* in your medicine cabinet, but don't use it unless you're instructed to do so by a physician or someone at the Poison Control Center.

Bathroom Safety

❑ Keep bathrooms blocked off with gates or install safety locks high enough so that your children can't reach them.

❑ Keep lids to toilets closed.

❑ Keep shower doors closed.

❑ Never leave water standing in sinks, bathtubs, or buckets.

❑ Keep cleaners, perfumes, deodorants, and any other *foofoo* stuff locked up.

❑ Always keep medicines in the medicine cabinet and away from children.

❑ Use child-resistant packaging for anything and everything you use.

❑ Keep small appliances (like hair dryers, curling irons, electric razors, and irons) unplugged and put away.

❑ Don't allow children to play in the bathroom.

❑ Never leave children unattended in the bathroom, especially while taking a bath.

Car-Seat Safety

❑ Always, always, always use a car seat when traveling. It's the law.

❑ Use only the type of car seat that is age and weight appropriate for your children.

❑ Fasten the car seat down with the seat belt.

❑ Always use the car seat's safety belt.

❑ Read the directions on the car seat and FOLLOW THEM!

❑ Don't put rear-facing car seats in the front seat where there is an air bag.

❑ Children weighing less than 20 pounds should always be facing the rear of the car.

Burn Prevention

❑ Put your coffee cup in the middle of tables or counters.

❑ Don't hold your children when you're holding a cup of hot liquid.

❑ Use your back burners to cook when possible.

❑ Turn pot handles toward the rear of the stove.

❑ Keep kids away from floor furnaces or area heaters.

❑ Hide your disposable lighters, or don't use them.

❑ Don't let your children use the microwave oven.

❑ Never hold your children while you're cooking.

Choking Hazards

❑ Grapes	❑ Nuts
❑ Hard candies	❑ Popcorn
❑ Deflated or bursted balloon pieces	❑ Pins
❑ Coins	❑ Small toys and toy parts
❑ Raw vegetables cut in circles	❑ Hot dogs cut in circles
❑ Buttons	❑ Plastic bags

Appendix B

Traveling

● ●

*T*raveling can be a relaxing, enjoyable event for parents, when you're prepared for it. Or traveling can be a royal pain in the behind if you're not
prepared. Whether it's a vacation to Walt Disney World or a quick run to the
grocery store, you can use the checklists below to ensure an easier and
better-prepared outing.

Important Baby-Bag Contents

- ❑ Diapers
- ❑ Diaper-rash ointment
- ❑ Changing cushion
- ❑ Eating utensils
- ❑ Pacifier
- ❑ Water
- ❑ Nipples

- ❑ Baby wipes
- ❑ Burp-up towel
- ❑ Food
- ❑ Change of clothing
- ❑ Blanket
- ❑ Bottles
- ❑ Bib

General Traveling Tidbits

- ❑ Allow yourself plenty of time to get to wherever you're going.
- ❑ Ask your travel agent about vacation sites that cater to children.
- ❑ Have snacks and toys close at hand.
- ❑ Take the phone number of your child's doctor with you.
- ❑ Take your medical insurance information with you.

Automobile Travel

- ❑ Make regular stops for rest, food, running around and burning off energy, and for gas.
- ❑ Clean up your car and bodies often.
- ❑ Exercise caution.

Airplane Travel

❑ Pack extra diapers and clothing.

❑ Be prepared for ear unplugging techniques.

❑ Take a car seat when you travel with your toddler. But you must pay for your child's seat on the plane.

❑ Take snacks and beverages with you. Don't allow small children to hold those flimsy plastic cups they give on airplanes. That is an accident waiting to happen.

❑ Limit your carry-ons. One bag is all you need.

❑ Don't let your kids walk the aisles during the flight.

❑ Reserve a bulkhead seat when flying.

Traveler's Supply List

❑ Diapers

❑ Baby wipes (or hand wipes)

❑ Spit-up towel

❑ Bottles and nipples

❑ Light blanket

❑ Eating utensils (cups, spoons)

❑ Plastic bags for dirty diapers and dirty clothes

❑ Change of clothing

❑ Beverages (juice, formula, water)

❑ Food

❑ Entertainment for the kids

❑ Current passport (when traveling outside the United States)

❑ Names and phone numbers of your doctor and medical insurance

❑ Medications

Family Vacation Guidelines

❑ Don't overschedule your time.

❑ Keep your kids on their eating and sleeping schedules (as much as possible).

❑ Plan plenty of free time for goofing off.

❑ Don't eat too much junk food.

Food-on-the-Road Guidelines

❑ Have enough eating/drinking supplies.

❑ Keep enough food on hand (no perishables).

❑ Keep plenty of liquids with you.

❑ Keep a bottle of water from home with you.

❑ Keep a supply of juice.

❑ Limit fresh fruit that you take with you (or buy it on the way).

Appendix C

Child Care

· ·

*O*f all the things that you, as a parent, need to research thoroughly, child care should be at the top of your list. Use the checkboxes and question-naires in this appendix to make your search easier.

You don't want to leave your kids with a sitter of any kind without giving the sitter permission to authorize medical treatment in case of an accident. Use the following slip. Fill it out and leave it with your sitter when you leave him or her alone with your children.

Medical Treatment Authorization

_____ has my permission to authorize medical

Fill in the complete name of your sitter

treatment to my child(ren) _____
in case of a medical emergency.

Signed,

_____

Sign your complete name

Sitters

Take time going over the following with your sitter:

- ❑ The evening schedule
- ❑ Naptime and bedtime schedules
- ❑ Household rules
- ❑ A list of emergency phone numbers and the phone number where you are going to be for the evening
- ❑ Favorite foods
- ❑ Allergies
- ❑ Favorite toys and the names your child uses for them
- ❑ Fears, along with things to help calm your upset child
- ❑ A list of *Do's* and *Don'ts*

After-School Program Questionnaire

1. Is the afternoon organized? ❑ Yes ❑ No
2. Is there a scheduled time for kids to do their homework? ❑ Yes ❑ No
3. Do kids get an afternoon snack or are
   they expected to bring their own? ❑ Yes ❑ No
4. How are the kids released to their parents?

Child Care–Hunting Questionnaire

1. May I have some names and phone numbers of parents who currently have their children attending here or of parents whose children you have cared for in the past? ❑ Yes ❑ No

2. Do you allow visitation during the day? ❑ Yes ❑ No

3. What kind of snack or lunch program do you offer?

4. May I see the play areas? ❑ Yes ❑ No

5. What is the procedure for releasing the children at the end of the day?

6. What are the rules regarding sick children?

7. Do you give out medications? ❑ Yes ❑ No

   What is your policy?

8. What will you do if my child gets injured?

9. If your caregiver calls only for an emergency, what constitutes an emergency?

10. What are your fees?

    Do you have a late pickup charge? ❑ Yes ❑ No

    What kind of payment schedule do you have?

    Do you allow uncharged time for vacations? ❑ Yes ❑ No

11. What is your teacher-to-child ratio?

12. What are your teacher qualifications?

13. What is the turnover rate of your teachers?

14. Do you do background checks on your employees? ❑ Yes ❑ No

15. How do you discipline children?

16. What kind of communication will I have with my child's caregiver?

17. How well does my child have to be potty-trained?

18. What is your daily curriculum for the children here?

19. Do you have a naptime during the day? ❑ Yes ❑ No

    What is your policy on children who no longer take naps?

20. Can I see your last licensing report? ❑ Yes ❑ No

21. Do you have NAEYC (National Association for the Education of Young Children) accreditation? ❑ Yes ❑ No

Rules for Child-Care Drop Off

❑ Don't rush getting ready in the morning.

❑ Spend some time together with your child in the morning at your child care center.

❑ Never sneak out while your child is doing something else.

❑ Make your good-byes quick and to the point.

❑ Don't scold a child who cries because you're leaving.

❑ Don't be too hard on yourself.

❑ When you pick up your child, don't be upset if your child isn't as tidy as when you left.

Appendix D

Medical Care

• •

*Y*ou have to do research if you want to pick the right pediatrician. Use the following questionnaires as guidelines to finding the right doctor for your family. And remember, you don't have to pick the first doctor you interview. Take whatever amount of time you need so that you can find someone with whom you'll be happy developing a doctor-patient relationship.

Questionnaire for Your Doctor Hunting

1. What are your open hours?

2. How do you handle follow-up visits?

3. Do you have bench checks or less expensive follow-up visits?   ❑ Yes   ❑ No

4. What are my payment options?

5. What do I do in case of an emergency?

6. Do you have additional doctors?   ❑ Yes   ❑ No

7. Do you have backup doctors?   ❑ Yes   ❑ No

8. How is your waiting room arranged?

Questionnaire for People Who Refer You to a Doctor

1. What do you like about this doctor?

2. What do you dislike about this doctor?

3. Does this doctor seem open to your questions?   ❑ Yes   ❑ No

4. Is this doctor kind and gentle to your children?   ❑ Yes   ❑ No

5. Do your children like this doctor?   ❑ Yes   ❑ No

6. Does this doctor take time to listen to your concerns and discuss problems with you?   ❑ Yes   ❑ No

7. Does this doctor have experience with mothers who have successfully breast-fed?   ❑ Yes   ❑ No

8. Does this doctor share your points of view on nutrition, starting babies on solids, weaning, and so on?   ❑ Yes   ❑ No

Pharmacy-Hunting Guidelines

1. Location:

2. A drive-up pharmacy?   ❏ Yes   ❏ No

3. Hours open:

4. Computer records?   ❏ Yes   ❏ No

5. Medicine summary for the prescription?   ❏ Yes   ❏ No

The Child-Doctor Relationship Rules

❑ **Do** be happy and relaxed when going to the doctor.

❑ **Do** greet the doctor cheerfully.

❑ **Do** use the doctor's name.

❑ **Do** thank the doctor after the examination.

❑ **Don't** use going to the doctor as a threat against your child.

❑ **Don't** tell your child that something is going to hurt, or that it won't hurt if you really know that it will.

Going to the Doctor

age	check-up
❑ 1 week	exam
❑ 2 weeks	exam and shots (if HepB is not received at the hospital)
❑ 2 months	exam and shots
❑ 4 months	exam and shots
❑ 6 months	exam and shots
❑ 9 months	exam and shots
❑ 12 months	exam (some providers will do shots at 12 months instead of 9 months)
❑ 15 months	exam and shots
❑ 18 months	exam (shots if your child is behind schedule and needs to catch up)
❑ 2 years	exam (shots if your child is behind schedule or missed appointments earlier, or if you have lived in a geographic area that recommends HepA shots)
❑ 3 years	exam (shots if your child is behind schedule or missed appointments earlier, or if you have lived in a geographic area that recommends HepA shots)
❑ 4 to 6 years (or right before starting school)	exam and shots
❑ every 2 to 3 years	general exams afterward
❑ 12 years	exams and shots
❑ 15 years	exams and shots

Vision Problems
(when to go see your doctor)

❑ Your child squints or rubs the eyes a lot (other than when tired).

❑ Your child's eyes move quickly either up or down or from side to side.

❑ Your child's eyes are watery, sensitive to light, or look different from the way they normally do.

❑ The pupils of the eyes have white, grayish-white, or yellow-colored material in them.

❑ The eyes stay red for several days.

❑ Your child's eyelids droop, or the eyes look like they bulge.

❑ There is pus or crust in either eye that doesn't go away.

A Good Dental-Hygiene Program

❑ Clean your child's teeth daily. Preferably twice a day.

❑ Floss your child's teeth when the molars start touching.

❑ Give all your kids, including your baby, water to drink.

❑ As soon as your child develops teeth, use a children's toothbrush and very gently brush the teeth for two minutes at a time.

❑ After age 3, use just a tiny amount of toothpaste (like baby pinky fingernail size) when brushing your child's teeth.

❑ Help your children brush their teeth until they are 7 or 8 years old.

❑ Don't forget to brush the tongue and the roof of the mouth.

Dental-Visit Guidelines

❑ Allow your children to go back to the dental chair by themselves.

❑ Always thank the dentist after the appointment is finished.

❑ Check out books on going to the dentist. Find one that has pictures of things your children may see in the dental office.

❑ Don't use going to the dentist as a type of threat.

❑ Don't talk about any possible pain or anything hurting.

Appendix E

Keeping Your Children Well

• •

*U*se this section as a reference to keep your children well.

Hot-Weather Guidelines

❑ Use sunscreen on your children anytime they're going to be in the sun (except for babies younger than 6 months old).

❑ Apply sunscreen on all body parts that are exposed to the sun (but avoid the eye area). Be careful not to put too much sunscreen on the forehead. A sweat-dripping head can cause sunscreen to go into the eyes. Better to wear less sunscreen but wear a hat with a bill to cover the forehead.

❑ Apply sunscreen liberally.

❑ Read the directions on your sunscreen.

❑ Don't go out into the sun between the hours of 10:00 a.m. and 3:00 p.m.

❑ Keep a hat on your children when they're in the sun.

❑ Keep a close eye on your kids when it's hot outside.

❑ Don't let your kids stay outside for more than an hour at a time without having them cool down.

❑ Provide your kids with plenty of liquids, preferably water.

❑ Go through extra measures to keep babies cool because they don't sweat well.

Cold-Weather Guidelines

❑ Never send your kids outside in the cold without proper clothing.

❑ Keep children's fingers and toes dry when they play outdoors.

❑ Make sure boots and other winter shoes are not too tight and do not have any holes or cracks in them.

❑ Limit the amount of time your children spend outdoors.

Signs of Illness

These are all problem signs that indicate your child may be getting ill. Keep this list close at hand. If your children display any of these signs, get them to the doctor immediately. Don't ever take chances on your children's health.

❑ Difficulty breathing

❑ Screaming loud with knees drawn up

❑ Pulling at ears

❑ Swollen glands

❑ Sleeping past feeding times or not eating as much as normal

❑ Changes in sleeping schedules

❑ Difficulty waking up from sleep

❑ Looking pale or gray

❑ Dark circles under the eyes

❑ Blue lips

❑ Acting limp and without any energy

❑ Bad breath (other than the fact that your child just ate three hard-boiled eggs)

❑ Smelly private parts, even after a bath

Preventing the Spread of Germs

❑ Don't share towels.

❑ Don't share cups.

❑ Don't kiss your pets.

❑ Don't sit on a dirty toilet seat.

❑ Don't eat raw meat or eggs.

❑ Don't smoke.

❑ Don't touch your face.

❑ Do wash your hands.

❑ Do disinfect your house often.

Your Medicine Chest

❑ Thermometer

❑ Suction syringe

❑ Eyedropper

❑ Medicine dispenser

❑ Children's or infants' Tylenol (acetaminophen)

❑ Ice pack

❑ Adhesive bandages (Band-Aids)

❑ Pedialyte

❑ Diaper-rash ointment

❑ Petroleum jelly

❑ Lip balm

❑ Moisturizing soap and lotion

❑ Anti-itch lotion

❑ Tweezers

❑ Scissors

❑ Syrup of Ipecac

❑ Flashlight or penlight

❑ Pad of paper and pen

❑ Cool-mist humidifier or vaporizer (okay, try under your medicine chest)

Index

• *C* •